MUSLIM WOMEN IN BRITAIN, 1850–1950

SARIYA CHERUVALLIL-CONTRACTOR and
JAMIE GILHAM (*Editors*)

Muslim Women in Britain, 1850–1950

100 Years of Hidden History

HURST & COMPANY, LONDON

First published in the United Kingdom in 2023 by
C. Hurst & Co. (Publishers) Ltd.,
New Wing, Somerset House, Strand, London, WC2R 1LA
© Sariya Cheruvallil-Contractor, Jamie Gilham and the
contributors, 2023
All rights reserved.

A Cataloguing-in-Publication data record for this book
is available from the British Library.

ISBN: 9781805260400

www.hurstpublishers.com

Printed in Great Britain by Bell and Bain Ltd, Glasgow

CONTENTS

v

CONTENTS

ACKNOWLEDGEMENTS

We would like to thank the contributors to this volume for their dedication to the project and Professor Sophie Gilliat-Ray for the excellent Foreword. Thanks also to the team at Hurst, especially our managing editor, Lara Weisweiller-Wu, for their support and advice.

For helping us to secure sources, images and permissions, we are very grateful to Zahid Aziz; Ahmet Ceylan; Abdul Hayee, Markfield Institute of Higher Education; Elen Jones, National Archives of Wales; Riordan Macnamara; Sarah Trim-West, Brunel University London Archives and Special Collections; and staff at the National Portrait Gallery, London. We also thank Abdul-Azim Ahmed and Arthur Magida for their help.

Jamie thanks co-editor Sariya for a very happy collaboration; Jason Brooke of The Brooke Trust for his help with research about Gladys Brooke; and Yen-Ting Cho for his advice and support. Sariya thanks the British Academy and the Leverhulme Trust for funding her research on historical British Muslim women. For giving this research an academic home, she thanks the Centre for Trust, Peace and Social Relations at Coventry University. She thanks co-editor Jamie for being so inspirational and for being a proper historian. Her family, Murtuza, Ahmed and Zaytouna, have encouraged her explorations and have accompanied her on travels to uncover the stories told in this volume—you enable my work. Thank you.

SCC and JG
January 2023

GLOSSARY

adab	Islamic etiquette, good manners, decency.
alim	Learned scholar qualified to offer Islamic legal opinions.
ayah	Nanny, lady's maid, historically from South Asia and working for Europeans.
burqa	Enveloping outer garment worn by women to cover the body and face.
Caliph	The successor of the Prophet Muhammad as leader of the *umma*.
Dayang Muda	'Little Lady', the hereditary title for the wife of the heir presumptive (Tuan Muda) to the British ruler (Rajah) of Sarawak.
fiqh	Muslim jurisprudence.
hadith	Report of the traditions (words, actions) of the Prophet Muhammad.
haham	Spiritual leader, learned in Jewish law.
Hajj	Pilgrimage to Mecca. The greater of the two pilgrimages to Mecca undertaken during the last month of the Islamic calendar; the fifth 'pillar' of Islam. *'Umra* is the lesser pilgrimage to Mecca, which can be made at any time of the year.
halva	Or *halwa*; a traditional Middle Eastern confectionary.

GLOSSARY

haram	Forbidden or proscribed by Islamic law.
harem	Women's quarters in a domestic space.
hijab	Headscarf.
'Id	Muslim religious festival.
imam	Muslim religious leader.
kalima	Islamic statement of faith.
karchobi	An elaborate embroidery of silver thread on silk.
kurta	A tunic-style shirt or dress worn by women, especially in South Asia.
madrasa	Islamic school.
mahr	The obligation, in the form of money or possessions, paid by the groom or his family to a bride at the time of marriage, which becomes the latter's personal property.
mahram	Male relative, spouse.
moulvi	Title used by an *alim*.
Nawab	Prince; Muslim nobleman, regional governor.
nikah	Islamic marriage ceremony.
Nizam	Hereditary ruler in colonial India.
pallu	The loose end of a sari, worn over the shoulder or head.
papadom	Or 'papadam'; thin, crisp bread.
purdah	Female seclusion, including physical segregation and covering the body to conceal the human form.
purdahnashin	A woman who observes purdah.
Rajah	Ruler in colonial India and South-East Asia, including Sarawak.
rajkufu	Princely rank.
Ramadan	Muslim month of fasting.
Ranee	Or 'Rani'; wife and consort of a Rajah.
sadaqa jariya	Acts of continuous voluntary charity, kindness.

Saiyid	Or 'Sayyid', 'Syed'; a signifier of eminence used by Muslims who are descendants of the Prophet Muhammad; title to denote a prince, lord or chief in Arab societies.
salwar kameez	Combination of trousers and long shirt/tunic worn by women, and some men, especially in South Asia.
shahada	The Islamic testimony of faith and first of the five 'pillars' of Islam: 'I declare that there is no god but God and I declare that Muhammad is His Messenger.'
shaykh	Or 'sheikh'; a religious leader, or the leader of a community or family/tribe.
shervani	A long-sleeved coat with a stand-up collar adopted by Indian men as formal dress in the nineteenth century.
Sufi	A follower of Sufism, or Islamic mysticism.
sura	A division, or chapter, of the Qur'an.
Tuan Muda	'Little Lord', the hereditary title for the (male) heir presumptive to the British ruler (Rajah) of Sarawak.
umma	The universal Muslim religious community.

LIST OF ABBREVIATIONS

AIP	American Islamic Propaganda
AQS	Abdullah Quilliam Society
LMI	Liverpool Muslim Institute
MSGB	Muslim Society of Great Britain
SOE	Special Operations Executive
WAAF	Women's Auxiliary Air Force
WIA	Western Islamic Association
WMM	Woking Muslim Mission

LIST OF ILLUSTRATIONS

Every effort has been made to identify copyright holders and obtain their permission for the use of copyright material. Notification of any additions or corrections that should be incorporated in future reprints or editions of this book would be greatly appreciated.

1. Fatima Sheir teaching the Qur'an at her home in Butetown, Cardiff, 1943. Photographed by Richard Stone for the Ministry of Information. © Imperial War Museum, London (D 15320).

2. A view of the interior of Cairo Café in Butetown, Cardiff, 1943. Olive Salaman (centre) serves customers whilst her husband, Ali Salaman, is just visible in the doorway in the background. Photographed by Richard Stone for the Ministry of Information. © Imperial War Museum, London (D 15292).

3. Abdullah Quilliam (standing, left) with his children and members of the Liverpool Muslim Institute, c.1893. The woman standing to the right of Quilliam is probably his wife Hannah Quilliam; the woman seated directly below Quilliam is his mother, Harriet (Khadijah) Holehouse. The identities of the other adults are currently unknown, but it is likely that one of the women is Fatima Cates and another is Quilliam's second wife, Mary Lyon. Photographer unknown. Private collection.

LIST OF ILLUSTRATIONS

FOREWORD

Since around the early 2000s, qualitative social scientific researchers carrying out projects involving living human participants have been bound by the requirements of institutional ethical approval panels. These bodies are usually concerned with protecting the anonymity of those who take part in research, to ensure all that is said or done remains confidential. There are good and important reasons for these requirements. The rigours of ethical approval provide necessary protection and remind researchers of the need for respectful, professional and sensitive approaches to their participants. In contrast, the work of researchers involved in historical work may require no formal ethical approval at all. The typical requirement of anonymity in relation to those about whom they are writing is lifted, and they perhaps have greater freedom to frame the representation of their subjects.

In this timely collection of essays, we read about some inspirational, pioneering and sometimes adventurous Muslim women in Britain in ways that reflect the kind of respect, professionalism and sensitivity that we accord to living human research participants, but with the benefit of knowing their identities. They are honoured, without being idealised. We gain a sense of their humanity, with no loss to their dignity. Without the benefit of contemporary interview transcripts, the authors of each essay have approached their subjects with honesty and intellectual rigour. Behind each account there lies meticulous new archival research.

FOREWORD

This collection reflects a winning editorial approach that combines the academic skills of a historian with a feminist Muslim sociologist. The outcome is a collection of essays that takes proper account of the cumulative intersections of religion, class, gender, geography, education, race and ethnicity. The changing and sometimes turbulent socio-economic circumstances behind each woman, and the impact on her 'journey', are brought to life. The stories of the women we read about are told with compassion and integrity, but with no academic compromises.

For the field of British Muslim Studies, the timing of this publication could not be better. In recent years, there has been an upsurge of interest about the history of Islam and Muslim communities in Britain, alongside the distinctive role that early converts to Islam in Britain might have played. Academic publishing in this field has flourished, often as the outcome of alliances between academics and British Muslim communities themselves. Some of the chapters in this collection reflect that collaboration. Bit by bit, aspects of British Muslim history are coming into view, revealing new and exciting understandings. But for many plausible reasons, the experiences and contributions of Muslim women in Britain have usually been in the shadows. The telling of their stories has presented greater challenges. Available sources are fewer or have simply been lost. These women have been subject to changing understandings about 'what counts' as important to preserve and remember. In some cases, their contributions to the flourishing of Islam in Britain were simply unnoticed or taken for granted at the time. Such is the benefit of hindsight.

This book is an important academic contribution to the field of British Muslim Studies, but it is also a gift to a Muslim readership, both male and female. Regardless of the different approaches and biographies that readers might bring to their engagement with this book, there are insights about the religious, economic, social, legal, administrative, educational and political agency of Muslim women between c.1850 and 1950. We learn about women who were forthright and vocal champions of women's rights in Islam and in public life more generally, alongside women who gave decades of unseen quiet labour that enabled the developing infrastructure of Muslim communities and organizations. The vibrancy of Islam in Britain today rests on their shoulders. Some of the women we read about had to make brave and costly choices. Others had a fluctuating relationship to Islam. In the humane and insightful accounts that follow, the stories of the women we meet arguably speak to women in the world today, everywhere, who are on their own journeys of discovery, sometimes in very difficult circumstances. This book is a reminder that within our midst, the most quiet and unassuming women may, in time, come to be known and appreciated as the heroines of tomorrow.

Professor Sophie Gilliat-Ray
Cardiff, January 2023

SECTION 1

WHY UNCOVER MUSLIM WOMEN'S HISTORY?

INTRODUCTION

WHY UNCOVER THE HISTORY OF
MUSLIM WOMEN IN BRITAIN?

Sariya Cheruvallil-Contractor and Jamie Gilham

Mrs Fatima Sheir: The woman on the cover of this book

First, the story behind the photo on the front cover of this book. Richard Stone took this picture in 1943 during his time as a photographer with the Photo Division of the Ministry of Information, a British government department responsible for publicity and propaganda during the Second World War which was dissolved in 1946. Established at the end of the First World War, it was revived in 1939 'to counteract the psychological offensives of the Nazi propaganda machine'.[1] Its main purpose was 'To promote the national case to the public at home and abroad in time of war'.[2] The Ministry also aimed to build morale and garner support for the war within the British Isles, using posters, broadcasts, news and books to foster a shared sense of British national self-identity and emphasizing 'shared values' such as resilience, pragmatism, humour, patriotism and unity. To this end, and no doubt to also rally support amongst Britain's many millions of colonized Muslim subjects, in 1943, the Ministry of Information commissioned a series of photographs depicting everyday life in the well-established Muslim community of Butetown (popularly known as Tiger Bay) in Cardiff, South Wales. The photograph of Mrs Sheir was taken for that series.[3]

3

What do we know about the woman in the picture? Not much, other than what we can glean from the image and the short caption that accompanies it:

> Young Muslim girls learn about Islam as they receive teaching in the home of Hussein Sheir, the Secretary to Sheikh Hassan Ismail. Mrs Fatima Sheir reads from the Koran to the girls as they all sit on the floor in front of the fire in the living room. All are wearing headscarves.[4]

Yet, in a clichéd manner, the image tells much to its viewer, especially if we juxtapose the photograph with what we know about Cardiff's Butetown in the first half of the twentieth century. The photograph is staged; it is an action image. Mrs Sheir is educating young Arab-Welsh (or Welsh-Arab) Muslim girls. The photo emphasizes the importance placed on the education of girls and women by the local Muslim community's imam (religious leader), Shaykh Hassan Ismail—a priority which was occasionally at odds with prevalent patriarchal attitudes of the time, British as well as Yemeni or Arab.[5] That Mrs Sheir, a visible Muslim, is teaching the girls in her community, challenges common perceptions or assumptions that Muslim women of the period were silent, invisible, and without agency or a voice within their communities. The different skin tones of teacher and students in the photograph is indicative of the ethnic diversity of wartime Butetown; that they are studying together, seemingly contentedly, reflects what we now know about the relative intra-ethnic cohesion of the Muslim community of Butetown during the war. Finally, Mrs Sheir and many of her students are wearing headscarves. The style of the headscarves and their dresses, as well as the fact that not all of the girls have their heads covered, suggests the ways in which these early British Muslim communities adapted and indigenized Islam, maintaining aspects of religious practice from overseas whilst also making it English, Welsh, and British. Yet, beyond what the photo indicates, we know very little about even the most basic facts of Mrs Sheir's life and work.

The image of Mrs Sheir represents a moment in time but also hints at the power dynamics behind its existence. Whereas much is known about the powerful organization that commissioned it, almost nothing is known about its subjects. This creative tension in the recording of history is central to the aim of the present book. It uncovers the stories of Muslim women who lived in Britain during the century from around 1850. In doing so, it recognizes and challenges the impact of societal hierarchies in how we know and tell history. Not much is known about Mrs Sheir, because as a Muslim woman she was not seen as a significant maker of history. The many aspects of her identity, as a woman, a Muslim, in all likelihood from a working-class background (Butetown was a working-class district), positioned her as unimportant in the annals of history. Incidentally, we have not been able to uncover much about Richard Stone, the photographer, who would have had his own intersectional identity.

That this image exists is partly because the Ministry of Information felt the need to curate images of model Muslims, in ways that mirror contemporary politics and debates around 'shared British values'. Although it was in existence for less than a decade, plenty has been written about the Ministry and its work.[6] While this book does not uncover Mrs Sheir's story, it does tell those of other Muslim women who lived during and before her lifetime. We have used Mrs Sheir's image on the cover of this book and dwelt on it here for two main reasons: first, to interrogate the power dynamics that have so far rendered Muslim women less visible in Western (and specifically British) history than men and non-Muslim women; and second, as an invitation to scholars, students, community historians—in fact, anyone interested in the history of Islam in Britain—to uncover the stories of Mrs Sheir and her female contemporaries. In the photograph of Mrs Sheir teaching the Butetown girls, there is a mirror hanging over the fireplace in which reflected images of both Mrs Sheir and her young students are clearly visible. Representations of history, indeed of Muslim women's history, are mediated—reflections of how they themselves, their societies, and their communities perceived them. Just as that mirror in Mrs Sheir's front room does, this book offers its reflections on a small number of Muslim women who lived in Britain between the mid-nineteenth and mid-twentieth centuries.

Uncovering the history of Muslim Women in Britain

Uncovering Muslim women's experiences and contributions to society is essential to building a full picture of Muslim life in Britain in the past. The history of Islam and Muslims in Britain is a growing area of study that garners much public interest. In recent years, numerous books and articles have been published about the general history of Islam and aspects of Muslim life in Britain in the late-nineteenth and early twentieth centuries.[7] However, whilst Muslim women feature in some studies, their lives and experiences remain obscure, if not hidden, both in academic and public discourse, which tend to emphasize the experiences of Muslim men. A research article by one of this book's editors has highlighted the significant social and leadership roles that women played in nascent British Muslim communities and also uncovered evidence of the challenges they faced.[8]

Ours is the first book to address the gap in the literature by documenting Muslim women's lives and experiences in Britain in the past. It includes women from the Victorian period to the years immediately after the Second World War, just before immigration profoundly affected the size and composition of Britain's Muslim communities. It reveals a variety of stories, of Muslim women who travelled to Britain or away from it, and many more who converted to Islam within the British Isles. Our knowledge and understanding about Muslim women in British history is currently very fragmented and incomplete. Consequently, rather than attempt to create a conventional—and potentially misleading—narrative by placing the chapters in chronological order, we have arranged them according to four broad themes:

1. Why uncover Muslim women's history? (Chapter 1)
2. Muslim women in the first British mosques (Chapters 2, 3 and 4)
3. British Muslim women and expanding spheres of influence (Chapters 5, 6 and 7)
4. Muslim women in Britain: sojourners, settlers, legacy-makers (Chapters 8 and 9).

INTRODUCTION

Many Muslim women lived in communities that evolved around the first prayer rooms, and later mosques, in ports such as Liverpool, Cardiff, Hull, Glasgow, East London, and South Shields, where from the nineteenth century onwards Muslim sailors (or lascars) settled, some of whom married local British women.[9] As the Victorian period progressed, Muslim women congregated around mosques in Liverpool and Woking, both of which were established in 1889, and then London and other urban areas in the early twentieth century.[10] Chapter One tells the story of one Cardiff port woman, Olive Salaman (1921–2007), who defied social conventions by marrying an Arab Muslim immigrant and converting to Islam. Salaman worked within and for her marginalized Muslim community, consistently demonstrating her agency and commitment to Islam. In the Liverpool and Woking mosque communities, the women were mainly British converts, who often encountered Islam through Muslim missionaries and their public lectures and publications. Some, especially upper- and middle-class British converts, discovered Islam abroad during their travels, primarily in the Middle East and South Asia. Two women connected to the Liverpool Muslim community led by the charismatic Abdullah Quilliam (1856–1932), Fatima Cates (1865–1900) and Nafeesah M. T. Keep (1844–1925), are discussed in Chapters Two and Three respectively. Both women were pioneers of Islam in Britain (and, in the case of Keep, her native United States) who endured great hardship and struggles due to their conversions to Islam. The Liverpool and Woking communities also hosted distinguished travellers from Muslim countries and scores of Muslim workers and students from across the globe; they attended services and events at the Liverpool Muslim Institute (LMI) and Woking Mosque, but their roles in these communities are still little known, and their women seldom accompanied them.

Muslim women played central roles in the establishment of Britain's first known mosques. Fatima Cates was the founding treasurer of the Liverpool Muslim Institute, and Shahjahan Begum (1838–1901), Muslim ruler of the Indian state of Bhopal, helped fund Woking Mosque. Chapter Four considers Shahjahan Begum's daughter and successor, Nawab Sultan Jahan (1858–1930), who, like her mother, was a patron of Woking Mosque and Muslim Mission (established in 1913). The chapter examines how Nawab Sultan Jahan's example and writings, both on their own and when considered alongside other Woking Muslim Mission discourses, reveal an understanding of Muslim femininity as both an issue of real importance and an essentially fluid concept during the First World War era. Until relatively recently, the roles of both Cates and Nawab Sultan Jahan remained largely unheard in historical accounts of the Liverpool and Woking mosques respectively and the Muslim communities that formed around them.[11] Their gender was a cloak that marginalized them at best or, in the case of Cates, rendered them almost invisible.

Of course, not all Victorian and Edwardian British Muslim women in Britain belonged to the more formalized Muslim communities in Woking or port cities like Liverpool. Contrary to popular belief, many of the Muslim women who had loose associations or were not connected with these distinct communities were from working- as well as upper- and middle-class backgrounds. Regardless of their class or social status, they converted to Islam for a variety of reasons, often after privately studying the religion or meeting Muslims (including future husbands) at home or abroad. The next three chapters of this book explore the lives of three such women, all of whom happened to spend a significant proportion of their lives overseas. Fatima Hannah Rodda Robinson (1854–1948), discussed in Chapter Five, was a working-class woman who converted to Islam after meeting an Indian Muslim trickster, whom she married. After separating from her husband, Robinson moved to Constantinople (Istanbul), where she received financial support from the Ottoman sultan's court. Robinson thereby escaped both the English class system and inevitable poverty in her homeland, living out her days as a relatively affluent socialite.

Bertha Cave (1881–1951) was also from a working-class English family. As discussed in Chapter Six, Cave was a woman ahead of her time; she attempted to join the legal profession when women were not permitted to do so. Like Robinson, Cave became a Muslim after meeting an Indian Muslim in London; they married and settled in India. Cave's marriage also failed; she returned to London and, in contrast to Robinson, without the support of the local Muslim community, her commitment to Islam faltered. Chapter Seven tells the story of a quite different Englishwoman: the aristocratic Gladys Milton Brooke (1884–1952), who married into the British ruling family of Sarawak on the north-west coast of Borneo. Whilst we know very little about the conversions of both Robinson and Cave, Brooke's unusual religious conversion ceremony—above the English Channel on a flight between London and Paris—was well-documented at the time, though her story has not previously been told in any detail. Like Robinson, Brooke left Britain, never to return permanently. She eventually settled in South Asia and, again like Robinson, retained her Muslim identity for the rest of her life.

Some Muslim women in Britain in the nineteenth and early twentieth centuries were visitors or temporary settlers from the British colonies and elsewhere. They came to Britain for leisure, work or studies, as discussed in Chapter Eight, which examines the fascinating stories of several Indian Muslim women who visited between the late nineteenth and early twentieth centuries. These women were highly educated, from elite or upper-middle-class families, who left published and unpublished accounts of their lives that enable us to partially reconstruct their experiences in Britain from the late-Victorian period through to the interwar years. The final chapter of this book examines the life of one of the most famous, and therefore well-documented, Muslim women in modern British history: the writer and spy, Noor Inayat Khan (1914–44). Indeed, much has been written about Noor, including several biographies, which have informed television and radio documentaries about her life and work.[12] Rather than replicate this material, Chapter Nine takes a fresh approach; written by Noor's direct descendant and drawing on family oral history, the chapter explores the complex and nuanced manner in which Noor inhabited the contested categories of Britishness, Muslimness and heroism.

How did the various signifiers within which this book identifies its subjects—British, Muslim, female—manifest in these women's lives? Crucial to this book are ideas of intersectionality that highlight the multiple realities and layered identities that shape individual identity.[13] Individuals and their complex identities also exist in social hierarchies that privilege and give voice to particular social actors. These same hierarchies marginalize and silence other social groups. An individual's identity is made up of their gender, ethnicity, religion, class, education, geographical location, and other characteristics that together determine how an individual is perceived and received by wider society, as well as how an individual perceives themselves. We suggest that theorization around intersectionality provides a useful lens through which to attempt to understand the complex identities of Muslim women in Britain's past.

While using the label or category 'Muslim women', this book aims to complicate and add nuance to understandings of what it means to be Muslim. The women in this book had different relationships with Islam and Muslim identity; some converted to Islam to marry their husbands—were these conversions of convenience or conviction? Where women were born into the faith, there is rich evidence of diversity in Islamic practice—what, if anything, did their Muslim identity mean to these women? Then there is the idea of the indigenization of Islam in Britain—how did these women negotiate a form of Islamic practice and identity that bridged their different cultural worlds? While this book by no means offers definitive answers to any of these questions, like the mirror in Mrs Sheir's front room, it offers reflections on these women and the historical, social and cultural contexts they inhabited.

Remembering and forgetting Muslim women: What can historical sources tell us?

The women (and men) of the pioneering Liverpool Muslim Institute are known through their writing or references to them in the Institute's core publications like *The Crescent* (1893–1908), a weekly newspaper that included brief commentary of everyday life at the LMI, reports of marriages, deaths and celebrations at the LMI, and *The Islamic World* (1893–c.1907), a more scholarly periodical that initially appeared monthly to document issues relating to Islam around the globe. Both publications were edited by the LMI president, Abdullah Quilliam, and through them, readers today are introduced to women such as Fatima Cates (Chapter Two) and Nafeesah M.T. Keep (Chapter Three), along with several others who wrote for or had formal roles at the LMI. We are also introduced to many more women only by name because their conversions to Islam were eagerly reported in the pages of *The Crescent*. These sources provide readers with a sense of attitudes towards gender in the Victorian and Edwardian period. Such everyday detail of life at the Woking Mosque and Muslim Mission remains beyond the reach of historians today, as its activities were, compared to the LMI, poorly recorded at the time. However, its monthly journal, *The Islamic Review* (1913–c.1971), includes brief vignettes about women, mainly British converts to Islam, and numerous articles written by women. The same is the case for the London Mosque Mission, which was based in the mosque in Southfields from the 1920s; its publications, including the monthly *Review of Religions* (founded in 1902), provide tantalizing glimpses, but frustratingly little more, of some Muslim women's lives in Britain during the interwar years and beyond.

Of course, as discussed above, not all Muslim women in Britain in the period covered in this book were affiliated with a community. Take for example Lady Evelyn Zainab Cobbold (1867–1963), an aristocrat who converted to Islam shortly before the First World War. She is well-known today as one of the first British women to make the Hajj (pilgrimage to Mecca), in 1933. Extraordinarily for her time, she performed the pilgrimage independently, albeit supported by some well-connected people in Arabia, and wrote a book about her experiences shortly thereafter.[14] Because her story is so well-known today, it may be assumed that this was always the case. But just twenty years ago, Cobbold's life and work had been nearly forgotten outside of her immediate family. The three books she published in her lifetime were long out of print. If remembered at all, Cobbold tended to be considered an eccentric character and/or relegated to footnotes in books about the Hajj, Western travellers to the Middle East, or the many tomes about the British soldier and writer, T. E. Lawrence (1888–1935), whom Cobbold first met in 1914. When the new sixty-volume edition of the *Oxford Dictionary of National Biography* was published in 2004, several (male) Muslims were included for the first time, but Cobbold was not. That Cobbold's story was subsequently uncovered (and she was finally included in the *Oxford Dictionary of National Biography* in 2007)[15] was due to historians discovering a cache of her personal papers, still held privately in her family, and reading her out-of-print books.

When showing the editors of this book Cobbold's personal papers, her great-grandson picked up a copy of a Qur'an that Lady Evelyn received during her Hajj in 1933. He noted that this was a free copy that the Saudi government gifted to all Hajj pilgrims at the time. It is extraordinary that this mass-produced and fragile copy of the Qur'an has survived. At the time of its publication, it had little monetary value and only limited social significance. Cobbold's is possibly the only copy that has survived, certainly in Britain, because it belonged to a wealthy woman who had the time and means to preserve it, along with other personal documents and artefacts from her long life. We found it intriguing and moving that the family still has a trophy from a pony race that Lady Evelyn won when she was eleven years old. That Cobbold's papers, albeit a fraction of them, exist facilitates the telling of her story, and it has now been told well.[16] It is possible that stories of other upper-class British Muslim women (for example, Gladys Brooke in Chapter Seven), and possibly some middle-class women as well, from the nineteenth and early twentieth centuries (and earlier) can still be uncovered and made accessible through such private papers, although there will of course always be gaps in the stories historians tell.

The surviving archival sources about working-class Muslim women, including those who lived in British ports, is much more limited, often snippets of information and anecdotes, as is discussed in Chapter 1 in relation to Olive Salaman. It has been possible to tell her story thanks to oral history interviews recorded with her at the beginning of the twenty-first century. As far as we know, the literal voices of all the other women discussed in this book have not been preserved and therefore cannot be heard. The unique recordings of Olive's voice underline the importance of this method to help record and preserve seldom heard and marginalized groups, not least Muslim women in Britain and elsewhere.

A note on our intellectual positionality

Historians can be shy of writing about methodology but, as a sociologist, Cheruvallil-Contractor's training demands that we present a short note on the methodologies we have employed. As this book is a joint endeavour between a sociologist and a historian, with contributions from scholars from various disciplines (history, sociology, law, international relations, literature and cultural studies) as well as community figures, in this section we reflect briefly on why we set out to produce this volume and what matters to us intellectually.

The editors of this book are a sociologist (Cheruvallil-Contractor) and a historian (Gilham). We work from within different academic disciplines but have a shared interest in applying a historical lens to Islam and Muslims in Britain. We both recognize a need from young British Muslims especially to understand the history of Islam in Britain. We both feel strongly that uncovering and reconstructing the history of Islam in Britain is essential to tell the complex history of Britain and its global empire. We also realize that, while the history of Islam is being gradually uncovered in this twenty-first century, Muslim women's stories have remained largely unexplored. Our aim for this book is simply that Muslim women's stories are known.

For this research, we largely work with a feminist historical approach to reinstate Muslim women as actors, storytellers and story makers who shaped the history of what is often described today as 'British Islam'. We draw upon the work of June Purvis and other scholars of women's history who argue that, as the authors of history in the past were largely men, women's contributions remain unrecognized.[17] Feminist historical approaches make women visible where they have been hidden within history, situating their contributions in wide societal contexts. Additionally, we use theories of lived religion to develop understandings of everyday religious life as messy, as entailing complex, untidy negotiations with textual religion, and as being a determinant of an individual's religious identity, which often differs from official doctrine.[18] The chapters in this book attempt to unravel and unpick the 'messiness' and 'negotiations with religion' in the lives of the women on whom they focus. The extent to which this is possible ultimately depends on the amount of archival and other resources available.

Uncovering the history of minoritized groups endows both them and their wider communities with agency. By understanding these stories, both sides of this artificial dichotomy are empowered with a better understanding of their roles in the past. History thus becomes political and agentive. Achieving such an empowering narrative of Muslim women's history is the overarching aim of this book.

Conclusions, or seeds for more storytelling?

This is the first book to focus solely on the history of Muslim women in Britain. As we write this conclusion, our hope is that it inspires more research using archival and, where possible, oral history methods to shed light both on those women who actively helped to build British Islam and also those women who happened to be Muslim in Britain in the past. As noted above, the history of Islam and Muslims in Britain is a relatively young subject, and there is much more to be uncovered, not least in relation to the lives, experiences and contributions of women.

This history is also being appreciated and acknowledged as part of the building blocks of British society more widely. Indeed, two English Heritage blue plaques—which are used 'to celebrate prominent individuals and mark other significant historical associations' (a complex and often controversial task)—have recently been installed in London.[19] They are dedicated to Noor Inayat Khan (2020) and a group of women known as *ayahs* (nannies or nurse maids) from South and East Asia, some of whom were Muslim (2022).[20] So much more needs to be uncovered and learnt about the women and their communities discussed in this book, as well as the great many others about whom we know little or nothing as yet.

Epilogue: Jane Digby, another story

As we were in the throes of editing this volume in autumn 2022, the BBC broadcast a new eight-part television adaptation of Jules Verne's classic novel, *Around the World in Eighty Days*. In episode three, when the protagonists are in Yemen, a white British woman in Islamic garb appears. Her name is Jane Digby—a scandalous woman who, the viewers are told, after multiple relationships married a Muslim Arab camel herder. The female protagonist of the drama wants nothing to do with this disreputable woman. As the drama proceeds, Jane proves herself to be a valuable and trustworthy ally. It then transpires that Jane's husband is not a camel herder, but a Bedouin prince.

Many viewers assumed that Jane was a fictional character. In fact, Jane Digby (1807–81) was a real English aristocrat who, as described in the drama, married four times and had numerous other relationships with some high-profile men. In Britain, she was derided as promiscuous, whereas the men in her life tended to keep their reputations intact. In 1853, at the age of forty-six, Digby travelled to the Middle East. In Syria, she met and married a Bedouin shaykh (leader of a local tribe) and took the name Jane Digby el Mezrab. Back in Britain, she was again much maligned in the press and, as the BBC drama indicates, her influential husband was described as a lowly camel herder. The marriage was, by all accounts, a very happy one. Jane Digby died in Damascus in 1881. She did not convert to Islam, but adopted Islamic cultural values, becoming known as the mother of her husband's tribe. That her story remains relatively unknown is symptomatic of the gap that this volume starts to fill.

1

UNEQUAL HISTORY

OLIVE SALAMAN AND (IN)VISIBILITY IN THE HISTORIES OF BRITAIN'S EARLIEST FEMALE CONVERTS TO ISLAM

Sariya Cheruvallil-Contractor

Introduction: Unequal history?

Olive Salaman (1921–2007) was a Welsh woman who fell in love with a Yemini sailor named Ali Salaman and married him in 1937— in her words, causing a 'stir' in her family and her community. In marrying her sailor, she 'swapped one culture for another'.[1] Far from leading a quiet or secluded life, she was visible in her community. In 2005, Patricia Aithie described Olive as the 'mother of the Yemenis' in Cardiff's *Bilād al-Welsh* (Land of the Welsh).[2] This chapter tells her story, positioning it within the socio-cultural context of her time.

In port communities like Butetown (popularly known in Olive's time as 'Tiger Bay'), South Shields and East London, visiting sailors tended to live in boarding houses that were run by people of their own nationality and/or religion. Gradually, communities that were transitory gave way to more settled communities. Due to socio-political reasons, the first generations of Yemeni sailors to settle down in Butetown, and elsewhere in Britain, did not usually bring their women.[3] As they settled down, some married working-class women who converted to Islam to wed Muslim sailors. As noted by Sophie Gilliat-Ray and Jody Mellor, a number of graves in the Muslim section of Cardiff's Ely Cemetery record the names of Welsh women who married Muslim seafarers and adopted new Muslim names.[4] Their conversions took place in social contexts that viewed Islam and Muslims with suspicion and ridicule.[5] In fact, these women's marriages were pejoratively described as acts of miscegenation.[6]

As noted in the Introduction to this book, women are often rendered invisible in historical narratives due to a devaluing of their social contributions on account of their gender.[7] For working-class women like Olive Salaman, social class added another layer of invisibility, further cloaking these women's lives. Class boundaries have transcended from their lives into history to determine what is possible to uncover about them. Against this backdrop, this chapter sheds light on Olive Salaman's life, showcasing her agency and the endeavours she embarked upon for her community. It departs from a trope that positions Olive and other working-class Muslim women of the time as mute and having been forced or coerced to convert to a foreign faith. In uncovering and telling Olive's story, this chapter considers the power imbalances that determine how history is recorded and why certain stories are forgotten while others are remembered.

Challenging historical invisibility: The lack of sources about the port women

Compared to what is available about some of the other women whose lives have been explored in this book, the comparative lack of material (written or otherwise) about working-class Muslim women from the port cities is stark. As we shall see in Olive Salaman's story, these women came from communities that experienced precarious and difficult challenges—racism, prejudice towards their marriages and children, wars, financial insecurity, patriarchy and the problematic citizenship status of their husbands. Preserving their records and life histories was perhaps the last thing on their minds. Existing literature about them and their communities equates the absence of their voices and their historical silencing with their lack of agency. The photograph of these women in Fred Halliday's book about the first Yemeni communities in Britain, with their bodies and faces fully veiled, has come to characterize these women as being hidden, repressed and forced to follow a foreign faith.[8]

However, the few stories that survive provide remarkable evidence of these women's agency. They often married in opposition to their families' and society's views. That these women persevered in their choices to marry is agentive in itself. There are more visible markers of these women's agency. After their marriages, they acted as advocates and 'interlocutors' for their men and for their communities.[9] They had had an 'integrative influence' upon their menfolk.[10] They liaised between these men and government as well as other institutions, securing opportunities for them by acting as translators and intermediaries.[11] Ceri-Anne Fidler tells the story of Mrs Mary Fayal who took charge of her husband's passport application and protested to the India Office on his behalf when he was considered an 'alien'.[12] In 1930, a 'wife of an Arab sailor' responded to negative coverage in a local newspaper in South Shields about Arab and Yemeni sailors:

> Half the Englishmen on the dole are there through their own fault, being too lazy to look for work [...]. They are forgetting it's the coloured man's country they depend on. What would England do if Arabs were to do the same to them as England is doing to the Arabs?[13]

From a feminist historian's perspective, it is important to recognize the intersectional social and cultural barriers that these women experienced on a daily basis and their agency in overcoming them. In addition to patriarchy and prejudice from within British society, after their marriages these women had to live with and challenge patriarchal attitudes from within their husbands' cultures too, which many of them had adopted. Despite this, these women displayed agency and leadership. When Shaykh Abdullah Ali al-Hakimi (a Yemeni Sufi teacher who was tasked by his spiritual mentor to visit Britain to serve and teach Muslims) arrived in South Shields in the 1930s, the British wives approached him for lessons in Islam, as they wanted to learn about their husbands' faith and culture. Al-Hakimi saw this as an opportunity for the intergenerational transmission of Islamic culture to the children of these families. He worked with these communities, including the men, to set up and deliver such sessions.[14] Halliday describes a twist to this narrative that highlights the patriarchy that women experienced from their husbands' cultures. As per Halliday's account, al-Hakimi's attempts to set up classes on the Muslim way of life for the British wives in South Shields were met with many obstacles, with the men ultimately blocking women's access to the educational spaces al-Hakimi had created for them. Halliday conjectures that this is what led him to leave South Shields and move to Cardiff, where he was successfully able to establish and sustain classes for Welsh-Yemeni women and their children.[15]

Olive Salaman's story takes us beyond these anecdotes and provides much needed detail to better understand the lives of the working Muslim women who lived in Britain's port towns, particularly Cardiff. Remarkably, there is around twelve minutes of audio-visual footage of Olive in a documentary produced by the BBC in 1968.[16] *Tamed and Shabby Tiger*, produced by Selwyn Roddren, documented Butetown residents' feelings regarding the redevelopment of their area and being moved elsewhere in Cardiff. In her interview for this documentary, Olive speaks about how she came to marry her husband and discusses her faith. We can actually hear and watch her speak, something that remains impossible for any of the other women discussed in this book. Olive's views and opinions are also preserved through three oral history interviews available at the National Archives of Wales in Aberystwyth. One was conducted in 2004 by Selwyn Roddren and Monique Ennis.[17] The second was conducted in 2006 by Monique Ennis.[18] And the third was a group interview conducted at some point in the 2000s (the record of the interview does not specify the date).[19] I have used this data in tandem with printed sources, such as an interview with Olive's son Daoud in which he talks about his memories of his mother, to attempt to tell Olive Salaman's story and situate it within the socio-political context of her time.[20]

Olive Salaman, the mother of the Cardiff Yemenis

Olive May Salaman was a Welsh woman who married a Yemini sailor, converted to Islam, lived through the Second World War, brought up her children, and ran a popular café with her husband in Cardiff's Butetown. She had ten children and went on to foster and adopt many more. According to her son, she fostered or adopted fourteen children, usually Muslim, but also others.[21] Through her mothering of these children and of her community in Butetown, she became known as 'the mother of the Cardiff Yemenis'—a legendary anchor of her community.

A cross-cultural marriage

Olive May Beverly Walls was born on 3 March 1921 to John Beverly Walls and Myfanwy Walls in Bedwellty in Rhymney Valley, South Wales. Her birth certificate lists her father's occupation as a Charabanc driver and an ex-army man. At some point, she and her family moved to Penygraig in the Rhondda Valley, and from there, aged fifteen, Olive went to Cardiff to train as a nurse in the Royal Infirmary. The Cardiff Olive moved to in 1936 was a divided city. In most parts, it was a 'well-laid out and spacious city', but Butetown had existed as a 'culturally, physically, socially and by legislation' separate town for over a century. Butetown was physically separated from Cardiff by a railway line, the docks, and the sea, only connected to it by a narrow tunnel under a railway bridge that led to Bute Street. Whereas Cardiff was elegant, respectable and safe, Butetown was characterized by disrepair and disrepute. While Cardiff was largely white, Butetown was a bustling, multicultural melting pot of sailors from different parts of the world that was viewed by outsiders with disdain and prejudice on one hand and seen as exotic and attractive on the other, hence its alternative name: Tiger Bay.[22] According to a 1941 report on Tiger Bay:

> Practically every race is represented here in an intricate pattern
> of inter-marriage and inter-illegitimacy. Half the whole coloured
> seamen population of Great Britain resides in Tiger Bay [...]
> largely inhabited by coloured seamen and their white wives and
> their half caste children.[23]

In 1919, riots broke out between unemployed white working-
class people from Cardiff and the residents of Butetown, with
the former accusing the latter of stealing their jobs and their
women.[24] The riots deepened cleavages between both sides of the
railway line. It was in this divided Cardiff, late one evening, that
Olive met a Yemeni man named Ali Salaman who was to be her
future husband:

> I'd been to the pictures in St Mary's Street. Came out and lost
> my way. [Mistakenly] making my way to the docks rather than
> to the town. I stopped and asked this boy, then, the way to
> Queen's Street and he said I was losing my way to the docks, and
> we started talking. I think we fell in love then and there. We got
> married when I was sixteen and three weeks, actually. I had five
> children before I was twenty-one. We had ten children, five boys
> and five girls.[25]

In 1937, Olive married Ali Salaman, transcending not just
ethnic, religious and linguistic boundaries, but also Cardiff's local
boundaries. She went from one side of the railway line to the other,
and the less desirable one at that. The marriage ceremony Olive
referred to above was likely to have been a Muslim ceremony, as
the marriage was not officially registered until 1940, at which
point Olive would have legally taken the surname Salaman. Olive
describes her husband as an orphan from Zabid in Yemen. He had
worked first with the British Camel Corps in Aden. After saving
some money, Ali moved to France, where he worked in a mint.
He then went to Cardiff. Olive's husband was not a sailor, but he
knew how to cook.[26] In Cardiff, he saw an opportunity to provide
boarding and food for Yemeni and other Middle Eastern sailors.
So, in rented premises at 236 Cairo Street in Butetown and using
second-hand furniture, Ali Salaman set up the Cairo Café and
Boarding House. Incidentally, the 1941 report on Tiger Bay cited

above, while generally disparaging and deeply critical about the environment, facilities, people, cafés and pubs of the area, rated the local 'Arabs' highly:

> The Arab Moslem [sic] community is [...] the best organised and most coherent racial group in Tiger Bay. The Arabs have a well-organised spiritual life, including daily services at 5 Arab boarding houses, so that visiting seamen are thoroughly contacted. The Arabs keep more to themselves than the other groups, and are less interested in the recreational life of Tiger Bay than the rest. They have their own lenders, societies and loyalties.[27]

After her marriage, Olive Salaman joined the Arab community of Butetown, working with her husband to run the Cairo Café, which became a hub for community life. She settled down in Butetown, living there for over thirty years. During the course of this time, Olive was an advocate and organizer for her community, fluidly moving between Welsh and Arab cultures. The BBC footage of Olive shows her walking through the café, comfortably greeting an elderly and distinctly Middle Eastern gentleman in Arabic, clearly at ease with the language and culture. In the interview, Olive reflects on her linguistic ability and her transcending of languages and cultures, reflecting on similarities between them:

> We only spoke Welsh at home and English. Now when I lived among the Arabs, I picked [up] Arabic. I think the Welsh and the Arabic language are very near to one another—that made it much more easier for me.[28]

In line with the socio-political attitudes of the time, the Salamans' marriage faced significant criticism. It caused a 'great stir' in Olive's family and wider community, and presumably, judging from the quote below, their marriage drew criticism from her husband's family in Yemen too:

> Their families were as much against them marrying Welsh girls as much as our families were against us marrying them. My family were very big Methodists. The priest told my mother I was marrying a heathen. They were not very happy. They finished with me, as far as I was concerned.[29]

Olive's family's criticism of her marriage was not unusual between the wars. By the mid-1930s, there had been a now infamous study of Liverpool's 'half-caste' children. The study had gained support from Cardiff residents, including from a Captain F. A. Richardson, who wrote to the *Western Mail* in July 1935 warning that:

> Hundreds of Arabs and other coloured seamen have settled in the city [...]. They construct their own places of worship in ramshackle sheds behind their boarding houses, and they mate with the type of women who are willing to accept them because there are none of their own kind to be had.[30]

In Olive's case, the estrangement from her family was not permanent, and she discusses how, 'years after when they saw I was happy and [Ali] was a good man they came round'.[31] In her 2004 interview, Olive adds that her grandfather, who was a deacon in the Methodist church, said that 'Ali was the best Christian he ever knew!'[32] Olive's narratives confirm that, while he was certainly not a Christian, Ali Salaman was a religious man who valued his faith, worked for the wellbeing of his community, and set up prayer spaces, including in the café:

> But my husband was a very, very religious man. During the war, the only mosque in Cardiff was bombed and he converted this [room at the back of the Cairo Café] into a mosque. It was the rear part of the restaurant. And it was his joy, the joy and pride of his life—his mosque and his religion.[33]

In another interview, Olive talks about the mosque at the back of the café as also having a 'little Arab school'. Here, the Muslim children of Butetown (and other children as we shall see later in this chapter) came to study Arabic or just to have fun. Olive describes her husband as 'living by his religion and not appearances'. In addition to the café mosque, he was instrumental in setting up other mosques and always gave to charity. Olive was proud that he was an honest man who made all payments on time and in full, leading a Jewish tradesman who received a payment from Ali Salaman to exclaim 'That's the first time an Arab paid a Jew'.[34]

Olive Salaman lived in an era that had quite different sensibilities to those in the twenty-first century, and she certainly considered the Jewish tradesman's comment as being complimentary towards her husband. In all the interviews and footage, Olive speaks fondly of her husband, explaining he never called her Olive, only 'Mrs'. Was this in keeping with Muslim *adab* (good manners), where one does not use first names either out of respect or as a form of endearment? From Olive's tone when she recalls this, it seems that it was the latter. On another occasion, she describes herself as lucky that she had 'a wonderful husband'. She recalls that Ali was ten years older than her, that he could not read or write, but that he could speak English and could count. She said that he had excellent business acumen and was careful with money, which was good for their café.

The video footage shows Olive Salaman walking inside the café that she ran with her husband, through a door to the back, and into the little mosque at the rear. This was not a ramshackle place of worship as described by Captain Richardson above, but one that was well-cared for. Olive tends to some flowers in the mosque. There is Islamic calligraphy in the background. A Middle Eastern man is reciting from what is presumably the Qur'an. Ali's mosque and faith are evidently dear to Olive, as we shall explore in the next section. After Ali Salaman died in 1965, Olive continued to run the café for a few years, until it closed down in 1968 due to 'regeneration' works in Butetown.

Olive's conversion, Hajj, and life-long commitment to Islam

Based on the evidence available, Olive had a happy and fulfilled married life. She accepted her husband's faith, raised a multilingual family, ran a successful business, and transcended two cultures. Olive converted to Islam at the time of her Muslim wedding ceremony. She does not dwell on her reasons for conversion in any of the recordings. Perhaps her conversion to Islam was inspired by her husband's clear and deep commitment to his faith. It is also possible she had no other choice—if she was to marry him, she had to convert. In any case, her family had made it clear that they wanted nothing to do with her if she married a man whom they described as 'Arab and heathen'. Despite not knowing her motivations for her initial conversion to Islam, it is clear that Olive developed an understanding and commitment to the faith that stayed with her for the rest of her life. In her 1968 interview for the BBC documentary, *Tamed and Shabby Tiger*, she states, 'I changed to Islam when we got married. Learnt the faith and really believe it's the one and only faith now.'[35]

Olive's commitment to Islam is displayed in various ways. In the same BBC interview, she states that 'of course my ambition is same as that of every Muslim to one day make the pilgrimage to Mecca'. Olive is alluding to the Hajj, which is a pillar of the Islamic faith—a pilgrimage that all Muslims must perform if they have the resources to do so. In her 2004 interview with Selwyn Roddren and Monique Ennis, she confirms that she did indeed perform the Hajj. It was a milestone moment in her life, as it is for most Muslims. By the time she had the resources to make the Hajj, her husband had died, and so she went with six Yemeni women. She combined her Hajj with a visit to one of her daughters who had married a Yemeni man and had settled in Ta'iz, Yemen.

The interview does not specify when exactly Olive made the Hajj, but she recollects that when visiting her daughter in Yemen she went to her husband's birthplace, Zabid. Here, she says, 'I bought a bag of earth. It is for my husband's grave. He died 20 years ago'. This places Olive's Hajj in the mid-1980s. She shares various details of her Hajj experiences, remembering the various Hajj rituals: sleeping in the open in Mina; picking up pebbles to perform ritual stoning of the devil; and running up the mountain before the sun rose to participate in this ritual. At the Ka'bah in Mecca, she proudly remembers pushing through a crowd of men to touch the black stone, which Muslims believe dates back to the time of Adam and Eve. From her memories, it is clear that the Hajj was an important moment in Olive's life, despite her husband's absence. Concluding her account of the Hajj, she reflects, 'You feel holy in Mecca'.[36]

From the sources we have, it is apparent that Olive was a reflective and articulate woman. The recordings of Olive Salaman are exceptional, in that they document her reflections, occasionally with intimate and moving detail around various aspects of her life, including her commitment to her faith. She speaks about how proud she was when her son Daoud was appointed as 'the Chairman of the Wales Islamic Centre at the Alice Street Mosque [in Cardiff]'. She recollects going to the mosque for '*Ids* (Muslim religious festivals) and then eating with her family. In the early 2000s, when she was in her eighties, Olive continued to fast and pray during Ramadan (the Muslim month of fasting) and celebrate '*Id* with her large family, whom she describes as 'Muslim, but not all practising'. John Bowen's distinction between 'practising' and 'believing' Muslims is useful in understanding the distinction Olive makes: whereas practising Muslims perform all aspects of Islamic worship and ritual, believing Muslims retain a Muslim identity but do not perform all aspects of Islamic worship.[37]

Other than not caring much for Arab food and her enduring love of chips, Olive does not allude to any conflicts between her Welsh and her Islamic identities.[38] Indeed, as mentioned previously, she almost seamlessly moved between and across the two.[39] While Olive does not discuss any conflicts between her birth and marital culture, adult children from other mixed-heritage families of the time speak about the everyday negotiations around culture that took place in their families. In the first episode of the 2011 BBC television series, *Mixed Britannia*, two adult children from marriages between white women and Middle Eastern sailors in another port town—South Shields—note the compromises that often characterized these marriages and family life. They recollected how their mothers ate pork or ham, despite their husbands considering this *haram*, or forbidden by Islamic law. In one case, the mother did this in hiding, while another woman ate pork with the full knowledge of her Muslim husband. As a compromise, the women ate these 'forbidden meats' only when their husbands were not at home and cooked them in pans used only for this purpose that were kept separate from other utensils.[40]

Olive does not mention conflict or compromise, but perhaps she negotiated between her cultures. From videos and images, it is evident that she did not wear a *hijab* (headscarf) that many Muslim women in her community wore. She is seen freely interacting with men in the café, which indicates that she did not conform to Muslim cultural norms around gender segregation that are likely to have been part of her husband's culture. Commenting on cross-cultural marriages in the 1930s, the broadcaster George Alagiah notes that families and couples found ways to navigate their cultural differences in ways that 'worked' for them.[41] In the case of the Salamans, that both of them ran the café together seems to indicate that this 'worked' for them. They were an entrepreneurial couple, who also had a strong sense of social responsibility. The café was a source of income as well as a way of serving their Butetown community through the mosque and the Arabic school. Incidentally, they also ran a business selling *halva* and other Middle Eastern sweets. Olive does not say when this was, but notes that they sold *halva* as far afield as Sheffield, 200 miles away in the north of England.

I was intrigued by what Olive had to say about the lack of provision for women in the café's small mosque. The interview offers insufficient context to understand whether she was issuing a complaint (feminist or not) about the lack of provision, which would be in line with contemporary debates in British Muslim communities. Only 28% of British mosques today have provision for women.[42] This is a regular focus of Muslim women's and men's activism in their calling for equitable access for both genders to mosques.[43] Alternatively, Olive's quote could also be viewed as a defence of Islam—that her mosque did not have access for women was not characteristic of Islam, and that mosques in the rest of the world did have space for women. Tantalisingly we will not know for sure what position, if any, Olive was taking:

> Of course this mosque is small because in Cardiff the women are not allowed to pray with the men, but in all other parts of the world, the mosques are built big enough to be divided so that the women and the men can hear the same Imam [Muslim religious leader], but not be seen by one another. We are hoping to have one in Cardiff like that.[44]

A final indicator of Olive's commitment to Islam is her narrative that, after her husband's death, she was comforted by the idea that he received blessings every time someone prayed in the little mosque he had established. Here, Olive alludes to the Islamic idea of *sadaqa jariya*, or acts of long-term charity or kindness, which continue to accrue rewards for the benefactor long after the initial act of charity. Such acts include planting a tree, providing someone with a source of livelihood, digging a well, or, as in Ali Salaman's case, building a place of worship. Olive Salaman's practice, belief and indeed her knowledge of Islam display a deep connection with her faith, as well as a developed understanding of its rituals and texts.

Family life during the Second World War

A key theme in Olive's 2006 oral history interview is her experience of the Second World War. Olive was seventeen years old when the war began in 1939. She had given birth to two children already and says that she had five more during the war. Her fourth child 'was born when the Japanese surrendered', i.e., in 1945. Just as it must have been for most families, this was a time of precarity, fear and austerity, with Olive and her family having to live with everyday risks to life and property. Food and other resources were scarce, and rationing was enforced by the government. Many British men, including immigrants, were drafted into the armed forces. Ali Salaman did not know enough English to join the British army. He also had a bad arm, from when a camel had bitten him during a previous job tending camels. Nevertheless, he joined the war effort. With a fellow Yemeni sailor turned Butetown resident, Mr Suttar, a Welshman named Arthur George, and the local parish priest from St Mary's Church, Father Garland, Ali Salaman became an air raid warden. The men went out together each night, watching for enemy planes and raising the alarm if any appeared, allowing residents to escape to the relative safety of bomb shelters.

During the war, business at the Cairo Café and boarding house continued as usual. At one point, Olive recollects that they had twenty-eight lodgers at the same time, all men from different nationalities working for the Merchant Navy. She and her husband had to expand the business to make space for the extra customers the war brought them in Butetown. Despite the business doing well, Olive remembers the war as a sad time, 'when you didn't know if you would wake up' the next morning.[45] She remembers that there was destruction all around Cardiff and that people were scared. On one occasion, a crew of fifty to a hundred Indian men, presumably from a merchant vessel, were at the boarding house. There was an air raid, and all the men rushed into the shelter. Olive and her children could not get in. Olive remembers that the men were hysterical, with some laughing and others crying. She could not do anything to help them. She was worried about her safety and that of her children, though, in the end, everyone was safe.

Olive describes the heavy bombing of Cardiff by German fighter planes: '[it felt as if] our houses were lifted and then came down again'.[46] She says, 'Cardiff retaliated with big guns'.[47] The Cairo Café survived the bombing, but other buildings and establishments did not fare well. A Norwegian sailors' home nearby was destroyed.[48] The block of houses next to Olive's house had a 'mine dropped on it'.[49] Another boarding house run by a Yemeni was bombed in an air raid and destroyed, except for its prayer room. According to Olive, nobody died on that occasion because at the time of the bombing, all the men were praying in the prayer room, which held up until the men escaped. Olive reflects, 'It was a miracle, like'.[50]

Family life was impacted by the severe uncertainties of war. Olive's husband was busy each night with his air raid warden role, leaving Olive to care for the children on her own. There was a bomb shelter opposite her house in Bute Street, where she and her children sheltered every time the siren signalled an air raid. The children were all well-trained on procedures during air raids, which they learned at school. They slept in their siren suits and had gas masks to use if necessary. Olive remembered the police station 'at the corner of our block—Bute Street Police Station' and the 'very kind police officer' who would help her usher her children into the shelter during air raids.[51] She, her children and the other residents had a bench to sit on and 'when the planes came we held our breath'.[52] Such was her fear during the war that even when air raids were not taking place, she slept with her children in the same bed, explaining, 'I pray to God that if they ever hit us that we will all go together'.[53]

According to Olive, the war was a hard time. Families had to live through the bombing in the night and then help clean up during the day. Food was rationed, and there was no recreation. Going to the cinema was out of the question, although Olive says that the radio was an important means of communication. She remembers listening to the radio for updates about the war: '... listening to Churchill's voice on the radio gave you spirit. All the different nationalities felt that way'.[54] And when Britain's and its allies' victory was announced, she recollects how 'very proud we were', emphasizing the pride that she and her multicultural Butetown community felt. While her immediate family was safe, Olive faced personal losses as a result of the war, including the death of two cousins. Olive's sister's fiancé who was in the Royal Air Force was also killed, and her enduring memory of the war was coloured by sadness: 'It was a sad time. Nothing is worth it'.[55]

Olive offers a few more reflections on the war that are worth noting. She explains that in Butetown, 'We all mixed', and during the war, 'We were a mixture. Everyone helped each other, whatever nationality or religion'.[56] Despite rationing, it was possible to get extra food, as the ships had supplies that sailors sometimes sold to Butetown residents. Another positive aspect about the war was that the Salaman's business grew. Regarding the enemy, Olive says, 'we didn't fight the Germans, we fought the Nazis', an astute reflection that does not stereotype an entire nation of people.[57] When asked about politics, wars and reducing violence, the solution Olive suggested is indicative of her confidence in her gender and in her own abilities to foster dialogue across barriers. Whatever underpinned Olive's thinking, we shall never know, but her idea certainly provides a sense of her personality. She suggests: 'Get all the men out and put the women in charge!'[58]

Diversity, pluralism, and conflict: Making a community

Writing about Butetown, Gilliat-Ray and Mellor note that it was set apart by 'an atmosphere of sociability, trust, and mutual assistance [...], largely deriving from the influence of women'.[59] This final section explores this sense of community and Olive's roles within it. Olive's reflection about the war as a time when people helped each other characterizes her perception of everyday life in Butetown during the war and before it. One particular story stands out: Olive remembers when 'an old Arab [who] was dying' wanted an apple, but there were no apples in the shops.[60] That evening, a group of American sailors came to dine in the Cairo Café. They were 'very generous' and because Olive knew that they would have supplies and rations on board their ship, she decided to tell them about the dying Arab and his last wish for an apple.[61] The next day, a bag of apples arrived at the café, which she took to the dying man straight away. She says he ate an apple 'like it was from heaven'.[62]

It is not clear whether this incident took place before, during or after the war, but two aspects of this story showcase the strengths of Olive's personality: first, Olive's concern about this old Arab man and his dying wish. She wanted to find him an apple and cared for this old man, just as she cared for the rest of her community. Second, she displayed her agency in asking the American diners for this apple, holding a belief in the kindness of humanity that is borne out in her comments about helping one another irrespective of nationality or religion. She was delighted to receive an entire bag of apples and rushed to take these to the dying man. Olive concludes her story by saying that there was 'a lot of goodwill' in Butetown.[63]

This 'goodwill' is reflected in a comment from historian and Butetown resident Neil Sinclair in the BBC documentary *Mixed Britannia*. At the time of the interview, Neil was an adult, but he reminisces about his childhood in Butetown, where, although not Muslim or Arab himself, he attended the Arab school at the back of the café:

> I used to go to the Cairo Café, and at the back of the Cairo Café, they had a little Arab school. And I used to go to the Arab School, and many of the kids used to go to the Arab school, even though we weren't Arabs or Muslims, for that matter. But because your friends were going, you wanted to go along. We were like a very integrated community.[64]

Throughout her interviews, Olive recalls the diversity in Butetown and in her café, where men 'from all the different nationalities' were residents at various times.[65] She remembers the gifts the men brought back. She felt that she and the other women were lucky to live in a seaport, as the men would bring 'things' back, special 'things' that were not easily available or too expensive in Cardiff.[66] During the war, these diverse people helped to keep each other safe as well as with 'clearing up after bombings'. Before the war and after, they tried to work together as much as possible. In addition to the positive and cohesive aspects of life in Butetown, Olive's narrative includes concerns around racism, rough behaviour, and having to keep the café closed whenever there was a big rugby match. She says that she 'was ashamed of drunk Welsh people. They came to the bay to look for trouble [...] we always get the blame'.[67]

Therefore, closing the café was safer. As noted previously, the Butetown Olive lived in (and which no longer exists) was separated from Cardiff. However, Cardiff Arms Park—a famous rugby and football ground—was only about ten minutes away from the town's entrance. After rugby matches, thousands of young Welsh men from the valleys who had come to watch the game would go to pubs along Bute Street for a drink.[68] Perhaps Olive is referring to young men such as these to be those looking for trouble.

There is a second salient point in Olive's quote—that she says 'we' always got the blame, suggests a sense that her sentiment of unfair treatment is also echoed by other minoritized people of the area. It is relevant here to reflect on the 1919 riots in Cardiff, which occurred only two years before Olive was born. A crowd of 2,000 people gathered outside Cardiff's Labour Exchange and began attacking non-white seamen. They also attacked a number of houses on Bute Street with shouts of 'fetch them out' and 'kill them'.[69] Halliday reflects on the abundance of Arab names in lists of those who were arrested and injured, although Arabs only constituted 20% of Cardiff's population at the time.[70] Halliday also describes the ways in which media coverage of the riots brought to the fore racist prejudices inherent in Welsh society.[71] Perhaps Olive's remark reflects her community's collective memory of this incident.

The latter years

Olive continued to run the café and live in Butetown until 1968. During this time, she remained an active member of the Yemeni community there. Olive describes intra-religious relations and frictions that arose in these latter years as the Yemeni Muslim community broke up into different religious factions. The *Daily Herald* hailed her as a peacemaker when she tried to mediate when a fight broke out between two rival Muslim Yemeni groups during Ramadan: According to the report, she tearfully said, 'This is a religious festival. It is a time for friendship'.[72] In 1968, she and most other Butetown residents had to move out due to regeneration works carried out by local government. Olive and her community did not have the money or the knowledge to effectively fight the local authorities. Most homes in Butetown were destroyed, and the residents were moved to different parts of the city. Olive's community was bulldozed. Sheikh Said, one of the leaders of the Yemenis in Cardiff at the time, lobbied the local authority, encouraging them to place all the Muslims together in particular residential areas. However, the council refused this.[73] Olive was moved to Grangetown, a different part of Cardiff. She had lost her community.

Olive was heartbroken. She felt in moving the residents out of Butetown and destroying their homes, the local government had 'broken the melody of the place'.[74] Olive recollects the story of an old man, Abdulla, who never left his home except to go to the bookmakers. She says 'demolition people' waited for him to go out, and then they demolished his house.[75] He too was heartbroken and never went to the bookmakers again.[76] Olive faced many changes.

She no longer had her community. '*Id* was different in that there were no big processions, and you could no longer slaughter a lamb in the street and have a communal '*Id* dinner. Indeed, in an interview for a local news outlet, she concludes:

> We were unique. They destroyed a beautiful community when they split us up. If they had built a street and re-housed them and went on like that we would have still been a community. But people had to move out to different parts of Cardiff and eventually they didn't want to come back.[77]

Olive died on 28 December 2007, leaving behind a large family that included sixty-two grandchildren and great-grandchildren.

Conclusion

Olive Salaman held multiple roles—as a wife, a mother and a restaurateur. Her son also fondly remembers a political position she had, as 'Chairman of the Conservative Club of the docks, which caused great problems among the community'.[78] Olive's is the story of many and one that she shares with her husband—it is *their* story. It is also the story of Butetown, the Yemenis and others. Finally, Olive's is the story of working-class women across Britain's many port towns.

Olive's story is different from others in this book, not just in the intersectionality her life represents between her gender, class and faith. She was Muslim, married to a Yemeni. Yet, in a moment that is reminiscent of Lady Evelyn Cobbold's declaration during her Hajj in 1933 that she was English, Olive recollects how she replied when during Hajj she was asked about her nationality. [79] She proudly responded: 'I'm Welsh'.[80] This statement demonstrates how Olive's Welshness remained important to her identity. Her story is also different in its charting of intimate, mundane and everyday detail of her life. This ordinariness positions Olive's story and agency as being unique to her specific circumstances while simultaneously being representative of working-class white Muslim women in Britain's ports—whose stories largely remain absent and unheard.

This case of Olive's heretofore absent story demonstrates the hierarchies and inequalities in how we record and tell history. Beyond this exposition on Olive's life, little exists regarding the lives of the working-class women from the ports. Where narratives of the port communities do exist, they are often by or about men. This imbalance in how history is recorded and the impact of class and gender (and other factors) needs to be more carefully considered as we reconstruct the lives of Muslims in Britain in the past.

SECTION 2

MUSLIM WOMEN IN THE FIRST BRITISH MOSQUES

2

FATIMA ELIZABETH CATES

THE LIFE AND STRUGGLES OF AN EARLY
VICTORIAN CONVERT TO ISLAM

Hamid Mahmood

Introduction

This chapter examines the life and struggles of Fatima Elizabeth Cates (1865–1900), one of the first known female converts to Islam in Britain. As a key early member of Abdullah Quilliam's (1856–1932) Liverpool Muslim community, Cates is often cited in discussions about the Liverpool Muslim Institute (LMI), yet little has been written about her life. She was born Frances Elizabeth Murray in Birkenhead on the Wirral, near Liverpool in 1865. Her father John Murray, an Irishman, was a porter at Birkenhead Market, which was within walking distance from their home, and her mother was Agnes Murray, *née* Mitchell.[1] From the outset, Frances' life was characterized by adversity and sorrow. John Murray died when Frances was just five years old, leaving her mother Agnes as the head of the family.[2] From then on, Frances looked up to her brothers, David and William. Three years after John's death, Frances' mother married Peter Cottam, a stone mason.[3] This union was blessed with a daughter, Clara, who later as a teenager was inspired by Frances to accept Islam.

Frances' route to Islam via the Temperance Movement

Understanding the cause of John Murray's untimely death at the age of forty-four may give insight into Frances' later journey to Islam. Her father died from presumed pulmonary tuberculosis and suffered from a skin infection, phlegmonous erysipelas, for the last six weeks of his life.[4] The skin infection was most probably caused by the tuberculosis, and it is possible that his immune system was further suppressed by the over-consumption of alcohol. This might have influenced Frances to join the Temperance Movement, which was thriving in late nineteenth-century Liverpool. The erosion of family life and rise in poverty in that city led to the promotion of temperance and teetotalism, or a complete abstinence from alcohol. Teetotalism was promoted by men as well as women who were keen to affect change and uphold morals. The Movement in Liverpool, as elsewhere, also gave women a public voice. Indeed, it was through the Temperance Movement that Frances found hers.

Across the River Mersey, Liverpool was described as 'the most drunken, the most criminal, the most pauper oppressed, and the most death-stricken town in England'.[5] The Temperance Movement began to address the large numbers of drunken sailors in the Liverpool docks. As a young woman, Frances was an advocate for teetotalism and regularly attended temperance meetings at the Birkenhead Workingmen's Temperance Association.[6] In the late 1880s, she heard about a local solicitor and prominent teetotaller, Mr Quilliam, and a lecture he had given under the auspices of the Liverpool Temperance League at Vernon Hall in the city. Frances attended a lecture entitled 'The Great Arabian Teetotaller' that Quilliam gave at the Queen's Hall in Birkenhead for the local Workingmen's Temperance Association.[7] Quilliam began by discussing well-known men in the spheres of invention and social reform—including the civil and mechanical engineer George Stephenson (1781–1848) and the campaigner against slavery William Wilberforce (1759–1833). Quilliam elucidated how 'each of these leading figures had resisted persecution and ridicule and had dedicated their talents towards their goals.'[8] He said that, 'in spite all of that opposition, the effects of their achievements and reform that have gained global recognition—they have spread and have benefited humanity a great deal.'[9] He then—to the surprise of Frances—continued his talk by introducing Prophet Muhammad to the audience:

> This master reformer came with a clear message inviting people to what is good and beneficial. In spite of this, he had to face harm and persecution, just like any other great reformers who have been dedicated to the welfare of people. Later on, when people realised the value of his message and believed him, they entered Islam in large groups and continued to do so until their numbers reached hundreds of millions, right across the world.[10]

Frances was intrigued by Quilliam's account of the Prophet of Islam and Islam's prohibition of intoxicants, including alcohol. As an inquisitive and questioning nineteen-year-old, following the lecture, she approached Quilliam and reputedly asked: 'Isn't it true, that the Muslim Prophet said that women do not have souls and will not go to Paradise?' Quilliam replied that '[It] is not true'.[11] Until this point, Frances knew only of Muhammad from negative Victorian propaganda: 'I always heard about Mahomet described as an imposter and a blood-thirsty man, who forced people to believe in his religion by threatening to put them to death, if they did not do so'.[12]

Quilliam gave Frances a copy of the Qur'an to read and discover Islam for herself. This was the beginning of a journey with many trials ahead. Frances would bring home many books to read, but her devotion to this particular book was intense and, according to her own account, raised the suspicions of her mother. When Agnes asked her daughter what she was reading, she replied: 'The Mahommedan Bible.' Agnes could not believe it: 'How dare you read such a vile and wicked book? Give it to me this moment and let me burn it. I will not allow such trash to be in my house'.[13] Enraged with anger, Agnes attempted to take the Qur'an from Frances so that she could burn it. Frances held onto the Qur'an and escaped to her room. This made her more devoted to reading what she later considered to be the most precious book that could be had:

> I was continually scolded and threatened with all kinds of punishments if I continued to read such a book, but all to no purpose; for I persisted in reading it, and finally I had to carry the Koran about with me, or during my absence it would have been destroyed.[14]

Frances wrote to Quilliam and joined some of his meetings at Mount Vernon Street. As Quilliam noted, at this time, the only people to attend were himself, two English converts and Frances: 'the ragamuffins of the neighbourhood broke our windows with stones or pelted us with mud and filth as we either entered or came out of the room'.[15] Frances was threatened and castigated at home and in the street, but this did not prevent her from attending Quilliam's meetings at Mount Vernon Street. On one occasion, as Frances made her way across the Mersey to attend a meeting, she was surrounded by a group of mobsters; they pinned her to the ground and rubbed horse manure on her face.

Despite this opposition, Frances converted to Islam in July 1887 and took the Muslim name Fatima. Taking the *shahada* (the Islamic testimony of faith) changed her life forever.[16] She lost the support of her family, friends and colleagues. Consequently, Fatima's life revolved around Quilliam and his small group of English converts. The community grew and, in 1889, moved to permanent premises at Brougham Terrace on West Derby Road in Liverpool. Fatima was elected first treasurer of what had become the Liverpool Muslim Institute.[17] That same year, Fatima married Hubert Henry Cates, a marine engineer by profession. The couple married at the Cathedral Church of St Peter in Liverpool.[18] When they first met, Cates was unfavourable towards Fatima's conversion. He was, she recalled,

> a Christian just as prejudiced and bigoted as my mother, and their views being the same both tried to keep me from the mosque, but in vain. He, seeing I was still determined to follow it up, and thinking there must be some truth in it, commenced likewise

to read the Koran, then to attend the lectures, and finally, I am happy to say, he has become one of the votaries of our faith.[19]

Fatima in the early days of the Liverpool Muslim Institute

For the first year after Fatima's conversion to Islam, she was the only female convert amongst a small group of men, mostly from Liverpool, who attended weekly meetings and explored passages from the Qur'an. Gradually, a few more women joined her in Islam at the LMI. Dr Henry Martyn Clark, a Christian visitor to the Institute in 1891, observed 'there is nothing of devotion about any of them, except some of the women'.[20] How were women treated at the LMI, and what role did Fatima play in its organization?

When Dr Clark, who was well-versed in the cultural and religious practices of the Muslims of India, interviewed Quilliam in 1891, he pressed the latter about the role of women at the LMI, questioning why members of the 'congregation' mixed freely, why the women were not veiled and wore their everyday clothes, and how it was that women were apparently involved in the governance of the Institute. When Dr Clark asked 'Is your treatment of women according to Islam?', Quilliam replied:

> We try to observe the spirit of the Koran. We maintain the spirit of Islam [which] gives women very large rights, larger in some instances than are given by the law of England. We do not try to put the women into an inferior position or anything of the kind; we should be loath to do it. We regard this rule the same as we do as to veiling; we take the words of the Koran literally to mean that they should hide their ornaments, but we do not insist on their being closely veiled.[21]

Dr Clark, however, shared the view of the two Indian seamen he had met earlier at the LMI, that its nature was '*behudgi* and *besharmi*', or absurd and immoral with an absence of modesty, though the men had concluded apologetically '*jaisa des waisa bhes*', or 'When in Rome, do as the Romans do'.[22]

When Clark visited Liverpool in 1891, the LMI was in its infancy. Within five years or so, the LMI was well-structured with a programme of weekly lectures, regular events and an educational programme. As treasurer, Fatima Cates submitted the Institute's first annual reports, which were then adopted subject to an auditor's report.[23] However, by 1893 she had been replaced and instead was demoted, for reasons unknown, to one of several female members of a new committee to oversee the development of a new initiative, an LMI day school for girls.[24] She then became a member of the LMI Ladies Committee and was re-elected to that position in 1895, when a male Muslim, W. Abdur-Rahman Holehouse, was elected LMI treasurer.[25] From 1896 onwards, Fatima was no longer listed as a member of the Ladies Committee.[26]

Writing and outreach

From the start, Fatima wrote on behalf of the LMI and about Islam in England to newspapers and other publications, presumably with Quilliam's blessing. In 1890, for example, she wrote to 'a native gentleman of Hyderabad' with 'a request for assistance in converting the British people [to Islam]'. Consequently, it was reported that 'the leading Moulvies [*alims*, or learned scholars qualified to offer Islamic legal opinions] of Hyderabad have opened a subscription list for that purpose'.[27] The following year, in April 1891, Fatima contributed to a lengthy correspondence in the *Liverpool Mercury* begun by 'Esperanza', who was later described as a 'learned married woman' about 'The Marriage Question'. For Esperanza, 'in the majority of cases the matrimonial bond does not bring with it the happiness, satisfaction and comfort anticipated by the contracting parties on entering it'.[28] The *Liverpool Mercury* inevitably received many responses to Esperanza, some in appreciation of her original statements, others severely rebuking her. To one female critic, Esperanza sarcastically recommended that they 'should join the new Mahometan cause now started in Liverpool. Their ideas of "forbearance" would probably be somewhat similar to hers—rather Eastern'.[29] The correspondence struck a chord with Fatima, partly because of Esperanza's evident disdain for the LMI and Islam but also because Fatima's marriage was in disarray after her husband began to physically abuse her.

Her lengthy response to Esperanza was published in the *Mercury* on 16 April and is important, not least because it is one of the few known published pieces by her:

> Gentlemen, Your correspondent 'Esperanza' in one of her recent letters recommended one of your other correspondents to join the Moslem Church of Liverpool, as their views with reference to the control of wives would be more in accordance with his, and thereby insinuated that the state of the marriage laws amongst Mahommedans was even more unsatisfactory than in Christian England.
>
> This is one of the vulgar errors into which persons whose whole knowledge of Mahommedanism is derived from reading books and pamphlets written by bigoted Christian missionaries and others, so often fall into. Therefore permit me, as a Moslem lady and wife, to at once say that Mahommedan ladies enjoy, and have done so ever since the time of the Prophet, much greater legal rights as to separate property and divorce than those enjoyed by Christians up to quite a recent date.
>
> The Mahommedan lady on marriage does not lose her personality, and is entitled to hold property in her own right to a far greater extent than married females in this country are allowed even under the various Married Women's Property Acts that have emanated from the Legislature within the last 25 years. Space will not permit me to give instances of these; but if your correspondent will study the article by the vice-president of our institute [Rafiuddin Ahmed, 1865–1954], which appeared in the last number of the *Asiatic Quarterly Review*, she will find the whole subject dealt with most exhaustively. And now with regard to the marriage question. The whole and sole trouble in connection with the marriage and divorce laws in this country is that they are modelled upon Christian ideas, and that marriage partakes to a greater or less degree of a religious ceremony. A calm consideration of the history of our marriage laws will show this to any unbiased student. Firstly, we find that England was primarily a Catholic country, and the Catholic Church regarded marriage as a sacrament and did not permit divorce. Then came the Protestant Reformation. Marriage was still looked upon as a part and portion of Christian worship, and divorce could only be obtained by means of a private Act of Parliament—a most expensive

process. Then came the jurisdiction of the ecclesiastical courts in matters of divorce and then finally the Divorce Act of 1857, which shook off many of the shackles of priestly interference, but still retained some of the objectionable features of the marriage law, purely the outcome of Christianity. [...] What is required to remedy this evil is to regard marriage solely and wholly as a civil contract between two parties, entered into with their mutual consent and which by the like mutual consent can be also dissolved, due care being always taken that the interests of any children there may be as issue of such marriage may be protected. This is the key of the whole difficulty.[30]

From her letter, it is clear that Fatima was well-versed in the history and legal discourse about marriage and divorce in England. Importantly, the letter gives an interesting insight into her growing understanding of Islamic jurisprudence and law. Fatima highlights the freedoms afforded to her and all Muslim women that are missing in English law or had only recently been enshrined in law.

The only surviving lecture script by Fatima was posthumously reproduced in the LMI's weekly newspaper, *The Crescent*, in 1900. Delivered at the Institute in 1890, prior to the establishment of the Institute's printing press, the lecture was entitled 'On the Folly of Heeding Scandal' and is just three pages long.[31] We do know that she gave other lectures at the LMI early on, but they were probably not published. She also attended many lectures with or without her husband Hubert between 1889 and 1895. On one such occasion, when Hubert had either accepted Islam or was still considering it, they were attending a lecture, and a large number of 'ruffians' made their way through to the hall. Hubert and other LMI members ejected the intruders, but, in the fray, one of the Muslims was stabbed in the cheek.[32] Fatima also attended many of the marriages that were celebrated at the LMI in the early 1890s, and she was also most probably amongst the few women who performed in the Institute choir.[33] In 1892, she wrote 'A Moslimah's Prayer', the only one to be written by a Muslim woman to be included in the hymnal of the LMI. It summarizes Fatima's life and experiences since she had converted to Islam:

Beset by numerous foes,
Concealed along the way,
We must those enemies oppose,
And ever work and pray.

They watch but to devour,
Like ravening beasts of prey,
If we in an unguarded hour,
But cease to work and pray.

Then may we ever heed,
The warning God has given,
That so we may in safety tread
The road that leads to Heaven.[34]

Another poem was dedicated to Shahjahan Begum of Bhopal (1838–1901),[35] which suggests that Fatima was inspired by this powerful female Indian Muslim ruler:

How *can* the feeble pen express,
How can the poet praise,
Thy noble acts of righteousness,
Thy virtuous deeds and ways?

Thou ruler of this happy State,
Thou noble Shahjahan fair;
How can this humble bard relate
Thy virtues, bright and rare?

Mercy, and Truth, and Equity,
Combine to spread thy fame;
As while thy magnanimity
Thy great soul doth proclaim!

With grateful hearts our thoughts we raise
Towards Heaven, in earnest prayer
That happiness and length of days
May be thy blessed share![36]

Few of Fatima's poems or other writings have survived. This is partly due to her absence from the LMI after 1895, when she moved away from Liverpool and her health failed. She no longer visited the LMI regularly but her interest in its activities and Islam

47

never flagged, nor was she forgotten at Brougham Terrace; she painted a beautiful vase with flowers and a text from the Qur'an and presented it to the LMI, and the vase stood on the platform in the lecture hall well into the twentieth century.[37] Why, then, was there no mention of Fatima in the many pages of *The Crescent* between her leaving the LMI in 1895 and her death in October 1900?

Life after the LMI

Fatima's work for the LMI and Islam in the early 1890s concealed the very real issues she was facing at home. She endured violent abuse from her philandering husband and, at the end of 1891, petitioned for a divorce, which was not recorded in *The Crescent*. It is unlikely that any of this was known to the LMI community beyond Quilliam and perhaps a few trusted confidantes. Fatima's petition for divorce offers a window into her troubled marital life.

Before 1857, divorce in England was essentially 'only for husbands'.[38] This situation changed with the Matrimonial Causes Act of 1857, an act of parliament that made marriage a matter of State rather than of the Church and made divorce more accessible. Women could file for divorce on the grounds of 'incest, bigamy and adultery with cruelty or four years' desertion'.[39] Fatima Cates petitioned the High Court of Justice Probate Divorce and Admiralty Division with fourteen points against her husband Hubert. She stated that her husband was a man of 'violent and uncontrollable temper'. His violent assaults 'caused her great pain and injury both physical and mental and seriously impaired her health'.[40] Fatima further petitioned that Hubert 'abused and struck her two violent blows on the head and locked her in a portion of the house and threatened her with other violence'; however, she had escaped from the house and found refuge at the residence of a 'mutual friend', most likely Abdullah Quilliam.[41] A period of 'agreed separation' ensued, then Fatima consented to resume cohabitation with her husband on the condition of 'his making promises of amendment and future good behaviour' and having expressed great regret for his past conduct agreed on the condition to 'occupy a separate bed room for a period of six months'.[42] However, the abuse continued and, after a series of violent attacks, Fatima was left with 'great discolouration of the flesh and grievous bodily harm' and, to 'escape his violence, was obliged to break several panes of glass in the window in order to attract the attention of the other persons in the house'.[43] In December 1891, Hubert threatened to kill Fatima with a knife. According to Fatima, he 'struck a violent blow on the side of the head causing the blood to flow from her ear and subsequently picked up a heavy iron weighing two pounds or thereabouts and threatened to "brain" her and raised the said weapon and attempted to strike Fatima therewith but was prevented from doing so by her sister Clara'.[44] Fatima reported the incident to the police, and Hubert was arrested and appeared at the Dale Street Police Courts, where he pleaded guilty to an aggravated assault and 'was bound over in his own recognizances in £20 to keep the peace for the period of twelve months'. Hubert, however, continued to threaten his wife with violence.[45]

Fatima drew closer to Quilliam, who supported his first female convert for the duration of the ordeal. In 1892, Fatima accompanied Quilliam to meet a group of Egyptian Muslim traders in Manchester. One of the notables from Alexandria stated that 'After we ate, [Quilliam] told us his [conversion] story and the arduousness of converting fifty people [to Islam in Liverpool] and that he was married to one of those Muslims in accordance with the Sharia'.[46] It seems that at this meeting Fatima was invited to visit Egypt. She left Liverpool for Alexandria in October 1892, accompanied by two other LMI Muslim converts, Mrs Amina Mokaiesh and Miss L. Zulieka Bankes. The group visited 'various Eastern Moslem Cities' over seven months, but currently further details about the trip are unknown.[47]

To further understand the latter part of Fatima's life and her absence from LMI affairs after 1895, it is crucial to read between the lines. Her divorce was kept secret from the LMI community, but her relationship with Quilliam grew stronger. Hubert Cates, who was suffering heart disease, died whilst he was working at sea on 2 January 1895.[48] As a member of the LMI, Hubert's passing was recorded in *The Crescent* with a poem:

Oh! Silent hearts, for ever passed.
  Beyond the reach of strife and care,
Lie calmly still in dreamless sleep,
  Nor know the grief we have to share.

While your freed spirits upwards fly
  On wings of love from sphere to sphere,
Until before Great Allah's throne
  You stand, and, trusting, answer 'Here!'[49]

Almost eighteen months after Hubert's death, in May 1896, Fatima gave birth to a boy named Hubert Haleem Quilliam. Hubert, long dead, was nonetheless recorded as the boy's father.[50] Notably, the boy's given name in the birth certificate is 'Hubert Haleem Quilliam', and his place of residence is recorded as 30 Elizabeth Street, the property next door to Quilliam's 'Crescent Printing Works'.[51]

The birth of Fatima's son was kept a secret from the LMI community. Notably, after her death in 1900, *The Crescent* stated incorrectly—yet, deliberately—that Hubert Cates had died in 1896 (not 1895) and that his marriage to Fatima 'was only blessed with one child, a boy, who was born about 5 months after his father's death, and who was therefore left parentless. After her husband's death Mrs. Cates removed herself and her son by keeping a boarding house and letting furnished apartments.'[52] The report claimed that, just half an hour before her death, Fatima stated that it was her final wish that Abdullah Quilliam 'be the guardian to her little boy'.[53] In his last will and testament, Quilliam indicated that Haleem Quilliam was his child and, indeed, Haleem was given a share in Quilliam's Trust Estate.[54]

It is likely that Haleem was in fact Quilliam's illegitimate son. Whilst Quilliam never admitted publicly that he had a sexual relationship with Fatima, he was a polygamist. Whilst married to his first wife Hannah (1858–1909), with whom he had four children, Quilliam had a long-term relationship with Mary Lyon (1864–1952), who bore him five children and whom he married shortly after Hannah died in 1909. The Ottoman journalist Yusuf Samih Asmay (d. 1942), who visited the LMI in 1895, noted that

Quilliam advocated polygamy and that he openly had two wives, both of whom lived in different homes and did not see eye-to-eye.[55] However, Asmay did not mention another 'wife' of Quilliam in his account of the Liverpool Muslim community. Fatima's relationship with Quilliam could not have remained a secret after she gave birth to his son in 1896, hence perhaps her retirement from the LMI when she became pregnant in 1895.

Fatima retired to the coastal town of West Kirby on the Wirral, where she started her life afresh as 'Mrs Fanny Kaitz' (i.e., Cates) and raised her son Haleem.[56] Her relocation would only have been possible with the support and financial assistance of Quilliam. It is possible that Quilliam married Fatima with a *nikah* (Islamic marriage ceremony) sometime between 1892 and 1895, just as he had done with Mary Lyon while he was legally married to Hannah.

The loss of an LMI stalwart

Fatima was not mentioned again in *The Crescent* until her untimely death from pneumonia caused by influenza at the age of thirty-five in October 1900:

> CATES.—On the 4th Rajab, 1318 [29 October 1900], at 6 p.m., at her residence, Sister Fatima Elizabeth Cates, widow, and relict of our late Brother Hubert Haleem Cates, deceased. (May Allah rest her soul in eternal peace!).[57]

A subsequent report in *The Crescent* claimed that, on hearing that Fatima's health had deteriorated, Quilliam rushed to her bedside:

> A few moments before she died Fatima raised the index finger of her right hand, and slowly, but clearly, repeated the *Kaleema* [*kalima*, Islamic statement of faith] in Arabic, then putting her hand in that of the Sheikh, she smiled a sweet smile and said, 'Goodbye; it is all over,' and without a struggle peacefully yielded up her breath.[58]

The *Daily Despatch* reported that, in line with her wishes, Fatima was given 'a Mohammedan Funeral': 'The first lady ever [to have] converted to Islam, in England, having died, was buried

51

yesterday at Anfield Cemetery, Liverpool, according to the rites of Mahomet'.[59] *The Crescent* noted that, since Fatima's burial was the first interment of a Muslim at Anfield Cemetery, a considerable number of Christians assembled to witness the proceedings.[60] 'There was no long procession of expensive broughams drawn by silver-bedecked horses; no clamouring crowd anxious to advertise their presence; no carriage laden with a wealth of flowers intended to convey feelings of condolence'.[61] Fatima's coffin was covered simply, with 'a green pall with [an] embroidered silver crescent and star'.[62]

George Henry Green noted in *The Crescent* that Abdullah Quilliam led the funeral ceremony: 'He was present in his official capacity, however he was more aptly there as the man who received the deceased lady into the faith, who throughout his valiant struggle for Islam was ever loyally aided by the woman whose soul had returned to its Maker.'[63] Quilliam later said that 'He could almost say of her as the Prophet said of [his first wife] Khadija: 'She believed in me and the Faith when all the world was against me.'[64] For George Green, 'The inspiring, pathetic, yet hopeful recitation by the tomb held the group spellbound, and as the Sheikh plaintively uttered the closing syllables his voice became almost inaudible, and the atmosphere was filled with a reverent solemnity that overcame the sensations'.[65]

> The Sheikh gazed down on the thin, plain coffin which encased the remains of a pious woman, a true wife, an adoring mother— remains of a woman who had fulfilled, if ever one did, God's mission on Earth; the tiny, parentless boy stood awed by the brink of the grave; the fond and aged mother sobbed and trembled as the daughter's corpse disappeared - there were a few dry eyes, but only a few.[66]

Back at the LMI, Quilliam recited the following original verses that he had composed for the occasion:

> 'Tis so our sister yielded
> The breath of mortal life;
> 'Tis so she ceased the struggle
> Of this fierce worldly strife;

And, saying, 'it is over,'
She winged her spirit flight.[67]

Postscript: Fatima Cates in contemporary Britain

Fatima lived on through the memory of Abdullah Quilliam and his community, and now lives on in the memory of British Muslims in this twenty-first century. In December 2014, I founded a *madrasa* (Islamic school) in London, the 'Fatima Elizabeth Phrontistery', named in memory of Fatima Cates. In founding the *madrasa*, I noted that:

> Being a Muslim who was brought up [in the UK], and having a *madrasa* aimed at children born here, who grew up here and spent all their lives here, I wanted to give them something that was from the country itself, and I found that in Elizabeth Cates. [...] They are taken aback by [Fatima's] story, they feel a connection, they feel that there are what we could call elders, pious predecessors or saints who lived here in England over 100 years ago.[68]

I was inspired by a desire to highlight Fatima's courage and the impact of pioneering Muslim women whose lives tend to be neglected by the stories of men. Fatima was a woman who refused to conform and stood up for what she believed in. I was drawn to her story because of her perseverance and determination. Fatima was a fighter: as a teenage Christian campaigner against alcohol, then within a difficult marriage and as she filed for divorce at a time when few women dared to; and, of course, as a Muslim woman in Victorian England. The *madrasa* I established aims to embody Fatima's vision, her virtues and her unwavering passion for and commitment to the Qur'an. As the academic Philip Lewis has noted, '[The founder] Hamid named it 'Fatima Elizabeth' after one of the earliest English Muslim women. This signals his aspiration to embody the best of English and Islamic cultures [...]. It is unapologetically non-sectarian and seeks to allow plenty of space for curiosity and questioning'.[69]

Fatima's life and struggle against persecution, violence and Islamophobia more than a century ago is now being rediscovered by British Muslims. In 2022, a stone was finally placed on Fatima's unmarked grave, commemorating her life and significance to British Muslims today. The headstone was funded by members of Liverpool's Muslim community.[70] It contains the following inscription:

> A faithful servant of Allah
> FATIMA ELIZABETH CATES
> 1865 ~ 1900
> Then may we ever heed,
> The warning God has given,
> That so we may in safety tread
> The road that leads to Heaven
> FEC 1892.

3

DYNAMISM AND DISCONTENT

NAFEESAH M. T. KEEP AND FEMALE MUSLIMS IN VICTORIAN LIVERPOOL

Matthew A. Sharp

Introduction

In the late 1990s, a group of British Muslims devised a plan to restore England's first mosque and promote the pioneering work of William Henry Abdullah Quilliam (1856–1932) and his Liverpool Muslim Institute (LMI).[1] The fruit of their dreams became the Abdullah Quilliam Society (AQS). Today, the AQS uses social media to bolster Quilliam's fame and garner financial support from the global Muslim community. For example, the AQS Facebook page includes a post with photographs of the Victorian kitchen with original cooking range at the LMI's Brougham Terrace premises, claiming it to be 'the famous kitchen used by Sheikh Abdullah Quilliam for making bread for the homeless' and thus portraying the act of service as being performed by him alone.[2] Posts like this resemble a larger issue in studies about Quilliam and the LMI that regularly ignore and downplay other Liverpool Muslims, especially females, who played a critical role in the Institute's activities.[3] This neglect is echoed in scholarly literature about Quilliam's American counterpart, Mohammed Alexander Russell Webb (1846–1916), who established the American Islamic Propaganda (AIP, 1893–1896) that mirrored the LMI.[4] Women were active members and contributors to both Islamic institutions in the late nineteenth and early twentieth centuries. This chapter discusses women's roles in these nascent Muslim communities, demonstrating the integral duties they performed in the establishment and operation of both the LMI and AIP. It examines the dynamic way women participated in these institutions, the rhetoric used in journals and pamphlets to positively portray female Muslim converts, and the examples of discontent from women that contradicted some of this rhetoric. The chapter draws on previously neglected non-English and non-LMI sources, such as material from the Ottoman archives and a Turkish travelogue, which present alternative perspectives and complicate some of the received narratives about these Islamic institutions and their founders.

An American convert named Nafeesah Mary T. Keep (sometimes spelled Nafeesa, 1844–1925) is a prominent figure in this chapter because she uniquely immersed herself in both the LMI and AIP between 1894 and 1895. She also epitomized the themes of dynamism and discontent. While serving in both Islamic institutions, she defied male leadership, which resulted in her expulsion. After she left Liverpool in 1895, there was a notable decline in the prominence of women in the LMI until its collapse in 1908. For this reason, the chapter concentrates on the contributions of LMI women in its first decade (1887 to 1897), with a particular focus on the life and Islamic ministry of Nafeesah Keep.

The earliest female converts in Liverpool, 1887–97

It is likely that Abdullah Quilliam first encountered Islam in Morocco in early 1883. After returning to Liverpool, he began independently studying Islam and publicly declared himself a Muslim in 1887. There were at least three important women in Quilliam's life between the time he visited Morocco and his religious conversion. First was his mother, Harriet (Khadijah)

Holehouse (1832–1901), from whom he received a religious upbringing in the Methodist chapel. Quilliam's mother had also taught him to be active in social issues, such as the Temperance Movement, which was very important to the Quilliam family. Harriet herself converted to Islam in 1893, and so too did her second husband and Quilliam's stepfather, William (Abdur-Rahman) Holehouse. The second important figure was Quilliam's first wife Hannah Quilliam (1858–1909), whom he married in 1879 and who bore him four children. Hannah never converted to Islam; however, she participated in the activities of the LMI and even held quasi-leadership roles there. Finally, there was Mary Lyon (later Quilliam, 1864–1952), who met Quilliam in the early 1880s. The two began a polygamous relationship that led to their legal marriage after Hannah died in 1909. Mary bore Quilliam five children between 1885 and 1897 and lived near the home of Hannah and her children. Mary's religious commitments and involvement in the activities of the LMI remain unclear; however, her children were mentioned in *The Crescent* as Abdullah Quilliam's children.

As a Temperance campaigner, Quilliam had access to crowds in Temperance halls where he lectured on Islam, resulting in his earliest and most loyal converts, James Jones (Djem Ali) Hamilton (d. 1899) and Frances Elizabeth Murray (1865–1900), later known as Fatima E. Cates (see Chapter 2). From the start, Fatima played a dynamic role in the LMI's management and its mission to spread Islam. For example, she was instrumental in the conversion of her sister Clara Murray, who married a Muslim from India and lived there for the remainder of her life. Similarly, Fatima's husband Hubert Cates (1859–95) converted to Islam. From the LMI's inception until approximately 1895, Cates was the acting treasurer, which was one of the highest posts ever held by a woman at the LMI. Unlike the other symbolic offices held by women in later years, Cates' title of treasurer was not an honorary one. Quilliam never hesitated to mention that he placed a woman in a prominent position within an Islamic institution in order to rhetorically show that LMI women were active and valuable to the life of the Muslim community, which contradicted Victorian perceptions that Islam subjugated and secluded women.

Cates was one of the most recognized names among the LMI members in the first decade because she published letters and responses in British and international newspapers and journals, including an English-Urdu monthly called *The Allahabad Review*. From 1890 until 1893, *The Allahabad Review* was the main outlet for LMI members to update the global Muslim community about their endeavours to spread Islam in Britain. In addition to Cates' articles and letters to the editor, another female convert named Bertha Amina Bowman (1854–1940) contributed poems that discussed nature and her reflections on the changing seasons, but had very little to say about spiritual matters or Islam. It was in *The Allahabad Review* that Cates published 'How I Became a Mahommedan', which was one of the earliest and most detailed conversion testimonies from any LMI member.[5]

From 1887 to 1895, Cates advocated for support from Muslims abroad and exhibited the essential virtue of hospitality to anyone that came to learn about the LMI.[6] Muslim travellers and merchants frequently docked at the port city of Liverpool, which meant that many Muslims visited the burgeoning British Muslim community at the LMI. In a moving obituary dedicated to Cates in *The Crescent*, H. Mustafa Leon praised her for hosting the first group of Indian Muslim students at the LMI and frequently entertaining Muslim travellers visiting Liverpool.[7]

In 1893, an anonymous author sent a defamatory article to the Arabic newspaper *al-Ustadh* accusing Quilliam and the LMI of supporting British imperialism in Egypt. In response, an Arab visitor to England described his positive experiences with Quilliam and the LMI, including the time he met Quilliam and a woman named 'Fatima', who accompanied Quilliam to Manchester to meet the Muslims there and discuss the LMI's mission.[8] This demonstrates the level of trust Quilliam had for Cates as well as her importance to the LMI's image and mission. Cates also welcomed and influenced other women towards Islam, including Hannah Robinson (1854–1948) when she visited Liverpool in 1891 (see Chapter 5).

Ottoman consul-general reports

Starting in 1890, Ottoman consul-generals in Liverpool regularly reported news about Quilliam and the LMI because high-ranking Ottoman officials and the Ottoman Sultan Abdulhamid II (1842– 1918) himself were curious about their progress, and they sought to cultivate relations that benefited the Ottomans' 'image management and damage control' agenda.[9] Quilliam also exhibited enthusiasm in line with Abdulhamid II's pan-Islamic ideology. In support of the growing Muslim community, the Ottoman Foreign Ministry appointed mostly Muslims to the Liverpool Ottoman consulate, which was uncommon for European cities. The first two Muslim consul-generals, İsmail Lütfi Bey (served 1891–3) and Esad Kenan Bey (served 1893–5), were responsible for the longest and most detailed reports that discussed the LMI. Both men noted the oddity of women not veiling, the lack of separation between sexes, and the use of an organ and singing during LMI gatherings, mostly performed by women. Whereas Lütfi learned to appreciate the efforts to make Islam more attractive to British people, Kenan rejected Quilliam's syncretic approach.[10] Instead, he insisted that 'these baseless innovations do not seem to be in agreement with the explanation they give and are contrary to the self-respect and religious sentiment of all good Muslims'.[11] There were many reasons for Kenan's negative assessment of Quilliam and the LMI, but he took particular umbrage with the intermixing of men and women, the active role women played in gatherings, and the fact that most women were unveiled. Thus, what LMI women wore, how they acted and practised Islam, and what they did in mixed gendered spaces became a litmus test for the authenticity of Islam in Liverpool.

The first two Muslim consul-generals also commented on Islamic marriage ceremonies (*nikah*s) performed in the mosque, the majority of which occurred during Lütfi's appointment between 1891 and 1893. Lütfi sent newspaper clippings about the *nikah*s, including the story about Hannah Robinson's marriage and conversion to Islam in 1891.[12] Oddly, Lütfi never discussed Quilliam's *nikah* to Mary Lyon, which, according to Kenan, transpired during Lütfi's time as the consul-general.[13] Several years later, Quilliam appealed to the Ottoman Shaykh-ul-Islam (the highest ranking official within the Islamic scholarly community and their religious bureaucracy) to certify his polygamous second marriage through the mediation of another consul-general.[14] Although Lütfi resisted sharing his personal opinion about the appropriateness of the *nikahs*, his general tenor implied support mostly because he objected to the British newspapers' disrespectful portrayals of the Islamic rite. Fatima Cates had also publicly addressed the disparaging accounts about Islamic marriages by non-Muslims in a letter to the *Liverpool Mercury*, decrying the 'vulgar errors' expressed by a correspondent and sharing her informed opinions 'as a Moslem lady and wife'.[15] The *nikahs* performed at the LMI were a source of controversy for many years because the British public generally disapproved of British women converting to Islam and then marrying non-English Muslims, not to mention the actual legality of the unions.[16]

When Shahzada Nasrullah Khan (1874–1920), the crown prince of Afghanistan, visited Liverpool in the summer of 1895, Kenan represented the Ottoman state for events hosted by the LMI. Nasrullah Khan was the most distinguished Muslim leader to visit the Liverpool Muslims, which helped to bolster the community's reputation and legitimize Quilliam's leadership. Kenan, however, expressed disappointment in the LMI members and ridiculed them. For example, he mocked them for dressing in 'oriental' clothing, especially the women who only wore veils for this occasion, and he chided them for shouting the *shahada* (the Islamic testimony of faith) and 'other cries inappropriate for the circumstances'.[17] Among the attendees was the American convert Nafeesah M. T. Keep. Her account of the visit, however, flatly contradicted Kenan's negative appraisal, as she thought veiling honoured Nasrullah Khan and deemed the occasion a successful representation of the LMI women's devoutness to Islam.[18]

Nafeesah M. T. Keep: A model of rhetoric, activism and controversy

Mary Theresa Klamroth was born to German immigrants in either West Liberty, Ohio or New Liberty, Indiana in May 1844.

Conflicting information in her passport applications obscure her actual place of birth.[19] Her parents died when she was a child, and she went to live with an uncle who exposed her to various religious creeds, although Catholicism shaped her general understanding of Christianity. She met and later married Charles Dwight Keep (1849–87) in a Catholic church in 1872. The couple had a turbulent marriage that resulted in a divorce in 1884. When Charles died in 1887, Mary refuted the legitimacy of their divorce and claimed that her former husband conspired with his new wife and a business partner to defraud her of inheritance by faking his death. Newspapers covered the ordeal and depicted Mary as deranged.[20] In the end, Mary failed to secure any financial compensation and was almost penniless. This was the first in a series of disputes between Mary and the men in her life, most importantly with Webb and Quilliam, characterized by suspicion and paranoia over matters of finance and fidelity.

We know little about Keep's life between 1887 and when she joined Mohammed Alexander Russell Webb's Islamic mission in 1894. One thing is certain: the injustice she felt over the disinheritance inspired her activism in social reform and gender equality. According to Keep, Islam was an attractive alternative to Christianity because Islam benefited women in matters of legal privileges and inheritance rights. Keep stated that she was 'interested specially in the position of Mohammedan women, for it was easy to see that under that religion alone does our sex know the real meaning of women's rights, in which I have always believed'.[21] For the rest of her life, Keep adamantly campaigned for women's rights. It was a hallmark of her social and religious advocacy, whether in Islamic institutions or in secular political organizations.

Keep joined the AIP in early 1894, just after Webb had discontinued its flagship journal, *The Moslem World*.[22] Through clandestine support from the Ottoman state, Webb was able to prolong the AIP's work from its office in Manhattan, New York. Using her background in journalism, Keep acted as the AIP's secretary and the editor-in-chief of the newly created *Voice of Islam*. However, she left shortly after the publication of the first issue, so we know very little about her contributions to the AIP. Initial collaboration between Webb and Keep turned to conflict when she locked herself in the AIP's office, demanding Webb compensate her for lost wages and threatening to disclose his financial malpractice. Convinced that Webb received funds through the Ottoman ambassador Alexandre Mavroyéni Bey, Keep wrote to the ambassador appealing for his assistance. Mavroyéni, however, lied to Keep, saying that 'the Sublime Porte had nothing to do with the accounts of Webb and his religious movement'.[23] Once again, Keep's plea for justice and financial restitution failed. Both Webb and the Ottoman ambassador dismissed her as hysterical and out to discredit Webb for her own financial gain. In the meantime, Quilliam heard about Keep's plight and an ongoing fight between Webb and his former colleagues, John Lant (1830–97) and Emin Nabakoff, who had formed a competing Islamic mission society in New York.[24] With Webb weakened by the dispute, Quilliam sought to position himself as the leader of the English-speaking Muslims. Quilliam even urged Lant, Nabakoff and Keep to form a new Muslim society affiliated with the LMI. Quilliam maintained correspondence with Keep over the summer of 1894, which opened the door for her to leave the United States and align herself with the LMI in England.[25]

Keep in Liverpool

Keep arrived in Liverpool in February 1895 and immediately found companionship amongst the Liverpool Muslims. Within a week of her arrival, she spoke at the LMI's Sunday evening meeting with a lecture titled 'An American Woman's Views of Islam'.[26] The LMI's two regular publications, *The Crescent* and *The Islamic World*, mentioned or reproduced four of Keep's lectures in a span of three months, all of which dealt with her understanding of Islam, the position of women and their rights within the religion.[27] No other woman in the LMI's history publicly spoke about Islam as often as Keep, nor did they address issues specifically about Islam in such depth. In multiple instances, Keep mentioned that her exploration of Islam led her to read a translation of *Hedaya*, a twelfth-century work of Hanafi *fiqh* (Muslim jurisprudence), and she later became versed in nineteenth-century works on Islam by scholars such as Sir William Jones (1746–94), Max Müller (1823–1900) and Sir Syed Ameer Ali (1849–1928). Her competence in Islamic knowledge confirms that 'she was more learned in Islamic legal rulings [...] than most converts of her generation and had developed stronger principles of Islamic orthodoxy than her convert counterparts at the LMI'.[28] Quilliam initially revelled in Keep's superior knowledge and discursive talents. Sariya Cheruvallil-Contractor has noted that Keep's lectures 'demonstrate a confident woman who was not afraid to share her views about Islam and who challenged Western perceptions of her faith'.[29] In fact, Quilliam wrote to Lant praising her first lecture and suggested that 'in New York she would only be the "woman who spoiled Webb," here she is a representative of American Islam'.[30]

Obviously, Quilliam believed that Keep's rhetoric bolstered the LMI's image and benefited its mission to spread Islam. The two shared a view that Islam and its teachings about women, marriage, divorce and a whole host of other issues could cure the social ills and disparities that plagued Western Christian societies.[31] Thus, they replicated the rhetoric of pan-Islamic Muslim writers of their day who argued that Islam would prevail over Christianity because it provided the answers for a modern society in terms of science, rationality and morality.[32] In her first lecture, Keep said:

> What most forcibly attracted my attention was the prohibition of intoxicants, the religious civil, social, and domestic rights accorded to women, the respect shown woman [sic] as the custodian of childhood, the temperance and frugality inculcated by Mohamet, and above all the absence of an aristocracy either ecclesiastical or political.[33]

Keep articulated her conviction that Islam not only resolved her internal spiritual dilemmas, but also promised societal reform. In 'The Position of Women under Islamic Law', Keep proved the genuineness of her pursuit of Islamic knowledge through a sophisticated collection of scholarly works on Islamic law and the legal rights of women. Keep never directly spoke publicly about her marriage and divorce, nor did she express her feeling of betrayal.

However, the many examples and scenarios she expounded upon in this lecture reveal why she found Islam to surpass Christianity. According to Keep, 'Every condition in which [a] woman was likely to be placed seems to have been provided for under the benign influence of Mohammed's teachings and practice', such that a divorced woman received financial restitution based on 'unqualified rights'.[34] However, Keep understood Islam and the position of women from the works of nineteenth-century scholars and a colonial translation of a twelfth-century *fiqh* text, so when she observed contradictions between her idealistic vision of Islam and the practices and behaviours of Muslims in Liverpool, she struggled to make sense of it. As much as she considered the position of women under Islamic law, she had never actually lived under anything remotely analogous to Islamic law and only later lived in a majority Muslim society.

LMI members generally rejected political quietism, and Keep was no exception. She was one of the few Muslim convert women to vocalize her political opinions in a public way. The only other woman that matched Keep's political rhetoric was Madame Terése Griffin Vielé (1831–1906), a French convert to Islam who adopted the Muslim name Sadika Hanoum. Vielé wrote for *The Crescent* and more frequently for *The Islamic World* on political affairs, often decrying the West's treatment of the Ottoman Empire and Abdulhamid II, especially in regard to the Ottomans' treatment of Armenian Christians.[35] Keep embraced Islam during the debates over the events known as the Armenian Massacres of the 1890s (incidents of violence against Ottoman Armenians in Anatolia) that inflamed many converts who lionized Abdulhamid II and accused Christians, especially politicians and the Western press, of fomenting hatred toward the Ottoman sultan-caliph instigated by Armenian conspiracies. In May 1895, Keep attended a rally hosted by the London-based pan-Islamic organization Anjuman-i-Islam to protest against Armenian aggression and to decry disinformation about the Ottomans.[36] Keep was the only Muslim woman present, and she spoke out during the meeting, asserting that 'the women of Turkey were by no means, in the abject, grovelling, and degraded condition generally represented'.[37] Her statement provoked the few Christians in attendance to anger, and they interrupted her before she could complete her speech. In an article about Nasrullah Khan's visit that had nothing to do with the Armenian issue, Keep reverted to diatribes against the 'clamorous Christians' who showed less 'tolerance' to the Shahzada than they did for 'the mythically persecuted Armenian subjects of Turkey'.[38]

Keep's letter to Sultan Abdulhamid II

Between February and August 1895, Keep dutifully served the LMI community. In addition to her many lectures, she worked countless hours in the LMI's Crescent Printing and Publishing Office and became the assistant superintendent of the newly formed weekly Sunday school to teach the Liverpool Muslim children the principles of Islam and the Qur'an.[39] Externally, it appeared as though Keep had found a community that empowered her to participate in Islamic endeavours through lecturing, writing and activism. Internally, Keep's relationships with Quilliam and other LMI members began to crumble. In early August 1895, Keep reached an inflection point and privately lashed out through a letter to Sultan Abdulhamid II.[40] Keep expressed frustration with Webb (although unnamed), blaming him for not teaching her how to perform the Muslim ablutions and prayers, which left her 'broken-hearted over the false teaching of Islam in America'.[41] However, she also levelled criticism at the Liverpool Muslims. Keep complained about poor living and working conditions in Liverpool, stating that, from February to June 1895, she had sustained herself on her own money, paying for her lodging, food and medicine, which had left her 'starving'. Even worse, she worked 'sometimes eight, sometimes ten, twelve, fourteen, even eighteen hours, per day' for Quilliam in the Crescent Office: 'The Doctor says that I am over-worked and that I am suffering with "Starvation of the Nerves and Muscles"'.[42]

According to Keep, 'True Moslems who come here from the Orient tell me that true Islam is not taught and is not practiced in the so-called "Mosque" in Liverpool'. She continued:

I have seen two (2) women stand shoulder to shoulder on the prayer-carpet with the men, then, when the prayers were finished, one (1) young woman always let some one [sic] of the men fasten her shoes on her feet for her. I objected to this. I saw this same young woman kiss two (2) of the young men in the so-called "Mosque." I objected to this. But the "Sheik-ul-Islam" [Abdullah Quilliam] says we cannot have Islam in England exactly as it is in the Orient.[43]

Although she had never visited 'the Orient' or studied Islam under any scholars, Keep believed that the Islam taught and practiced in Liverpool was unorthodox. Furthermore, she doubted Quilliam's credentials to lead the British Muslims. Her letter was more than a list of grievances and allegations. She humbly petitioned Abdulhamid II to relocate her to Ottoman lands: 'I want to reach a country where the people are true Muslims. I want to learn the Moslem prayers and ablutions. I want to live and die among true Believers'. She was a widow with no remaining family, no wealth and poor health, who felt 'broken' from fighting 'false teachers of Islam in America and England'.[44]

Keep's letter is notable for many reasons. First, there are so few examples of letters, diaries, personal accounts or other private materials from Victorian Muslim converts, specifically LMI women, which makes her letter a rare survivor. Second, as a consequence, scholars tend to rely on public-facing publications that underwent considerable editorial control by Quilliam and male leadership. However, in her letter, we see Keep wielding agency through an unfiltered account of the conditions in Liverpool. Third, through her petition to Abdulhamid II, Keep showed her dedication to Islam and her determination to be an 'authentic' Muslim, which she argued was impossible to achieve under Quilliam's leadership.

The Ottoman Grand Vizier's office sent a translated copy of Keep's letter to the Sultan's Yildiz Palace, but there is no record of Abdulhamid II's response. Despite this, Keep persisted, frequently visiting the Ottoman consulate in Liverpool in search of benevolence to the point that Hassan Tahsin Bey, the newly appointed consul-general (served 1895–8), requested advice from Rüstem Pasha, the Ottoman ambassador, on how to deal with her. Tahsin showed a level of sympathy for Keep because she was at the 'end of her resources' and simply wanted to travel to Constantinople (Istanbul) to learn the real doctrines of Islam and become 'an accomplished Muslim woman'.[45] The ambassador refrained from interfering in the affairs of the Liverpool Muslims and only assured Tahsin that he had forwarded Keep's letter to Constantinople. Perhaps the most revealing part of the ambassador's response is a crossed-out line in which he told Tahsin to refrain from engaging with Keep at the consulate office.[46] Once again, Keep failed to garner support from Ottoman officials in her pleas for justice as she strove to become a devout Muslim.

Keep's collaborator

Another Ottoman Muslim in Liverpool at the time attentively listened to Keep's complaints and shared her concerns about Quilliam and the Liverpool Muslims. His name was Yusuf Samih Asmay (d.1942), a journalist and intellectual who had travelled to Liverpool in the summer of 1895 on a fact-finding mission that resulted in his travelogue called *Liverpool Müslümanlığı* (1896).[47] Asmay's account is salient on several fronts. First, it corroborates observations made by foreign Muslims and includes information relevant to how British Muslim women participated in the LMI. Second, it potentially exposes some of the more unsavoury aspects of Quilliam's personal life. Finally, together with Keep's letter and appeals to the Ottoman officials, it clarifies why Keep's name disappeared from LMI publications after the summer of 1895. It is likely that Asmay was among the 'true Moslems' who told Keep that 'true Islam' was not taught and practiced at the LMI.

Like consul-general Kenan, Asmay found the innovations at the LMI to be bizarre and even unorthodox. To his surprise, he observed the pronounced role played by women during the Sunday evening meetings, including Miss Nelson who played the piano, Miss Gibson who accompanied her, and another important young woman named Rosa Warren (1862-1925) who played the organ and became a pillar in the LMI's female community.[48] After Keep, Rosa Warren was one of the few women to speak at the LMI's formal events, lecturing on non-Islamic topics such as modern poetry, music and dance. Asmay also recounted a story from a friend who attended Friday prayers and claimed that both the men and women were ignorant of the essential rites and rituals for prayer. As Asmay described it: 'What was even more peculiar is that out of respect for the fairer sex, they had the ladies take the front row and the men the back row, because these fair creatures were not able to prostrate, [i.e., perform] prostration, due to their [brimmed] hats and [stiff] corsets, so they sat prostrated with their eyes while bowing their heads slightly, and various other similar [indicative] gestures happened'.[49] Asmay heard similar accounts about Nasrullah Khan's visit and the 'bizarre costumes' British Muslim women wore 'at Quilliam's direction to imply that they follow the Islamic code', but which Asmay felt showed 'the people of Liverpool that this is how strangely Muslim women wear religious dress out on the street'.[50]

While in Liverpool, Asmay also interacted with the LMI's first imam (Muslim religious leader), Maulana Muhammad Barakatullah Bhopali (also commonly spelled Barkatullah, 1854–1927), an Indian scholar who joined the LMI in 1893 and later became a globetrotting pan-Islamic activist.[51] In *Liverpool Müslümanlığı*, Asmay shared Barakatullah's letter from 15 August 1895 that revealed Keep's accusations against both Quilliam and Barakatullah. He told Asmay that Keep had written to Nasrullah Khan, attacking them for being 'irreligious and indecent and that we were visiting ladies in their houses at night for wantonness and debauchery'.[52] Barakatullah denounced Keep as a liar and said that he felt betrayed because 'I have always been kind to her. I wrote letters to India and other places in praise of her [...] And this is what I get in return'.[53] Unfortunately, Keep's portrayal of Quilliam's behaviour was not unique. Asmay wrote that 'Mr. Quilliam has a regard for the fairer sex as much as he loves money, so he made a name for himself in Liverpool: they say that once he sets his eyes on a dove, she cannot escape his clutches even if she flies away'.[54] In addition to Quilliam's womanizing, Asmay even speculated that he owned a brothel.[55]

Aside from Barakatullah, Keep acted as Asmay's main collaborator for gathering information about the LMI.[56] When people queried the numbers of LMI members and converts, Quilliam consistently refused to share exact figures. Through Keep, Asmay obtained a list that totalled 'no more than seventy-five, out of which forty-two are women and girls', which was far less than the 200 that Quilliam recounted to Asmay in 1895.[57] Although *The Crescent* made no direct mention of why Keep left the community, Asmay provided details about her expulsion. He referred to a special meeting convened to denounce Keep 'because she was accused of saying inappropriate things about the converts, especially the young ones, of denigrating the [Liverpool] Muslim community to Muslims coming from the East to visit the mosque, and of writing letters against Quilliam and Maulana Barkatullah to His Highness Nasrullah Khan'.[58] Asmay claimed that the LMI members rejected Keep's requests to go to a Muslim country because they feared she would spread gossip about them. The most damaging account from Asmay was a story of Quilliam's stepfather, William Holehouse, beating Keep in the Crescent Office and kicking her out because she disparaged Quilliam and the LMI in correspondence with Muslims outside Britain.[59]

The LMI's annual reports expose the community's antipathy for Keep and supply possible answers to why other prominent LMI members vanished from the LMI's publications and memory.[60] In Quilliam's opening statement for the LMI annual meeting on 12 August 1895, he reminded the LMI members that an injury to one Muslim was an injury to all. Although they could tolerate differing opinions with good intentions, 'when the conduct of a person professing Islam may be blameable and not conducive to the welfare of the general community', disciplinary action was necessary. Without naming Keep, Quilliam lashed out, stating:

> There is no room in Islam for the profligate, the traducer, the slanderer and backbiter, the evil-minded, the unjustly suspicious, and the self-aggrandiser. The place of such an [sic] one is not amongst us. Islam condemns in no unmeasured terms such conduct, and the perpetrator thereof cannot be a true Muslim. No amount of mere profession can constitute a person a Muslim, there must be the consistent practice of Islamic virtues, 'Actions speak louder than words.'[61]

Informed by Keep's letter and how Asmay portrayed her experiences, it is obvious to whom Quilliam addressed his tirade. At the next year's LMI annual meeting, Quilliam reiterated the LMI's commitment to root out fomenters of discord. He reminded them that in the previous year, the LMI confronted 'the unpleasant but necessary step of suspending from all the privileges of the institution an individual who claimed to have become a Muslim in another land, but who by actions—which ever speak louder than words—had shown that the lip-profession of our faith was strangely inconsistent with her conduct'.[62] Quilliam carefully crafted his words, but when he described a woman who claimed to become a Muslim in a foreign country, it was a clear indictment of Keep. Ironically, some Muslims wrote to Arabic newspapers alleging that Quilliam was either not a true Muslim, had converted for financial gain or was spying for the British government.[63] Quilliam used his own religious authority to denounce Keep as a hypocrite and as never being a true Muslim.

In the same 1896 LMI annual meeting, a British Muslim convert named T. Omar Byrne (1856–1901) berated 'one foolish and ill-informed person in Egypt' who wrote 'a ridiculous book' that misinformed the Muslim world about the LMI. Here, Byrne criticized Asmay for supposedly never attending a Friday prayer and insinuated that Asmay's association with Keep explained his false testimony.[64] The statements issued by Quilliam and Byrne show that they rejected, in no uncertain terms, any signs of disloyalty, especially if someone targeted Quilliam and his legitimacy. Stressing Muslim solidarity and the duty to maintain harmony, Quilliam wielded significant control over what LMI members said privately and publicly. At the 1897 LMI annual meeting, the honorary secretary declared that 'the motto of our leader has ever been, "A place for everyone and everyone in his proper place"', and he alluded to their problem of finding qualified persons to fill important positions at the LMI.[65] With so few people joining the LMI, it is likely that they struggled to find suitable people. However, Keep's experience and the relative disappearance of other significant figures who presumably questioned Quilliam's leadership indicates that it was not a matter of finding qualified people. Instead, the 'proper place' for LMI members was complete adherence and conformity to Quilliam's teaching and leadership of the LMI. When qualified people like Keep questioned or rejected his authority and legitimacy, they were expendable.

Keep after Liverpool

Keep's activities between 1895 and 1899 remain somewhat mysterious. Asmay stated that, after she left Liverpool, Keep met an Egyptian in London who invited her to stay with his family in Cairo.[66] This confirms what she later said in an 1899 interview that discussed her religious conversion, time spent in an 'Egyptian harem', and her new plan to establish an Islamic mission in America.[67] At the time of the interview, Keep lived in a small flat in west London. In Cairo, Keep had the opportunity she longed for, to live among 'true Muslims' and learn the tenets of Islam. Now as an expert on 'harem life', she rhetorically debunked negative Western tropes about repressed Muslim women in Islamic societies. Her stay in Cairo lasted a short time because she caught cholera, but she supposedly travelled to Cairo again after her recovery. Documents indicate that a 'Mrs. Nafeesah Keep' boarded the steamship *Circassia* from Glasgow to the United States in August 1896. Then, in 1898, she applied for another passport, declaring New York as her permanent residence, journalism as her occupation, and her intention to return to the United States in two years.[68] It is difficult to ascertain if in fact she travelled back to Cairo, or if after she contracted cholera and returned to the United States in 1896 she remained there until she arrived back in London in 1898. During her second trip, she claimed to meet Hajji Mohammed Dollie (1846–1906), a South African Muslim and friend of Quilliam, who had established a temporary mosque in London in 1895. An article in *Thamarat al-Funun*, an Islamic newspaper in Beirut, noted an event in London hosted by Dollie in September 1898 to celebrate the anniversary of Abdulhamid II's accession to the throne, and among the attendees was someone mistakenly referred to as 'Mister Keep' from the 'Islamic settlement in America'.[69] So, presumably Keep left New York in mid-1898 and arrived in London to join the Muslim community formed by Dollie, despite his amicable relationship with Quilliam.

By 1899, Keep conceived of a scheme to purchase 50 acres of land to establish a colony of Muslims in the United States to spread Islam 'in precisely the same spirit as that in which benevolent persons in the two great English-speaking countries send missionaries to China and to Africa'.[70] She anticipated difficulties raising support from the Muslim world because of the rumours of financial mishandling by both Webb and Quilliam. Keep never mentioned her association with the two leading male converts and only briefly insinuated that her rival (probably Quilliam) concocted stories of her death at sea. Her plan to return to the United States to establish a new Islamic mission never materialized. Had she succeeded, Keep would have become the first female Muslim to create and lead an Islamic mission and organization in the United States.[71]

Instead, sometime in the early 1900s, Keep settled in Perth, Australia. There was a Muslim community in Western Australia, but it is unclear what, if any, affiliation she had with them. In Australia, Keep remade herself and seemingly rejected Islam. Now known as Mary T. Keep, she engaged in charitable works with the Sisters of the Good Shepherd (a Catholic organization) and rose to prominence in women's rights activism as a member of the Women's Auxiliary of the National Liberal League. Keep died in Australia in December 1925 at the age of 81. In a bewildering obituary that appeared in *The Mirror of Australia*, the author eulogized Keep with extraordinary tales of her many travels and accomplishments in the Middle East, most of which were fanciful at best. At no time in the obituary do we read of her conversion to Islam, or of her connection to Webb, Quilliam and the LMI.[72]

Conclusion

At the 1896 LMI annual meeting, Quilliam told the story of how he welcomed into his home a young child whose mother had fallen on hard times. This laid the groundwork for the LMI's next ambitious charitable project, the Medina Home for Children, which became a mainstay in their Islamic ministry for the next decade. Based on initial reports, articles and subsequent advertisements, LMI women were major contributors in the Medina Home's administration. They created a Ladies Sewing Committee and *The Crescent* recorded a rotating list of women who served on the Medina Home Committee. Further investigation points to some patterns of how women served at the LMI in the final decade. For one thing, not all the women involved in the Medina Home were Muslims, most notably Quilliam's first wife Hannah, who held the title of orphanage treasurer. For another, no matter which women participated in the Medina Home's committee or other programmes and events, there was always a male figure over them. In the case of the Medina Home, Abdullah Quilliam always served as the president, and some other man held the position of honorary secretary. Frankly, we know next to nothing about the inner workings of the Medina Home. Perhaps Hannah and the other women asserted authority and Quilliam simply acted as a figurehead. Regardless, the Medina Home became the main outlet for women to consistently serve in the LMI's activities, albeit mostly under male supervision and oversight.

In the last decade of the LMI, members mourned the death of three distinguished women in the span of two years. First, Elizabeth Leylah Warren, the mother of LMI members Rosa Warren and Henry Nasrullah Warren (1866–1930), died in December 1899. Recounting Elizabeth's role in the community, *The Crescent* stated: 'It was no uncommon sight to see our sister sitting in the Lecture Hall surrounded by little girls, the daughters of Muslims. In fact, she was deservedly regarded and looked upon as a "Mother in Islam"'.[73] Then, in October 1900, the LMI learned that their beloved sister Fatima Cates, the first female convert to Islam in Liverpool, had died. The following year, in April 1901, Quilliam's mother died, and this received considerable attention in *The Crescent*. The LMI members deemed all three women, in one way or another, to be notable matriarchal figures in their community. After Keep left the LMI and with the deaths of these three important British Muslim women, no LMI women took up the mantle of leadership and influence through rhetoric or activism. The 'proper place' of

LMI women in the final decade became increasingly isolated and relatively invisible compared with the first decade, which may partially explain the demise of the Muslim convert community after Quilliam left Liverpool in 1908.

4

SULTAN JAHAN AND THE WOKING
MUSLIM MISSION

REPRESENTING ISLAMIC FEMININITY DURING THE
FIRST WORLD WAR

Diane Robinson-Dunn

Introduction

In 1916, Khawaja Kamal-ud-Din (1870–1932) presented a moving
description of his decision to establish the Woking Muslim Mission
(WMM) to a group of friends in Lucknow, India, which was later
reproduced in the pages of its monthly publication, *The Islamic
Review.*[1] According to Kamal-ud-Din's account, in November
1912 he visited the abandoned mosque in the town of Woking,
just outside London.[2] He found amid 'straw and other rubbish
the accumulations of the many years during which its doors had
remained closed' an old copy of the Qur'an. He then turned to
a passage so inspiring that he prostrated himself upon the cold
floor and, with tears in his eyes, prayed that he would be able to
transform that place into a '"Mecca in the West"'.[3] Yet the creation
of that Muslim missionary organization in 1913 also owed much to
the patronage of Nawab Sultan Jahan (1858–1930), the Begum, or
ruler, of the Indian princely state of Bhopal, who upon travelling

75

to England in 1911 for the coronation ceremony of George V and Queen Mary was reminded of the mosque in Woking that her mother had helped to fund a generation earlier. She pledged to resuscitate the building which, by that time, had been closed and neglected for over a decade. This chapter examines how her example and writings, both on their own and when considered alongside other WMM discourses, reveal an understanding of Muslim femininity as both an issue of real importance and an essentially fluid concept during the First World War period, a time when the WMM established itself on a firm footing.

Sultan Jahan, the Woking Muslim Mission and Muslim femininity

Sultan Jahan was the fourth in a succession of female Muslim sovereigns who had ruled Bhopal in central India since 1819. While each Begum differed in personality and approach to her role, all promoted the importance of Islam within the British Raj. In an effort to educate an English readership about that dynasty, Sultan Jahan wrote two books and had them translated and published in London: an autobiography, *An Account of My Life*, which appeared in 1912, and a biography of her great grandmother Qudsia, entitled *Nawab Gauhar Begum alias the Nawab Begum Qudsia of Bhopal*, published in 1918.[4] Through these two works, Sultan Jahan brought a wide range of historical actors and circumstances to life, presenting the Begums as formidable and admirable Muslim women, an example to others.[5]

Qudsia (r. 1819–37) set the precedent for female leadership in Bhopal. After wresting power from male contenders, she used her own arguments and the sway she held with religious authorities to secure the legal right of a woman to rule the kingdom. Both Qudsia and her daughter Sikandar defended Bhopal from aggressive neighbours, maintained an alliance with the British and promoted Islam. As her daughter's Regent, from 1819 until 1837, Qudsia led troops in military manoeuvres and funded the construction of new religious buildings, most notably mosques in Bhopal and houses in Mecca and Medina for her subjects to use while on pilgrimage.[6] Sikandar further strengthened Bhopal's alliance with the British when she helped to suppress the uprising of 1857; in part because of her loyalty during that crisis, she was able to convince the British to reopen Delhi's historic mosque, the Jama Masjid, an act which earned her the respect of Muslims throughout India. In addition, Sikandar became the first ruler, male or female, from the subcontinent to make the Hajj, or pilgrimage to Mecca.[7]

Shahjehan (r. 1844–60 and 1868–1901) and her daughter Sultan Jahan (r. 1901–26) continued the tradition begun by Qudsia and Sikandar of advancing Islam in the British empire; yet, unlike their predecessors, they extended that interest to include the metropole.[8] Shahjehan initiated the construction of the largest mosque on the Indian subcontinent, the Taj-ul-Masajid in Bhopal, and contributed the necessary funding for the erection of the first purpose-built mosque in the British Isles, later named in her honour, in Woking; both buildings were designed in the same Indo-Saracenic style, a contemporary interpretation of seventeenth-century Mughal architecture. Although Shahjehan could not have realized it at the time, her decision to support the publication of Mirza Ghulam Ahmad's (1835–1908) 'first and most celebrated book,' *Barahin-e-Ahmadiyya* or *Proofs of Islam*, contributed to the rise of that Punjabi religious reformer and thus the eventual missionary career of his student, Kamal-ud-Din.[9] Her daughter and successor Sultan Jahan would provide patronage for Kamal-ud-Din, the revival of the Shah Jahan Mosque, and the WMM, serving as the Mission's 'primary benefactor' until her death.[10] In fact, in 1925, just prior to the end of her reign, she travelled England for the first time since 1911, making a highly publicized appearance in Woking and contributing towards the cost of building an extension to the mosque for which she laid the foundation stone in an 'informal and private ceremony', adhering bricks and mortar with a silver trowel.[11]

In her writings intended for the WMM and an English-speaking audience more generally, Sultan Jahan emphasizes the strength and competence of the previous Begums, qualities shared by other female Muslim leaders, past and present. Taking the helm of government as a teenager, Qudsia led Bhopal for almost two decades, bringing peace, justice and general good order to her subjects. Sultan Jahan describes her great-grandmother as liberal and charitable, while at the same time dedicated to running a fiscally sound state and building a fine army.[12] Likewise, Sikandar proved to be an extraordinary ruler and excellent administrator, initiating beneficial reforms in agriculture, the economy, infrastructure, the justice system and the military.[13] According to Sultan Jahan, Sikandar showed the world that she could 'rise superior to the weakness of her sex' and develop the 'qualities that only men are supposed to possess'.[14] In that respect, the Begums joined the ranks of female Muslim leaders who, while relatively unknown in the West, nevertheless made significant contributions in their day: Shujarat-ud-dar of Egypt; Razia Sultanah in Delhi; Ummul Majd of the Vilam dynasty; Chad Sultanah of the Deccan; and Eshkhtoon of the Atabag dynasty in Shiraz.[15]

In addition, Sultan Jahan's publications also make clear that when women govern, they do not simply acquire male attributes or act like men. Rather they become *superior* leaders by tapping into feminine qualities that they already possess such as 'mercy, sympathy, toleration, fidelity, and firmness'. Based upon extensive historical study, Sikandar's biographer even came to the conclusion that the 'administrative capacity is more inherent in women then in men' and that therefore 'nature specifically intended them for rulers'.[16] Relating this idea and elaborating upon it, Sultan Jahan explains how, while it is relatively easy to govern during times of war when a common enemy unites the people, it is ten times more difficult to rule a peaceful kingdom when every law passed is perceived by someone as an infringement on their personal liberty. Fortunately for Bhopal, its three successive generations of Begums possessed 'that softer quality, the love of peace and mercy, which only attains its full development in a woman's heart, and by which alone true happiness can be spread'.[17]

Yet while Sultan Jahan valued maintaining peace, she also understood conflict as an unavoidable part of the human condition and wrote with pride about the Muslim women who fought for their people. She related how the thirteenth-century ruler of the Delhi Sultanate, Razia Sultana (r. 1236–40), courageously commanded her army in numerous battles and regularly took to the field dressed as a soldier, and how even the *purdahnashin* of Bhopal defended the city's gate against invaders during a four-month siege in 1812–13.[18] There, at the age of fourteen, her great-grandmother Qudsia watched her own mother Zeenat Begum galvanize the other women who, in turn, fired canons and threw homemade explosives.[19] Even Sikandar, to whom Sultan Jahan refers as having the love of peace and mercy in her heart, nevertheless also had the 'blood of her warlike ancestors' coursing through her veins, as evidenced by her effective response to the 1857 uprising.[20] In the same spirit as in Sultan Jahan's books, female warriors occasionally appear in the pages of *The Islamic Review*, such as in the story of the women who accompanied Muhammad in battle for the original purpose of nursing the wounded but became so inspired by the sight of Umi Nasibah, who 'wielded sword and drew bow' in defence of her beloved prophet, that they too decided to take up arms and charge the enemy.[21]

While the female figures in Sultan Jahan's biographies play a number of heroic and praiseworthy roles, the males appear unimportant by comparison, and when they do emerge, often it is to act as a foil to the wise government of the Begums. After Qudsia's secure and prosperous reign, Nawab Jahangir managed to gain control of Bhopal for seven years, bringing tyranny to the country and allowing the capital city to be sacked and plundered by his political allies.[22] Similarly, the golden age of Sikandar's rule and the early years of her daughter Shahjehan's effective government were followed by 'disastrous results' when Shahjehan's second husband, Sidik Hasan, began to exercise illegitimate influence in affairs of state, overstepping the legal boundaries of his position as Nawab and consort.[23] For while the husbands of the Begums received that royal title, they were not allowed by law to hold or exercise any actual political power.[24]

In order to prevent Sultan Jahan's future husband from attempting to usurp her position, as Sidik Hasan and Nawab Jahangir had done, Sultan Jahan's grandmother Sikandar selected a young boy 'of tender age' from a noble family to be brought to Bhopal. There, the child, Ahmad Ali Khan, received the training and education that would prepare him for his destined role as 'counsellor' and 'helpmate' to the Begum.[25] In addition, he signed a prenuptial contract stipulating that he would not interfere with Sultan Jahan's personal property; that he would not take a second wife unless she granted him permission to do so; and finally that his wife and her mother would make all future decisions with regard to any children the couple might have.[26] When Ahmad Ali Khan died of a heart attack in 1901, just six months after Sultan Jahan assumed the throne, the latter decided not to remarry, believing that it was the will of Allah for her to rule alone.[27]

Given Sultan Jahan's own independent spirit and a dynastic legacy characterized by female power, it might come as a surprise that, for most of her life, she embraced a seemingly conservative view with regard to veiling and seclusion. After all, by the early twentieth century, a number of Muslims had rejected those practices as backwards, unenlightened and a barrier to social progress generally.[28] Sultan Jahan was well aware of the debates surrounding those issues in the Muslim world, especially in India and the Ottoman Empire, and understood that she had a choice in the matter, as had the previous Begums.[29] In fact, had she based her decision regarding purdah (female seclusion) on the lessons learned from studying the lives of her predecessors, it seems that she would have rejected the practice. In her biography of Qudsia, Sultan Jahan explains how, at the age of thirty-four and after fifteen years as Begum, her great-grandmother came to the conclusion that ruling from behind the veil was like 'working in the dark' and abandoned the practice both for herself and her daughter Sikandar.[30] While the third Begum, Shahjehan, may have taken the opposite tack by going into purdah at the age of thirty-three in order to follow the wishes of her second husband, Sidik Hasan, Sultan Jahan considered the results to be disastrous, as noted previously.

Yet inspired in part by the 'acrobatic' use of the curtain, or the ability of Muhammad and his followers to fashion barriers that protected privacy without hampering the ability of women to participate fully in and contribute to the life of the community, Sultan Jahan sought to use her own vast resources and influence to recast purdah as a vehicle for female empowerment.[31] Like Muhammad's wife Ayesha, who spoke to disciples from behind a screen while they listened in respectful silence, Sultan Jahan employed a similar device when discussing affairs of state with political officials, and on her tours of the Bhopal countryside she met directly with rural women, thereby gaining valuable information and addressing their concerns.[32] In addition, by establishing female-only educational and cultural institutions complete with 'covered conveyances and segregated boarding houses', Sultan Jahan created new spaces in which both Western and secluded Indian women could gather to share ideas and converse about issues of social and political importance, building strength and solidarity in the process. Through a variety of associations and activities, which could range from philanthropic societies to female-only sports tournaments and an All-India Ladies Art Exhibition, Sultan Jahan made Bhopal 'a centre for the reform of India's Muslim woman'.[33] In part because of these efforts, Sultan Jahan's close and long-time friend, Sarojini Naidu (1879–1949), the esteemed Hindu feminist, suffragist and political leader, told an audience at the Lyceum Club of London that Muslim women would be a 'great force in progress and freedom' and a 'sword of victory, to every world-wide women's movement'.[34]

Readers of *The Islamic Review* could read Naidu's praise and learn about Sultan Jahan's efforts to create female spaces for intellectual development in the context of Muslim history. One article from that publication entitled 'Behind the Purdah' reproduced the inaugural address given by Sultan Jahan for the First Annual All-India Ladies Conference held in Bhopal. The introduction to the address explained how seclusion need not serve as a barrier to progress and that for centuries Muslim women 'behind the veil' had been able to grow and excel in various branches of learning in ways that their Western counterparts, despite their relative freedom, had not been allowed to do, at least not until the past fifty years. In addition, the new female-only clubs, associations, meetings and conferences in India provided 'every opportunity' for 'culture and elevation'. In the address itself, Sultan Jahan spoke of the genius of Muslim women to which 'the whole world is indebted' and the many contributions that they had made in the past and still may make in all realms from the arts of peace and arts

81

of war to administration, science and literature.[35] Echoing these sentiments later in the same issue, Sheikh Mushir Kidwai (1878–1937), an Indian Muslim writer closely associated with the WMM, noted that history was 'full of brilliant Muslim women', including poets, philosophers, jurists and physicians.[36]

As women from the British Isles began to accept Islam through the WMM, they too joined this international Muslim sisterhood.[37] Violet Ebrahim of London, reportedly Kamal-ud-Din's first convert to Islam, even experienced for herself the feminine spheres of activity that Sultan Jahan had created in Bhopal. Ebrahim, whom Kamal-ud-Din described as both English and Scottish, was the daughter of a British army colonel and married an Indian Muslim man. After listening to Kamal-ud-Din's arguments, Ebrahim gradually came to believe that she was a 'Muslim at heart', as she explained in a letter to her 'sisters in India'.[38] In Bhopal, she attended a garden party in her honour hosted by Sultan Jahan and gave an inspiring speech at the Princess of Wales Ladies Club, of which that ruler was patron. In her speech, reproduced in *The Islamic Review,* Ebrahim emphasized the importance of women's missionary work, at one point calling for a modern Rabia Basri, referencing the female Sufi saint and mystic from the eighth century, to come to England to teach Islam.[39]

While Ebrahim was the exception rather than the rule in terms of her ability to visit Bhopal and meet Shah Jahan and other *purdahnashin* in that country, it would be surprising if other members of the WMM, particularly female ones, were not aware of that ruler's practice of wearing a burqa, an enveloping outer garment worn by women to cover the body and face, at official functions and during her travels, which, in addition to India, included Arabia, France and England.[40] Given Sultan Jahan's commitment to employing purdah as a means to develop and ultimately widen female spheres of activity beyond the confines of domestic life, her use of the burqa perhaps can be interpreted as another means of extending feminine space. In photographs from the Delhi Durbar in 1911, she appears entirely enclosed in royal splendour, from the crown on the top of her head to the shawls and gowns of silk and brocade that flow to her feet. It is almost as if she inhabits a small, mobile palace of her own creation, allowing her to travel anywhere and see others while remaining in a majestic state of occultation. Even Sultan Jahan's grandmother Sikandar, who chose not to wear a veil in Bhopal, understood the theatrical power of such a display, becoming the 'star' of the durbars as the only female ruler among princes and wearing a burqa of white silk with 'dazzling jewelry' on top of it.[41]

However empowering Sultan Jahan's use of purdah might have been to her and other women in India, WMM members did not see veiling and seclusion as equally applicable or even appropriate for women in the West. Rather they accepted Kamal-ud-Din's understanding of it as a cultural practice, not a requirement of Islam.[42] Even when defending purdah, writers for *The Islamic Review* took care to state that its observance in India was the result of the 'environment', for both non-Muslims and Muslims, not 'Qur'anic injunctions'.[43] Muslim women who visited the Shah Jahan Mosque in Woking chose if and to what extent they wanted to veil, and the converts all wore Western clothing, with males and females praying together and mixing freely amongst each other as was conventional in Edwardian society.[44] In a photograph taken of a group of converts at the mosque in 1913, both sexes appear together, side by side, dressed modestly but with faces exposed.[45] Similarly, a full page portrait of 'A British Muslim Family', published in *The Islamic Review* in 1916, serves as a testament to the ease with which the inward transformation of conversion could accompany the outward appearance of middle-class respectability; other than the title and the new Islamic first names underneath the photograph, the image itself contains no visual cues to indicate that the people in it are Muslims. Finally, even Sultan Jahan, despite her strong beliefs about purdah and building an Islamic sisterhood across geographic and cultural boundaries, seems to have understood that her arguments expressed in *Al Hijab: Or, Why Purdah is Necessary* (1922) were far more suitable for an Eastern audience than a Western one, thus choosing to have that book published in Calcutta (Kolkata) but not in London like her biographies.[46]

Yet just as Muslims in the East debated the value of purdah, converts to that faith in the West could come to very different conclusions with regard to seclusion and veiling. Lady Evelyn Cobbold (1867–1963) and Marmaduke Pickthall (1875–1936), for example, both resided in Britain and made the decision to embrace Islam during the First World War period.[47] Both also produced representations of Islamic societies for an English audience: Cobbold in her travel memoir *Wayfarers in the Libyan Desert* (1912) and Pickthall in his novel *Veiled Women* (1913).[48] Yet while Cobbold depicted the secluded harem as like a prison, even a kind of 'living death', the female protagonist of Pickthall's novel, an English convert to Islam called Barakah, describes the separate 'world of women' that she found in Egypt in much the same way that Shah Jahan understood the potential of purdah, as capable of creating a 'great republic' with 'something of the strength which comes from solidarity'.[49]

Interestingly, Cobbold would grow to find value in seclusion and veiling over the course of several decades.[50] However, Sultan Jahan decided to abandon those practices at the end of her life in order to serve as an example for the next generation of Muslim female leaders, particularly her daughter-in-law Maimoona and her granddaughters, Abida, Sajida and Rabia, all of whom had accompanied her in England and been educated by her in such a way so as to be able to comfortably straddle the worlds of East/West and masculine/feminine.[51]

Inconsistent views towards purdah appeared in the pages of *The Islamic Review* as well. For example, in 1914, soon after the outbreak of the First World War, when enthusiasm for the war effort was at its height, an article on the topic of seclusion appeared in which the author, known to us only as 'The Occident', maintained that Islam could not possibly favour that practice given how historically Muslim women had accompanied troops in battle, providing encouragement and nursing services.[52] Yet a very different perspective was put forward in 1918 when, after years of attrition and devastating losses, anxieties about the impact of war on changing gender roles had become inseparable from fears for the future of civilization itself.[53] In that context, Shaykh

Kidwai stated that if English women had practiced purdah like the 'ideal Indian Muslim woman' and stayed in their homes rather than working in munitions factories, fewer men would have had to go to the front and 'much valuable human blood would have been saved'.[54]

While both Kidwai and Sultan Jahan understood that purdah remained an issue of debate in the Islamic world and that they were not obligated as Muslims to support a particular view of it, Sultan Jahan approached the topic with a degree of depth not found in Kidwai's *Islamic Review* articles. She had spent most of her life considering how to work for the betterment of the female sex and came to the conclusion that seclusion and education were the two most important issues facing them.[55] She eventually changed her mind with regard to the former, but she did not make that decision lightly. Rather, it followed decades of gradual liberalization.[56] Kidwai, on the other hand, could put forward contradictory representations of seclusion without feeling the need to reconcile them. Less than six months after his above quoted statement about the ideal Muslim woman keeping purdah instead of going to work in a factory, he wrote of the courage and heroism historically displayed by Muslim women on the battlefield, noting that it should come as no surprise that Ottoman Turkish women had joined a female military organization equivalent to the British Women's Army Auxiliary Corps.[57] For him, the multiple and disparate views on purdah amongst Muslims, past and present, meant that he could employ whatever interpretation supported his argument at any given time, an approach most likely justified by his conviction that finding ways to enlighten an English readership on the truth of Islam was more important than maintaining a consistent position with regard to that contested issue.

Like purdah, polygamy, or more accurately polygyny, also was a subject of debate in the Muslim world as a number of contemporary reformers in India and the Ottoman Empire sought to eliminate it.[58] In her writings made available to the WMM community, Sultan Jahan described the practice as rare but legitimate under certain circumstances. In her book *Muslim Home* (1916), dedicated to the enlightenment of 'My Muslim sisters in the West' and distributed at mosque events, she explains that it was never intended as a goal, but rather originated as a remedy to other social ills by providing security to widows who had lost husbands in tribal warfare and prevented children from being labelled as 'bastards'. Potential abuses of the institution could be checked through regulation by, for example, adding clauses to marriage contracts, as she herself did.[59] One interesting and novel argument presented by Sultan Jahan in both *Muslim Home* and in the pages of *The Islamic Review* is that if polygyny had been allowed in Europe during the early nineteenth century, Napoleon would not have had to divorce his first wife Josephine.[60] Rather, he could have remained in that love marriage while still satisfying his imperial ambitions by also marrying Marie Louise of Austria, thus gaining both a Hapsburg alliance and eventually an heir to the new Bonaparte dynasty. This idea reflects Sultan Jahan's knowledge of European history and her interest in thinking creatively about how Islamic traditions regarding family and gender relationships could be seen as appealing in the West.

Shaykh Kidwai also presented polygyny as beneficial to Westerners in *The Islamic Review*, and, as with purdah, his discussion of it related to wartime concerns. In 1917, after the catastrophic loss of life in the Battle of the Somme in 1916 and over the course of the war more generally, Kidwai described polygyny as a 'boon' that 'saves the nation from disease' by checking a falling birth rate. He then went on to relate how the great German philosopher Arthur Schopenhauer (1788-1860) had expressed his support for that type of familial social organization and that a 'certain German military officer' sought to introduce polygyny into that country, an issue soon to be discussed in the Reichstag.[61] Given the wartime context, compounded with increasing anxieties about the ability of the nation to reproduce itself, Kidwai's description of polygyny would have sounded almost like a type of national defence, a way that Islam could come to the aid of the British Empire during a time of crisis.[62] In fact, according to Kidwai's sources, even the French, Britain's most important ally on the continent, were considering polygyny since the war had left only one marriageable man for every six women.[63]

As with purdah, individuals associated with the WMM did not need to remain consistent with regard to their understanding and/or representations of polygyny. In the case of the latter, however, it was not Kidwai, but rather Kamal-ud-Din who took a situational approach. Kamal-ud-Din tried to disassociate polygyny from Islam in response to publicity surrounding a circular issued by the Australian government warning white women that, if they married Muslim men, they would find themselves confined to a harem with 'native' wives who would hate them and endeavour to make their lives miserable.[64] However, in the opening speech of a debate at Cambridge University, also published in *The Islamic Review*, Kamal-ud-Din stated that the 'solitary female life' was the underlying cause of the 'heinous' tactics of militancy exhibited by the suffragettes. As he explained, those women were Eves in need of Adams; without husbands and children to occupy them, their minds were prone to temptation. Therefore, since women in England outnumbered men, polygyny was necessary.[65]

The issue of women's suffrage is a particularly important one with regard to gender politics in British society and the British Empire, and when WMM leaders and supporters expressed an opinion of it for the benefit of an English audience, it tended to be favourable.[66] After all, the belief in 'votes for women' was consistent with their position that, as Muslims, they supported female emancipation and empowerment. Even Kamal-ud-Din's Cambridge University speech criticized the militant tactics of the suffragettes, but not the idea that women should have the vote. For in that same speech Kamal-ud-Din also stated the following with regard to the suffragists: 'They have a laudable object before them as far as their demands are concerned, and I see no reason why every honest man interested in the betterment of the fair sex should not sympathize with their noble cause'.[67] Given the intense and violent opposition that the suffragists often experienced at the hands of their male opponents, whether in the street or as a result of official policy regarding the forced feeding of hunger-striking suffragettes in prison, Kamal-ud-Din's statement on their behalf should be understood as a way of presenting Muslim male attitudes as more just and chivalrous than that of their British Christian counterparts.

In the same vein, the British convert and active member of the WMM, Marmaduke Pickthall, related a story of how one evening in 1914, he and two other men were having dinner together in a hotel restaurant in London. After they finished eating, one of them, an English Member of Parliament, began to rail against the suffragettes, even going so far as to say that they deserved the violence that a number had recently experienced at the hands of a mob. The MP, no doubt labouring under the assumption that Muslim men were oppressive or even barbaric with regard to women, assumed that their Ottoman Turkish dinner companion would agree. Yet much to his surprise, the Turkish man responded not only by condemning the British government as 'both wicked and foolish' for allowing 'such cruelty', but by stating that the just alternative was, in fact, to give women the vote. Pickthall presented Islam as essentially progressive with regard to gender issues, even stating that taking historical context into consideration, the 'Prophet of Islam was perhaps the greatest feminist the world has ever known'.[68]

While there is no reason to doubt the sincerity of Kamal-ud-Din's statement in support of the suffragists or Kidwai's understanding of Muhammad as a feminist, it is important to note that these men tended to identify with feminist causes only insofar as doing so furthered their primary objective, which was to present Islam in a positive light. Kamal-ud-Din's suggestion that the militancy of the suffragettes could be remedied through polygyny would have alienated most Western and, in fact, growing numbers of Eastern and Muslim feminists at that time who opposed the practice and saw it as contrary to their faith. His statement, therefore, should be understood not as a step towards creating coalitions in pursuit of feminist goals, but rather as a way of countering and reversing dominant Orientalist imperialist discourses in which English men liberated women from patriarchal Muslim systems that oppressed them.[69] Pickthall's story does the same by presenting the (Christian) Englishman as the one who condones violence against the suffragettes, while the Muslim man objects to it. Indeed, the repeated insistence from both women and men associated with the WMM that, unlike in the West where women had to fight and in the case of the suffragettes endure great hardship in hopes of obtaining their rights, Islam simply granted them those that they were due, could be interpreted as reinforcing a conservative, apolitical position.[70]

Still, the 'sacred' rights that women had under Islam, particularly those within marriage and the family, remained a topic of real importance to the WMM, both for its learned authorities and new converts. In her publications intended for that community, Sultan Jahan calls Muhammad the 'Benefactor and Emancipator' of the female sex, in part because of the material guarantees his teachings provided them both during marriage and in the event of divorce.[71] Kidwai discusses the same issues in his 'Women under Islam' series, at one point describing child custody laws as recognizing the 'superiority of women over men'.[72] Both in that series and to an 'appreciative' audience at a marriage ceremony held in the Shah Jahan Mosque, Kidwai explained the institution of *mahr*, which stipulates that the bride is entitled to receive a dowry from the groom, or his family, which then becomes the personal property of the wife to use however she likes. In addition, she may demand it in the event of a divorce.[73] These types of representations resonated with both male and female converts in Britain, a number of whom expressed delight in the belief that their newfound faith sought the emancipation and equality of women.[74]

In fact, one point emphasized repeatedly by and for the benefit of those involved with the WMM was that Islam elevated the position of women in a way that no other doctrine or legal system could, past or present. Time and again, WMM members were reminded that the rise of Muhammad put an end to the practice of female infanticide common in pre-Islamic Arabia. Sultan Jahan pronounced female inheritance rights in Islam to be superior to those of any other civilization 'modern or ancient' and described her faith as less restrictive to women than Chinese, Japanese, Indian, Jewish and Christian traditions.[75] In a paper presented to the London women's social and intellectual organization, the Lyceum Club, and reproduced in *The Islamic Review*, Kamal-ud-Din compared the rights of women in Islam favourably to the principle of coverture in English law. As he explained, by fusing the legal identity of husband and wife into one person, coverture put the latter under the complete power of the former, making her legal condition no better than that of an enslaved person in the Americas or ancient Rome.[76]

In addition to their exposure to the legal rights of women under Islam, WMM members were given ample opportunity to read about Muhammad's relationship with his wives and benefit from his and their words and actions. His kind, respectful and chivalrous behaviour made him a role model for his followers. In addition, the vast majority of Muslims whose marriages were monogamous could look to the example set by Muhammad and Khadijah, his first and only wife for twenty-five years until her death. To her, he was 'An ideal husband', demonstrating great love, esteem and devotion, and the two had such an intimate bond that she was able to understand his true character in ways that no one else could fathom.[77] Even towards the end of his life when wartime circumstances dictated polygyny, Muhammad remained a good husband. According to his third wife, Ayesha, a great jurist and creator of *hadith*, or reports of the traditions (words and actions) of the Prophet Muhammad, and thus an authoritative source in Islam, he still provided a praiseworthy example and told his followers that 'The best man among you is he who is best to his wife; and I am best among you in respect to my wives'.[78]

The Muslim wife and mother was understood and presented to the WMM community as an ideal role, one that, like the Victorian 'Angel in the House', promised a kind of blissful domesticity within the private sphere.[79] Sultan Jahan described the Muslim home as 'a paradise' in which husbands and wives have different but equally important functions and abilities characterized by complementarity, an idea echoed in Muhammad's statement that women are the 'twin-halves of men'.[80] According to Sultan Jahan, women are physically weaker and more delicate and therefore better suited for the private sphere, where their natural tenderness of heart nurtures the next generation. Men, on the other hand, are endowed with strength to enable them to face the challenges of the outside world in order to protect and provide for the family. Because of their different roles in society, the Qur'an gives men a 'superiority' over women that is 'by no means prejudicial to the equality of the sexes'. This gradation is further mitigated by the mutual dependence of each upon the other and the belief that the 'two great divine attributes—the Maintenance and the Nourishment of the universe found their epiphany in mankind through father and mother'.[81] Praise of motherhood appears in *The Islamic Review* as well, such as in the oft-cited comment by Muhammad that 'paradise lies under the feet of the mothers' or the statement by 'an Indian Muslim lady' that 'the destiny of future generations lies in the lap of women'.[82]

Representations of the devoted mother and wife fulfilled in her separate sphere would have been as familiar to the WMM's British audience as the middle-class respectability of the dress of the mission's converts.[83] Certainly the idea of female clubs, organizations and educational institutions would have had resonance as well. Yet less recognizable, and in some cases dramatically different, views of Muslim femininity also were available to the WMM community: from that of Sultan Jahan in full burka to the idea that nature intended for the female sex to rule to the suggestion that polygyny would strengthen the English nation. Attempting to shed light on how those involved with the WMM understood Muslim womanhood during that organization's early years can seem like a study in contrasts. For the Muslim woman could be represented as so committed to purdah that she would not venture out of the house even when wartime crisis called her to the factories or, conversely, as heroically charging the enemy on the battlefield brandishing weapons in hand. Along the same lines, she could come to the conclusion that her faith prepared her not only to participate but also to assume a leadership role in contemporary feminist movements, such as women's suffrage, or, on the other hand, decide that since Islam granted females sacred rights, they had no need for secular ones.

Conclusion

In short, during the early years of the WMM, when the organization first established itself on firm ground in Britain, it did not produce one fixed or stable image of Muslim femininity. Rather, the concept remained continually in flux.[84] Sultan Jahan, Muslim missionaries at Woking, and other contributors to the *Islamic Review* may have believed that Islam empowered females and understood the importance of presenting positive depictions of Muslim gender roles in order to counter the negative ones already existing in British society, but that did not mean they agreed with one another on exactly what 'empowering' or 'positive' meant at any given time. Not only did those associated with the WMM, its female patron, male leadership, and writers for *The Islamic Review*, who were both male and female but primarily male, disagree with regard to issues debated in the Muslim world, most notably purdah and polygyny, but an individual Muslim might change his or her mind about or present contradictory views of those practices. It is worth noting, however, that Sultan Jahan's writings regarding those issues and Muslim gender roles more generally tended to be characterized by considerably greater depth and reflection than did those of her male counterparts.

While the unstable nature of Muslim femininity put forward by Sultan Jahan and others involved with the WMM during the early years of its establishment could be interpreted by some as resulting from an essential incongruence between the position of women in Islam and the culture of modern Western society, I would suggest the opposite. Those representations surrounding the proper role and status of women in Islam may have been characterized by numerous inconsistencies and contradictions, but so too were ideas about women in England more generally. After all, the nineteenth century had seen a rise in feminist movements of all types, including the demand for the vote, property rights and access to higher education, and gender tensions and debates continued into the early twentieth century with the militancy of the suffragettes reaching a point of crisis prior to the outbreak of the First World War.[85] That war further complicated ideas about 'proper' gender relationships as women began to assume a variety of new responsibilities in the public sphere. The fluid nature of Muslim femininity as portrayed by Sultan Jahan and the WMM from roughly 1913 to 1918, then, reflects that organization's modernity and affinity with the larger English and British imperial culture of which it was a part.[86] In addition, the ambiguity of that concept, within certain parameters, allowed individuals to create and re-create meaning for themselves, a valuable process for both lifelong Muslims and recent converts.

SECTION 3

BRITISH MUSLIM WOMEN AND
EXPANDING SPHERES OF INFLUENCE

5

'FATMA *HANIM* OF THE ENGLISH CONVERTS'

HANNAH RODDA ROBINSON AND THE OTTOMAN COURT

Gareth Winrow

Introduction

Until recently, very little had been written about the life of Hannah Rodda (1854–1948). This is surprising given that she was one of the first women in Victorian England to convert to Islam. The lack of interest in the life of Hannah Rodda is more puzzling given her later impact on the Ottoman court after she relocated to Constantinople (Istanbul).[1] The life of Hannah Rodda Robinson, also known as Fatma *Hanım*, is an intriguing and remarkable one in which fact is certainly stranger than fiction.[2] This chapter seeks to explain why Hannah converted to Islam and notes, in particular, the importance of her marriage to the supposed Afghan warlord, Dr Gholab Shah. The key roles played by the British Muslim leader Abdullah Quilliam (1856–1932) and the Ottoman authorities in the months of turmoil following the collapse of Hannah's marriage are examined. In the face of terrible circumstances for herself and her young children, Hannah chose to remain in Constantinople and maintained her commitment to Islam.

From Bethnal Green to India

Hannah Rodda was born in Stepney, east London, in 1854. Life was not easy for the young Hannah. The youngest of three girls born to Benjamin Rodda and Mary Ann Rodda (*née* Russell), Hannah was raised in the slums of Bethnal Green. The Russells were an impoverished family of bricklayers from the East End. Hannah's father was a merchant seaman born in Cornwall. Benjamin Rodda died at sea (of tuberculosis) while Hannah was an infant, and, in her first years, Hannah spent periods of time in the local workhouse with her mother and two sisters.

Entering into domestic service, in her youth Hannah worked for Dr Geoffrey Pearl (c. 1806–84), a former mayor of Windsor and one of Queen Victoria's personal physicians. It seems that Hannah had an illegitimate daughter with Dr Pearl; Gertrude, born in December 1875, was certainly a major beneficiary in the will of Dr Pearl when he died in 1884. After the birth of her daughter, Hannah left Dr Pearl and worked as a housekeeper in Lambeth, south London. At the time, this was an area notorious for its squalor, petty crime and prostitution.

Hannah's situation dramatically improved when she married Spencer Robinson (1838–89) in St Pancras, London in March 1880. Robinson was a former well-to-do tenant farmer from Lincolnshire who had emigrated to India after the death of his first wife. Spencer was a co-proprietor of three tea estates in Bengal and later became a traffic manager for the Darjeeling Himalayan Railway. It is not clear how Hannah met Spencer, although in the early 1870s Spencer had briefly lived in West Firle in Sussex, which was near to Dr Pearl's summer residence in Ripe. Spencer returned to India almost immediately after marrying Hannah, while Hannah left for India several months later in November 1880. In general, Hannah lived a happy life in India raising a family, even though her husband was imprisoned for several months because of bankruptcy. The Robinsons recovered and, when Hannah returned to England in 1890 or 1891 after Spencer's death, she was a wealthy woman. She could afford to open a superior boarding house at a prestigious address in Brighton on the south coast.[3]

Religion did not appear to figure prominently in Hannah's early years. Her parents had married in the local Anglican church of St. Matthew's in Bethnal Green. Interestingly, though, Hannah's family would develop Jewish connections. In 1864, her aunt, also called Hannah, married John Patrick Netto, a bootmaker and later a publican. John Patrick was a direct descendant of Rabbi David Nieto (1654–1728), the renowned Torah scholar and *haham* (spiritual leader, learned in Jewish law) of the Spanish and Portuguese Jewish community in London in the early eighteenth century. This Jewish connection, though, had been almost severed by the time John Patrick married Hannah's aunt because John Patrick's father, Phineas, had previously married a Catholic.[4]

In 1901, Hannah's illegitimate daughter, Gertrude, married a German Jewish businessman, Max Eisenmann, who was a Hamburg-based car dealer. This was when Gertrude was becoming well-known as a racing motorcyclist in Wilhelmine Germany. After her marriage, Gertrude became a famous car rally driver. It seems that Hannah and Gertrude maintained minimal contact, exchanging only a few letters. Fearful of Nazi threats to seize control of her husband's business, Gertrude Eisenmann apparently committed suicide in early 1933.[5]

Prior to relocating to India, Hannah's first husband, Spencer Robinson, had got on well with the local vicar in the Lincolnshire village of East Keal. He had organized the lavish celebrations held in the village when the Reverend Joseph Spence returned from his marriage tour with his wife. The Robinsons were seen as respectable church-goers. Spencer Robinson's father, John Wheelwright Robinson, had been a churchwarden in East Keal and had contributed greatly to the restoration of the village church; a stained-glass window was erected in his memory in St. Helen's church at Saxby near Market Rasen in Lincolnshire. It was not unusual, therefore, for Hannah to have inscribed on Spencer Robinson's gravestone in Kalimpong the words of Jesus as cited in the Gospel of St. Matthew: 'Come unto me all ye that labour and are heavy laden and I will give you rest'.[6]

A convert to Islam

Given this background, why did the widow, Hannah Robinson, convert to Islam less than two years after her husband's death? According to a popular but erroneous narrative which evolved in modern Turkey, Hannah, for some unknown reason referred to as Sarah, had converted after witnessing the plight of Muslims in British-ruled India. Eager to help the Muslim population, 'Sarah' and her husband converted to Islam and then later moved to Constantinople. They took the names Fatma and Abdullah. According to this account, the origins of which are unknown, both 'Sarah' and her husband were highly educated and influential in their community in India.[7] Hannah and Spencer's son, Ahmet Robenson (1889–1965), also spoke of his mother's supposed privileged upbringing in a 1965 interview with a Turkish journalist. He noted how his mother's family was ostensibly renowned in the fields of art, education and literature, and was linked to the British businessman and politician Cecil Rhodes (1853–1902).[8] Here, Ahmet Robenson seemed to have consciously played upon the similarity between the 'Rhodes' and 'Rodda' surnames.

Why did such an error-strewn account become popular in Turkey? A supposedly important family converting to Islam was good propaganda for the Turkish state. Two of Hannah's sons became well-known in Turkey. Ahmet Robenson and his brother, Abdurrahman (1887–1915, original name, Eugene Robinson) founded the Scouting movement in the Ottoman Empire. Ahmet Robenson became a successful goalkeeper for the Galatasaray football team and introduced basketball and other sports to the Ottoman Empire. The family also provided martyrs for the Ottoman cause. Abdurrahman and another son, Yakup (1884–1916, original name, Spencer John Bernard) fought against the British and died in the First World War.

An alternative account to explain Hannah's conversion was provided in *The Crescent*, the newspaper published by the Liverpool Muslim Institute (LMI) established by Abdullah Quilliam in 1887. Hannah had apparently visited Quilliam's wife, Hannah Quilliam (1858–1909), in Liverpool and had then decided to renounce

Christianity and become a Muslim together with her children.[9] This may have occurred in 1891, prior to Hannah's marriage to Dr Gholab Shah in November of that year. It is not clear, though, how Mrs Quilliam would have convinced Hannah to convert to Islam given that she herself, unlike her husband and mother-in-law, remained a Christian throughout her life.

One needs to be cautious when attempting to understand Hannah's behaviour because of her propensity—as will be observed—to exaggerate or to distort the truth. However, it does seem that Hannah's relationship with a supposed Afghan warlord was key to her decision to convert to Islam. Accounts from Hannah herself, as well as reports from the British and Ottoman authorities, appear to substantiate this. Nevertheless, although Hannah may have abandoned Christianity to marry Dr Gholab Shah, the evidence also suggests that, after her conversion, Hannah/Fatma became a devout, practicing Muslim.

Fatma married Dr Gholab Shah at the LMI on 26 November 1891. The ceremony, which took place according to the rites of Islam, was performed by Abdullah Quilliam himself. It was reported that Fatma and her children—but apparently not Gertrude—had converted to Islam some time before the wedding. Gholab Shah was depicted as a distinguished warlord, the eldest son of Sheikh Mohammad, who had fought against the British in the Second Anglo-Afghan War. In that war, Gholab Shah was reputedly one of the leaders of a company of Ghazis—fanatical warriors and devout followers of Islam. After the war, he had established himself as an eye doctor based in London. Immediately after the marriage, the couple left the country to begin a new life in Constantinople.[10]

In her later correspondence with the British Prime Minister's Office, Fatma described how she had first encountered Dr Shah when he was living and working as an oculist in Greenwich, south-east London.[11] This must have been after the April 1891 Census, when Gholab Shah was registered as living at Mornington Crescent in north-west London. It appears that this was a whirlwind romance, as news of the impending marriage was announced in late October 1891.[12] Engagement to a supposed former Afghan warlord and previous enemy of the British may have seemed odd. However, Fatma informed the British authorities that she had thought that her marriage could be 'greatly instrumental' in improving ties between the Afghan and British governments.[13] This was at a time when Afghanistan was strategically important for the British in the so-called 'Great Game' in Central Asia.[14]

Fatma noted how Gholab Shah had represented himself to her as a Muslim, and stated that she had accepted his offer of marriage 'after due consideration'.[15] Details from the Ottoman Archives are more explicit. A letter from the Ottoman Sultan's Yildiz Palace Secretariat, dated 4 February 1892, bluntly stated that Fatma had converted to Islam to make possible her marriage to Gholab Shah.[16] According to the Ottoman Embassy in London, the newly-wed couple had moved to Constantinople so that they could raise their children according to Islamic tradition.[17]

Fatma's marriage to Gholab Shah was one of the earliest at the LMI involving a female convert to Islam. The first such marriage was probably in April 1891 when Charlotte Fitch wed Mohamed Ahmad, a London-based barrister. On that occasion, a Christian ceremony had taken place in London before the wedding in Liverpool.[18] This set a precedent for what appeared to become a common practice of having a legally recognized and recorded wedding in London (or elsewhere) before performing a religious Muslim marriage in Liverpool. The legality of marriages carried out at the mosque in Liverpool would be later questioned by the British Home Office.[19] In the case of Fatma and Gholab Shah, however, no marriage was registered in the official records of the General Register Office.

Marriages of female converts at the LMI encountered fierce local and national opposition, and Fatma's wedding was no exception. People were shocked at British women who converted to Islam and then married primarily Asian Muslim men from the colonies. There was a belief that for a strong nation to rule an empire, it was essential to preserve the 'cultural and racial homogeneity' of the 'British patriarchal structure'.[20] Marriage to a Muslim man conjured up images of the harem (women's quarters), female enslavement and violence against women. Commenting on Fatma's marriage, one newspaper reported that it would be a pity if this set an example which would lead to 'our free, Christian women' being 'transplanted to Mohamedan harems'.[21] However, social and class distinctions were also important in late Victorian England. For example, a marriage to an 'honoured guest' such as to an aristocrat from India might be looked upon more favourably.[22] As a supposed famous warlord, Gholab Shah would seem to fit in this category. But Fatma was also criticized in the media for marrying to secure the title of 'Mrs Dr Gholab Shah' as this 'sounded better than Mrs Robinson'.[23] The marriage between Fatma and Gholab Shah turned out to be a disaster, and they soon separated. Stranded in Constantinople, Fatma's links with the Quilliams proved to be of vital importance to her securing a divorce from Gholab Shah.

The importance of Abdullah Quilliam

A colourful, charismatic and controversial character, Abdullah Quilliam had a reputation for being a womanizer (see Chapter 2).[24] Interestingly, at the time of writing he was a figure much respected by the governing Justice and Development Party in Turkey for his promotion of Islam in Victorian England.[25] Moreover, a narrative has developed in contemporary Turkey which asserts that Quilliam was actually the father of Fatma's children. Reports found in the Ottoman Archives are largely responsible for this portrayal. An account referring to the execution of Yakup Robenson in December 1916 for passing intelligence to the British noted that he was the son of 'Abdullah Gevilyan', the Turkish for 'Quilliam'.[26] And, according to Ottoman records, when Ahmet Robenson was registered as a student at the Galatasaray Lycée in 1899, he was listed as the son of Quilliam.[27] The Turkish football historian, Melih Şabanoğlu, has also argued that Quilliam was the father of Fatma's offspring.[28] Such a story would perhaps make sense for many in Turkey, with Fatma supposedly coming from a distinguished family and Quilliam regarded as an important Western Muslim. But it is not true; Quilliam never visited India and so he could not have fathered Fatma's children. However, given Quilliam's reputation for philandering, it is quite possible that he may have had a relationship with Fatma.

The Ottoman authorities probably first became fully aware of Quilliam in October 1890, when he successfully protested against the staging of the play *Mahomet*, with its depiction of the Prophet Muhammad, which was about to open at the Lyceum Theatre in London. That month, the Ottoman ambassador in Britain informed Prime Minister Lord Salisbury (1830–1903) of Sultan Abdulhamid II's (1842–1918) opposition to the planned production.[29] Quilliam heard of the Sultan's support for his protests in a letter sent to him by Woods Pasha (Sir Henry Felix Woods, 1843–1929), an admiral in the Imperial Ottoman Navy and a key public relations advisor to Abdulhamid II.[30] Contacts between Quilliam and the Sultan quickly developed. In April 1891, Quilliam and his eldest son, Robert Ahmad (1880–1954), were invited to Constantinople and remained there for over a month. The young Robert was appointed lieutenant-colonel in the Sultan's elite *Ertuğrul* regiment (the Imperial Guard).[31] This was the first of several visits made by Quilliam to the Ottoman Empire. By 1894, the ties between the Sultan and Quilliam were such that Abdulhamid II apparently raised no objections when the Liverpool lawyer declared himself 'Sheikh-ul-Islam of the British Isles', effectively the leader of British Muslims.[32]

The activities of the small community of Liverpool Muslims were closely monitored in Constantinople. It was not surprising, then, that Fatma's marriage to Gholab Shah at Liverpool in November 1891 attracted the attention of the Ottoman authorities. A letter from the Ottoman Embassy in London to the Ottoman Ministry of Foreign Affairs confirmed that the marriage had taken place and added that Fatma *Hanım* owned a fortune—around 20,000 Ottoman liras (which would amount to over £500,000 today). The letter noted that, at Quilliam's request, passports had been issued to enable the couple to begin their new life in Constantinople.[33]

Within months of their arrival in Constantinople, the marriage was in ruins. By early February 1892, Gholab Shah had squandered all of Fatma's money. Ottoman officials authorized the payment of a stipend to Gholab Shah to support him and his family, which was personally approved by the Sultan.[34] In her later accounts to the British authorities, Fatma revealed details of the abuse she and her children had suffered at the hands of Gholab Shah. Trapped alone in a hotel room in Constantinople, Fatma was physically threatened by her husband, who declared that he was 'Jack the Ripper', the name given to the notorious serial killer who stalked the streets of London in the late 1880s. She said that Gholab Shah attempted to marry off her young daughter, Adile (original name, Maud) to an Indian merchant.[35] British officials provided information that revealed that Gholab Shah was actually called Elahie Bosche. A known troublemaker from India, Bosche had become infamous for attempting to marry British women for their money. He also dabbled in politics and had sought to curry favour with the Russians with regard to their interests in Afghanistan and Central Asia.[36]

By June 1892, Fatma had successfully secured a divorce from 'Gholab Shah' through the ruling of a local court in Constantinople. Her British lawyer had provided testimony from an English woman whom Gholab Shah had earlier married in England in a Christian ceremony.[37] The supposed Afghan warlord had married a Miss Edith Mary Lait from Hull in 1888. Edith had swiftly left Gholab Shah upon discovering that he was already married. This would have made Fatma's later marriage to Gholab Shah illegal in the eyes of the British authorities. There was some speculation in files now stored in the Ottoman Archives that Fatma had secured the divorce because at the time she still believed in her previous religion and was not a 'true' Muslim. In court, Gholab Shah had perhaps accused Fatma of not being a Muslim in an attempt to damage her case. Following the court's ruling, Gholab Shah was despatched to Izmir with a group of security guards and from there was deported to the United States. Fatma continued to receive the stipend previously allocated to Gholab Shah and was allowed to live in rent-free accommodation in a well-heeled neighbourhood of Constantinople.[38]

Fatma's connection with Quilliam had most probably also helped her in the court proceeding. At around the time of the court hearing, on 13 June 1892, Fatma had written a letter to the Grand Vizier, Ahmed Cevat Pasha (1851–1900), pleading for further financial support for herself and her children. Together with her petition she enclosed a letter of backing from Quilliam himself.[39] Being an early member of the LMI seems to have worked in Fatma's favour. She would continue to maintain close ties with Quilliam in the following years while living in Constantinople. In the aftermath of the court ruling, Fatma, as a single woman with a young family to feed, became increasingly dependent on the largesse of the Ottoman court.

The role of the Ottoman court

For a period after her divorce, Fatma continued to seek financial support and assistance from both the Ottoman and British authorities. Although she had converted to Islam and resided in Constantinople, Fatma remained a British subject. Ultimately, Fatma succeeded in obtaining more assistance from the Ottoman court. She would become known generally as 'Fatma *Hanım* of the English Converts'.[40] It was the significance of her conversion to Islam rather than her nationality which enabled Fatma to continue to receive considerable backing from the Ottoman authorities in the months after her divorce. Only one week after despatching a letter to the Grand Vizier, on 20 June 1892, Fatma sent a missive to the British Prime Minister's Office urging the government in London to lobby on her behalf to secure more funds for her from the Ottoman Sultan.[41] In a follow-up letter, she boldly requested British officials to inform the Sultan that she was willing to be of service to him, 'being practical, energetic and from England' and 'hoped that his Majesty will attach me to his family in this way'.[42] She had obtained a further £50 from the Sultan, and her sons had secured free places at a school in Constantinople. Fatma added that she wished the Sultan to be notified that she came from a European family accustomed to 'civilised refinement' and that it was impossible for her to continue to live in her present condition.[43] Here was a clear example of an extremely forward and determined Fatma not being entirely honest.

The response from the British authorities was not very helpful. The Foreign Office declared that 'Mrs Robinson' was 'very lucky' to receive anything from the Sultan, and if the British Ambassador to the Ottoman Empire, Francis Clare Ford (1828-99), pressed for more support, this could rebound against her. Concern for the fate of Fatma's children was expressed with officials voicing alarm at the 'grave scandal' if the children of the late Mr Robinson had converted to Islam. The Foreign Office noted that if the Embassy in Constantinople interfered and the children were removed from their Ottoman homes, they would probably starve unless some Christian religious or charitable society intervened.[44] Surprisingly, the Foreign Office did not seem to be aware of earlier newspaper reports of Fatma's second marriage and most of her children's conversions to Islam.

In his message to the Prime Minister, Ambassador Ford noted that 'Mrs Robinson' lived in Constantinople as a 'Turkish woman' and as a Muslim, and that she had told British officials that she did not want to leave the Ottoman Empire.[45] There was perhaps little incentive for Fatma to return to Britain. Having renounced Christianity and then having lost all the wealth accumulated by her first husband, it would not have been easy for her to settle in England. It was not clear to what extent Fatma had maintained ties with her relatives in London. At least one branch of her family still lived in poverty. After the death of her father, her mother had married a cow keeper living in east London. The daughter from this marriage—Annie Sarah Radley—was living on parish relief in Bow in a one-room dwelling according to the 1911 Census.[46]

Finding little support from the British authorities, Fatma became more dependent on assistance from the Ottoman court. It was customary in the Ottoman Empire to provide welfare for foreign women left single and destitute. Sultan Abdulhamid II seemed to take a particular interest in Fatma, a woman who had converted to Islam and who knew Quilliam well. However, 'Fatma *Hanım* of the English Converts' still retained her British nationality. The Foreign Office stated that 'Mrs Robinson' had not ceased to be a British subject given that Gholab Shah was already a married man at the time Fatma wed him.[47]

According to Ottoman tradition and Islamic law, conversion to Islam on Ottoman territory automatically made the convert a subject of the Sultan-Caliph. Other converts to Islam were also looked upon favourably. However, this changed with the adoption of the Ottoman Citizenship Law of 1869. Conversion to Islam was no longer a sufficient condition for Ottoman citizenship. Each case had to be judged on its own merit. The Ottoman Empire had become a place of refuge for 'suspicious characters', including individuals who were looked upon as possible spies.[48] Article 3 of the 1869 Ottoman Citizenship Law stated that foreigners could become Ottoman citizens by petitioning the Ottoman Ministry of Foreign Affairs after they had resided in the Ottoman Empire for five years. But Article 4 of the same Law noted that the Ottoman government reserved the right to confer nationality on exceptional individuals who did not meet the residency requirement. In certain circumstances, the Ottoman state did facilitate long-term residency for foreigners. This included providing social welfare for single and destitute women who could eventually gain citizenship through marrying an Ottoman subject. Fatma was a convert-migrant seeking to belong to the 'well-protected domains' of the Sultan.[49] Given her conversion to Islam and her association with Quilliam and the LMI, Fatma could have eventually secured Ottoman citizenship by the terms of Article 4 of the Ottoman Citizenship Law. However, it appears that after a period of time, Fatma finally secured Ottoman citizenship by marrying an Ottoman subject.

After securing her divorce, Fatma continued to receive support from the Ottoman authorities in spite of British officials' reluctance to press her case. Receiving regular stipends, she continued to live rent-free, and her sons obtained free board and tuition at the prestigious Kuleli Military College in Constantinople. Fatma's daughter, Adile, was rescued from the clutches of Gholab Shah and was housed with the family of Mustafa Zeki Pasha (1849–1914).[50] A close associate of the Sultan, the Pasha was the Field Marshal of the Imperial Arsenal of Ordnance and Artillery and was in charge of all military schools in the Ottoman Empire.

However, in order to continue to benefit from the generosity of the Ottoman court, it seems that Fatma had to convince the local authorities of her sincerity in her adoption of Islam. Quilliam again came to her support, providing a letter of reference. On 28 January 1893, Fatma wrote again to the Grand Vizier. In her letter,

1. Fatima Sheir teaching the Qur'an at her home in Butetown, Cardiff, 1943.

2. A view of the interior of Cairo Café in Butetown, Cardiff, 1943. Olive Salaman (centre) serves customers whilst her husband, Ali Salaman, is just visible in the doorway in the background.

3. Abdullah Quilliam (standing, left) with his children and members of the Liverpool Muslim Institute, c.1893. The woman standing to the right of Quilliam is probably his wife Hannah Quilliam; the woman seated directly below Quilliam is his mother, Harriet (Khadijah) Holehouse. The identities of the other adults are currently unknown, but it is likely that one of the women is Fatima Cates and another is Quilliam's second wife, Mary Lyon.

The Position of Women under Islamic Law.

By Madame Nafeesa M. T. Keep.

IN considering the position of woman under Islam, I shall not take up your time, nor distract your attention, by a lengthy account of who and what woman was under other dispensations; suffice it to say that there is undoubted evidence of woman having been in the most degraded and humiliating social and moral subjection to man at the period when Arabia's great prophet began his mission, which has now the proofs of more than thirteen centuries to attest its success as the emancipator from idolatry, inhumanity, and a host of other evils, which some six centuries of non-Islamic teaching had *not* eradicated from the race of mankind.

4. 'The Position of Women under Islamic Law' by Nafeesah M. T. Keep, published in Abdullah Quilliam's *The Islamic World*, March 1895, pp. 342–51.

5. Nawab Sultan Jahan, the Begum of Bhopal, at the Delhi Durbar, 1911.

A BRITISH MUSLIM FAMILY

From left to right :—1. Mrs. Mubarakah Welch ; 2. Master Yusuf ; 3. Mr. Ahmad Welch ;
4. Mrs. Hajarah Phillip, aunt to Mubarakah.

6. 'A British Muslim Family' as featured in *Islamic Review and Muslim India*, vol. 4, no. 3 (1916), frontispiece.

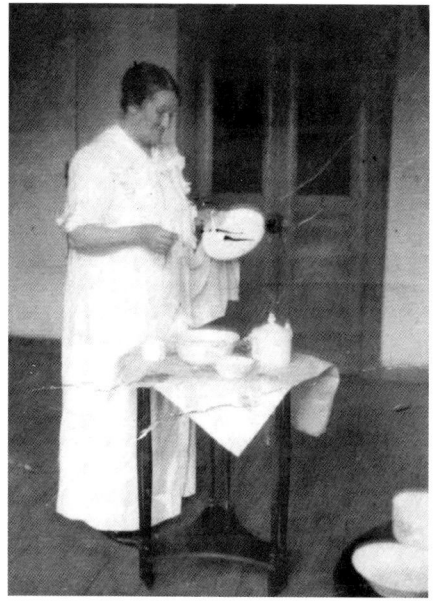

7. Hannah Rodda
Robinson, date unknown.

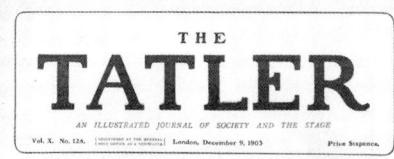

8. Front cover of *The Tatler* featuring Bertha Cave, 9 December 1903.

9. Gladys Milton Brooke, the Dayang Muda of Sarawak, with Khalid Sheldrake at Croydon Airport prior to her conversion to Islam, 18 February 1932.

10. Students and staff at Maria Grey Training College, London, 1905–7. Atiya Fyzee is seated on the ground in the front row, third from the right.

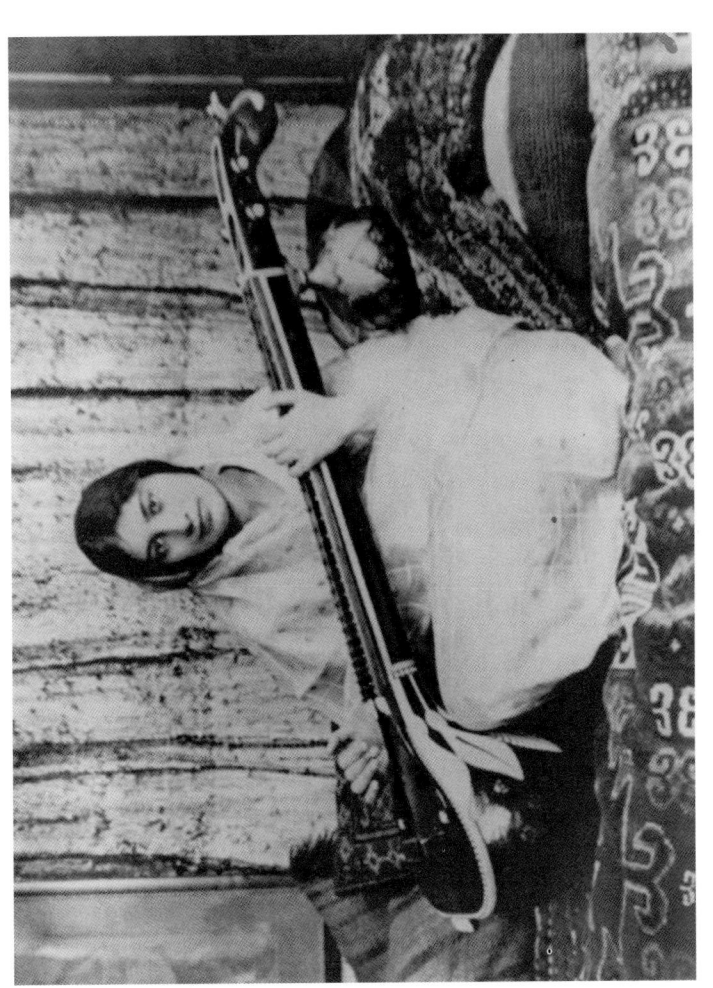

11. Noor Inayat Khan, 1937.

she stated that she had written to Quilliam and that he had replied confirming that Gholab Shah was an imposter. More significantly, Quilliam testified that he was 'well-acquainted' with Fatma. Fatma went on to explain how she had corresponded fully with Quilliam over a lengthy period concerning 'doctrinal points' of 'my Holy Faith upon which I had doubts'. Fatma insisted that 'my joining the Moslem faith was a free action of my own prompted by conviction'.[51]

One will never know how sincere Hannah/Fatma was when she initially converted to Islam. However, in her second letter to the Grand Vizier, it appeared that Fatma was forced to explain her reasons for converting to Islam in order to continue to receive welfare support. The significance of this letter, together with Quilliam's reference, should not be under-estimated. The letter may have finally dispelled any lingering doubts the Ottoman authorities had concerning the sincerity of Fatma's conversion to Islam.

The past months would have certainly been stressful for Fatma. As early as June 1892, in a petition to the Ottoman Ministry of the Interior, Fatma noted how she was 'in pain for having changed her religion', but she had no intention of giving up Islam.[52] In another petition forwarded to the Ottoman authorities in the same month, Fatma explained how she had left all her friends in England and had nobody to turn to for support.[53]

Fatma's situation improved immeasurably when she later married Ahmet Bahri, one of the Sultan's young military officers. The marriage probably took place in 1894, as the couple had a child, Fevzi, born in March 1895.[54] Fatma had become an Ottoman citizen. No longer 'Fatma *Hanım* of the English Converts', she would still be able to enjoy the benefits of the generosity of the Ottoman state and maintain close ties with Quilliam and the Muslim community in Liverpool.

The later years

After her marriage to Ahmet Bahri, Fatma did not disappear from public view but instead became somewhat of a celebrity in the last years of the reign of Sultan Abdulhamid II. Likely through a bureaucratic mix-up, Ottoman officials at one time attempted to claim rent payments from Fatma, who had moved. The authorities demanded the payment of 90,750 Kurus in back-payments— quite a substantial sum of money. Responding in a petition, Fatma reminded officials that she had been given the accommodation free of rent. On 12 February 1907, the Ottoman Minister of Finance himself, Mehmed Ziya Pasha, was obliged to send a letter of apology to Fatma.[55] In that period, the only other person to live in rent-free accommodation on the same street as Fatma was Fausto Zonaro (1854–1929), a famous Ottoman court painter.

Fatma and her family were guests of honour in May 1898 when Abdullah and Hannah Quilliam visited Constantinople. The Bahris were invited to be part of a distinguished welcoming committee, which also included Woods Pasha and Ibrahim Hakki Bey (1862– 1918), then the principal legal councillor to the Sublime Porte (the Ottoman government), who would later become Grand Vizier. Fatma and her daughter were veiled when they met the Quilliams at the famous Pera Palace Hotel.[56] Later, in the same month, the Bahris accompanied the Quilliams to the boat that would take them to Izmir. As a parting gift, Ahmet Bahri's father, Captain Mustafa Effendi, presented Quilliam with a picture that had quotations from the Qur'an written in Turkish characters.[57]

There is evidence that strongly indicates that the Bahris and the Quilliams remained on close terms as late as 1908, the year that Abdullah Quilliam permanently left Liverpool and the LMI closed.[58] In November 1917, in a communication to the British Foreign Office, Martha May Thompson (1880–1952) made inquiries about the whereabouts and wellbeing of her fiancé, 'Ahmed Robinson Bey'. In her correspondence, Martha May gave details about the 'Robinsons', which proved that she was well-acquainted with the family. She noted that her fiancé's mother was known at the British Embassy in Constantinople as 'Mrs Robinson' and added that all the family were known at the Yildiz Palace to officials and members of the 'royal court'. Somewhat despairingly, Martha May asked the Foreign Office if there was any hope that her fiancé would come to England after the end of the war.[59]

This was the same Martha May Thompson who had been involved in a notorious divorce case that had resulted in the end of Quilliam's legal career in 1908 and precipitated his leaving Liverpool and the closure of the LMI. Martha May and Quilliam were accused of conspiring to frame the former's husband to obtain a divorce by using a former employee of Quilliam to set up a meeting between the husband and a prostitute in Glasgow. There were rumours that Quilliam was involved in a relationship with Mrs Thompson and that the two had gone to Constantinople in 1908 at the time when full details of the arranged rendezvous with the prostitute were revealed in court.[60] It is quite possible that Quilliam had arranged for Mrs Thompson to stay with the Bahris in Constantinople. An assistant in a tobacco stall, Mrs Thompson would have not previously travelled abroad. Fatma's household would have been able to put Martha May at ease in a strange environment. There is no record of Ahmet Robenson visiting England, so it is difficult to imagine in what other circumstances Martha May could have met Fatma's son. It is currently unclear, though, if the two were ever officially engaged.

Fatma was certainly appreciative of the support she received from Abdulhamid II and would become a staunch advocate for the Sultan. This was seen in a letter from her which was published in Quilliam's *The Crescent* in 1907. A fire had destroyed part of the Galatasaray Lycée, the school where Fatma's sons had studied and where Ahmet Robenson became a sports instructor. Fatma warmly praised the Sultan for rapidly ordering repairs to the school. According to Fatma, the school was 'the very best in the country', and many of the pupils were placed there by 'our beloved Caliph's generous benevolence'. She added that, in the school, pupils who were Muslim, Jewish or Christian worked 'side-by-side', and all benefited from the 'generous assistance' of the Sultan, who was truly 'a living Father of his people'.[61]

Following the 'Young Turk' Revolution of 1908 and the removal of Sultan Abdulhamid II from office in April 1909, the Bahris would have lost the benefits they had previously enjoyed through their close connection to the Ottoman court. Their rent-free accommodation would have been terminated. However, there is no evidence that Fatma suffered as a consequence of the Sultan's demise. Indeed, she would be able to bask in the favourable publicity enjoyed by her sons, Abdurrahman and Ahmet, who had established the Scouting movement in the Ottoman Empire by 1911. By this time, Ahmet Robenson was considered to be the finest goalkeeper in the country, playing for the championship-winning team, Galatasaray. With the deaths of two of her sons in the First World War, Fatma became especially close to Ahmet. With Ahmet's wife, Nina, they lived together in Izmir in the 1920s, before Ahmet Robenson decided to emigrate to the United States in 1929. In her last years, Fatma lived quietly in the Buca district of Izmir, an area popular with the British expatriate community.

According to information provided by relatives, Fatma was a practicing and devout Muslim throughout her life, although the family itself was quite secular. Her great-granddaughter (the granddaughter of Adile) remembered how she prayed five times each day and was only seen in public wearing a scarf and long dresses.[62] Although she never completely mastered the Turkish language, Fatma had clearly fully adapted to life in the Ottoman Empire and the Republic of Turkey. Dogged by ill health throughout her later years, she died in May 1948. Her passing was briefly acknowledged in the national press.[63]

Conclusion

Undoubtedly, the life of Hannah/Fatma was a fascinating one. From a humble background, she travelled widely. Her life had its share of misfortune, but also adventure. Converting to Islam was certainly a key turning point in her life, which led to her move from Brighton to Constantinople. She only lived as a Muslim for a few months at most in England before relocating to the Ottoman Empire. Nevertheless, her membership at the LMI helped her during her greatest time of need in the months following her arrival in Constantinople. And it was her close connection with Abdullah Quilliam that enabled her to continue to secure support from the court of Sultan Abdulhamid II.

It is difficult to give a definitive answer as to why Hannah/ Fatma decided to convert to Islam. Taking her at her word, she changed her religion due to a genuine belief and conviction in Islam. However, Hannah/Fatma was prone to exaggerate and not always tell the truth. It would seem, though, that her encounter with Gholab Shah/ Eliahie Bosche played a fundamental role in her decision to renounce Christianity. The supposed Afghan warlord was, upon first impression, a charming, vibrant and persuasive individual, and he may well have insisted that Hannah/Fatma and her children should convert to Islam as a condition for marrying him. What is clear, though, is that after her divorce, Hannah/ Fatma was a devout Muslim. Her new religion became a part of her identity. However, it seems that she did not completely forget her roots. Christmas was evidently celebrated in the family. Her children were fluent in English, and Ahmet Robenson made use of his language skills to work as an interpreter between the Ottoman and British authorities at the end of the First World War. A born survivor, resolute, determined, supremely adaptable and able to overcome extreme adversity, Hannah/Fatma was clearly a formidable woman.

6

'NO ROOM AT THE INN'

BERTHA CAVE, A WOMAN BEFORE HER TIME

Judith Bourne

Introduction

Bertha Cave (1881–1951) was an important feminist campaigner.[1]
She fought to open the legal profession to women in 1903 by
making a daring application to join one of the four Inns of Court,
Gray's Inn.[2] Women were blocked from formally practising law in
England and Wales until the Sex Disqualification (Removal) Act
1919, so in 1903 it was men, and men alone, who were allowed to
join such an institution. These Inns of Court were the only places
where men studying for the Bar were able to eat the thirty-six
dinners required as part of the qualification system to be called
to the Bar of England and Wales. Without such membership,
a man could not practise as a barrister. Cave's application was
rejected, attracting much press comment. She was not the only
woman to apply (and fail) to join the Inns of Court at this time;
however, none of the other women challenged their rejection, and
this is what set Cave apart and made her so extraordinary.[3] Cave
appealed her rejection by Gray's Inn, which also failed. It was not
just her sex that made Cave's application exceptional, but also her

class; she was a servant's daughter from Kent, while the majority of barristers were from the middle and upper classes.[4]

Cave's life story furthers our understanding of women's entry into the legal profession and our knowledge of the culture surrounding the Bar in the early 1900s, but she is also noteworthy for more than her very public struggle to open the legal profession to women. She converted to Islam and in 1905 married Colonel Ali Altof Khan (known as Altof). Altof was a barrister, an Indian and a Muslim. Her conversion and marriage tell us an alternative narrative of women's agency and autonomy at a time when women had extremely limited legal rights.[5] Although there are many gaps in Cave's biography, this chapter partly reconstructs her story and shines some light on her Muslim life. Her story is also helpful to our understanding of attitudes towards Islam, Muslims, mixed marriages and white Muslim women in early twentieth century Britain.

Marriage to Colonel Altof

Bertha Cave married Altof in December 1905. Little is known or has been written about Altof, but some details of his life can be gleaned from private family papers. Son of Bahadur Altof Hussain Khan, the sometime assistant commissioner of Lahore, Altof was the chief of forces for Kapurthala State, a princely Sikh kingdom that had treaties with British India. Altof fought in the Second Afghan War of 1878–80, and his bravery was honoured with an Afghan medal. He was then sent by the government to further his education in London, and in May 1884 he received an honorary membership of the Royal Artillery Institution. Simultaneously, Altof was admitted to Lincoln's Inn on 16 May 1884, but he left London suddenly and returned to India, where he became the highest-ranking officer of the Kapurthala State Artillery Forces.[6] In 1900, by now a widower and grandfather, he returned to England and was readmitted to Lincoln's Inn on 1 August that year.[7] He was then called to the Bar in June 1903.[8] We know from press reports that this was the same year as Bertha Cave's application to join Gray's Inn.[9] It is possible that they met in London's legal circles during this period.

Although Cave's application to join Gray's Inn was reported in many newspapers, by November 1904 she had vanished from all public record, and therefore the circumstances of her marriage remain obscure. Cave was not included in the 1911 Census of England and Wales, probably because she was in India with her husband, and only reappeared in England in June 1920 as an elected Fellow of the Royal Microscopical Society. Her marriage was, however, commented upon in the Islamic press:

> On December 1 1905, Col. Ali Altof Khan of Kapurthala, a member of the Pan-Islamic Society, was married to Miss Maryam Bertha Cave. Both the bride and bridegroom being Muslim, the ceremony was performed by Imam Redjai Effendi of the Imperial Ottoman Embassy according to Muslim rites. The bride's name is not unknown to the public, as her application a few months ago, for admission to Gray's Inn, had caused some stir in the legal world.[10]

Despite searches, the marriage does not appear to have been legally registered. Whilst we know that the wedding reception was held at the Savoy Hotel in London, it is not clear where the actual marriage ceremony took place.[11] In 1905, there was only one purpose-built mosque in Britain, at Woking in Surrey, not far from London. Its founder, G. W. Leitner (1840–1899), claimed that the mosque was designed to demonstrate British religious 'tolerance', but it was a problematic space for those wishing to use it for Islamic rites; it was only open to men approved by Leitner and could not be used for conversions or Islamic propaganda, nor for marriages between English women and Muslim men. However, after Leitner's death in 1899, the mosque fell into disuse and was not reopened until 1912/13.[12] It is possible that Cave and Altof were married at the Liverpool Muslim Institute established by Abdullah Quilliam (1856–1932) in Brougham Terrace in 1889; however, extensive searches of the Institute's weekly newspaper, *The Crescent*, have failed to find any record to confirm this. The Altof family's understanding is that Cave had converted to Islam prior to her marriage and that her conversion was not dependent on or consequent to her marriage; this was corroborated by

The Islamic Review and Muslim India in 1914: 'Miss Bertha Cave became a Muslim [...], subsequently marrying Col. Ali Altof'.[13]

There is no evidence as to why Cave and Altof did not marry legally. There could have been many reasons for this, such as, for example, a fear of the loss of Cave's nationality.[14] If Cave had married Altof in a legally binding ceremony, she would have lost her British nationality immediately according to Section 10 of the Naturalisation Act 1870. Unless she became naturalized in India, she would have become stateless.[15] Any children of the marriage would have gained their nationality through their father.[16] In such circumstances, the couple's subsequent separation would have been difficult for her, as she would have had to reapply for British citizenship. The narrative behind the 1870 naturalization legislation was that marriage had become a choice; it was a personal contract and was considered voluntary.[17] Of course, this ignored the fact that women were subjected to coverture and thus had limited legal rights.[18] As a woman who had demanded gender equality, Cave may not have viewed marriage as necessary; like some feminists in 1905, she might have rejected marriage as a concept.[19] Moreover, Cave might not have legally married because her relationship with Altof, an Indian, might have already subjected her to familial or social disapproval. In early twentieth century Britain, women in 'mixed race' marriages were generally seen as immoral and irresponsible.[20] Perhaps there was reluctance on both sides; Altof was widowed and had two daughters in India, and Cave might have feared further scrutiny after her very public legal challenge. We can only speculate as to their reasons for not legally marrying. We do know that the year of Cave's marriage to Altof saw numerous headlines expressing outrage at a non-legally binding Islamic marriage between a young Englishwoman and a Moroccan circus performer at the Liverpool Muslim Institute.[21] Public opinion suggested that white women needed protecting from these types of marriages.[22] Fears ranged from sexual deviance to the wife's slowness picked up from her husband or mentally deficient children.[23] What is clear is that without a legal marriage, no maintenance could be demanded if Cave and Altof separated, and any children they had would be illegitimate.

There was an almost forty-year age gap between Cave and Altof, but this was not necessarily unusual at the time.[24] We know that many of those who were present at the wedding were men who had been called to the Bar of England and Wales and who would return to India to become prominent lawyers or politicians. Guests included Muhammad Iqbal (1877–1938), Mian Fazl-i-Hussain (1877–1936), and Abdul Qadir (1872–1950).[25] Muhammad Iqbal had recently arrived in England; from humble beginnings, he became a prominent writer, poet, philosopher, politician, and advocate for the independent state of Pakistan. Mian Fazl-i-Hussain was from a military family and had travelled to Britain in 1898 to further his education; admitted to Christ's College, Cambridge in 1899, he graduated in 1901 and was called to the Bar at Gray's Inn the same year. He returned to the Punjab to work as a lawyer and became a member of the Indian National Congress, but left in 1920 upon disagreeing with Gandhi's Non-Cooperation Movement. He became a politician and was promoted to the Viceroy's Executive Council in Delhi in 1930. Abdul Qadir was also called to the Bar (1907) and was in favour of a separate Muslim state. Upon his return to India, he served as a member of the Punjab Legislative Council.

Bertha Cave was clearly mixing with the Indian Muslim intellectual elite living in London.[26] Although Britain ruled India, the British allowed Indian men to practise as barristers, but not British (or Indian) women such as Cave. The contradiction is apparent: British women could not practise law, but Indian—and other non-British, non-white—men could.[27] Male Indian law students, such as Altof, were therefore not unusual in Edwardian England. They had been travelling to England to study law since the 1860s.[28] They were usually sons of wealthy families who were studying abroad because of the intellectual, social and financial benefits associated with a British education.[29] A British education almost always guaranteed a job in the Indian civil service, which led to its 'Indianizing' in the early twentieth century. Before 1914, it was estimated that one in every three Indian students was studying at the Bar because of the advantages it offered upon their return to India.[30] Indian students were greeted with a mixed reception in England at this time. The National Indian Association in Aid of Social Progress was established to help ensure such students received a warm welcome.[31] Many Indians disliked English food and the cold and wet climate, which often led to ill health.[32]

Life in India

Private records of the Altof family show that after their marriage in 1905, Bertha and Colonel Altof travelled to India, where in 1907 the latter was admitted as Advocate to the Chief Court of the Punjab at Lahore by Henry Duffield Craik, the Registrar of the Court. Altof practised law in Lahore, as well as Murree, Calcutta (Kolkata), and Lyallpur (Faisalabad). The couple lived their married life on a large estate in Lyallpur. We have no evidence of their life together in India, but it would have been difficult, especially for Bertha. Miscegenation was condemned by both Indians and the British, so the relationship would have been frowned upon. Presumably only the strongest relationships survived, and theirs did not. In the Victorian and Edwardian period, white men in India were discouraged from 'inter-racial' relationships.[33] White women in a sexual relationship with an Indian man were seen by the British as an abomination and violating the 'natural order'.[34] British fears abounded about incompatible cultures: Christian monogamy versus potential Muslim polygamy.[35] There was a fear that overtly sexual Indian men would seduce white women.[36] Women were seen as the custodians of racial purity, and therefore a woman like Bertha Cave would have been seen to be betraying her 'race'.[37] Examples included the 1893 marriage of Maharaja Sir Rajinder Singh of Patiala (1872–1900) to Miss Florry Bryan, an Irishwoman.[38] Lord Curzon (1859–1925), who became viceroy and governor-general of India, was disturbed by the union because the Maharaja was a ruling Indian, and Bryan was from the working classes.[39] By the turn of the century, Indian officials feared that there was an epidemic of deviant or sexually perverted white women who were seeking and marrying Indian men.[40]

Cave and Altof would not have been well-received in India by either the ruling British or Indians.[41] Cave would have been seen as transgressing the social distance expected and demanded between rulers and the ruled, which was mandated by imperial ideology.[42] Since Altof was wealthy and of a higher social status than Cave, their relationship would have confused racial, sexual and class hierarchies.[43] Altof's family would have expected him to have married someone from their own religion and Islamic culture, and it is unlikely that they welcomed Cave. Even if she had adopted their lifestyle and conformed to their ideals, she ultimately did not come from their cultural background. She was a young twenty-four-year-old in 1905. Although she had limited legal personhood in England, she had managed to make a very public challenge to the British establishment before her departure for India, one that had demanded rights for women and entrance to the Bar. When in India, Cave would have been confined to the estate and within society. She was a woman in a foreign country, with little of her own money, control or autonomy. We do not know why the couple's marriage failed, but it is possible that a woman such as Cave found life difficult, and both she and her husband would have found society's attitudes towards them difficult to manage. It is possible that Cave, who had demanded rights for women, might have criticized the position of women in her new country, which may have caused problems. Additionally, they did not have children, which may have also been an issue in a society where children were seen as a necessary part of married life, and the birth of a son was desirable.

Return to London and emigration

Altof and Cave returned to England together in 1912. They both settled in London, albeit separately: he in a boarding house in Bayswater, and she in Shepherd's Bush. We have evidence that, for Altof, the marriage was over. Altof's descendants have in their possession a four-page letter written by Cave to her husband at his Bayswater address, in which she begs to see him. Unfortunately, the postmark is missing, but that address dates it to around 1912. It is a sad and distressing letter. Cave addresses Altof as, '[M]y own darling husband', and she signs it, 'love from [your] own poor little wife'. She writes that she did not wish to give him 'trouble or waste your time'. She requests the favour of seeing him for a few minutes as he had promised that they could be friends. She speaks of having lost everything and of being 'too sad'. Anticipating his departure, she wrote: '[W]e may never, perhaps meet again so I ask you not to grudge a little time to me'. She concluded that she would not 'worry' him or talk about anything 'unpleasant'. It is clear that she understood that the marriage was over, but it appears that this was not her choice; she still seemed to be very much in love with her husband.[44]

It is not known what exactly happened next. Records show that Bertha Cave lived unmarried in Hackney, east London between 1918 and 1920, and in this period she became a Fellow of the Royal Microscopical Society. In 1922, Cave emigrated to Canada with her mother. She declared herself a widow (even though Altof was alive) and a bacteriologist, who intended to practise that profession in Canada. Cave stated that she and her mother would join her brother in Innisfree, Alberta. She was in possession of £50, and her religion was described as Church of England, not Islam.

Cave arrived with her mother in Innisfree and remained there until at least the early months of 1922. In January of that year, Cave wrote to Simon Flexner, the Director of the Rockefeller Institute for Medicine, New York, enclosing a research paper, which he unhelpfully returned. In 1930, Cave was recorded as living in Montreal, where she wrote again to Flexner regarding an unpublished paper, 'The Lifecycle of the Filterable Viruses', again to no avail. By 1933, she had moved to Toronto, where she was recorded in the 1935 electoral register as 'Mrs Alec Altof', a widow. She died in Canada in 1951.[45]

Religious beliefs

There appears to be a contradiction in Cave's professed religious beliefs. We saw earlier that Cave had converted to Islam before her marriage to Altof in 1905. We have also seen that Cave declared on her immigration form in 1922 that her religion was 'Church of England'. Did she lose her Islamic faith? Did she convert to Islam in order to marry Altof? Did she feel that the practise of Islam was not socially acceptable, although she carried her husband's name to her grave, a name that was Muslim? Did she lack the facilities to practise her Islamic faith in the West? As a divorced woman, was she excluded from Islamic spaces? We have no evidence that can definitively answer these questions, or explain why she denied the religion that she had freely converted to or returned to the religion of her birth. However, we are able to draw some conclusions if we follow the clues left by her behaviour prior to her marriage to Altof.

Life before marriage

We have seen that Bertha Cave's pre-married life has been enshrined in historiography as the woman who, in March 1903, applied to join Gray's Inn and was rejected because of her sex. Her subsequent appeal against that decision was used thereafter as a precedent for preventing future female would-be lawyers from entering the legal profession.[46] Her name is 'visible', and yet the woman remains fairly invisible; for example, her conversion to Islam did not appear in the press at the time and has been little commented on since. Many books mention her name, but only for a couple of sentences or at most a paragraph.[47] Often, the material is incorrect.[48] The spotlight that has been shone on Cave so far has been in relation to her campaign to open the legal profession to women, rather than focusing on her interactions and the social, political and religious context in which she lived. She became decontextualized, simply the would-be female lawyer, a 'failure', 'unsuccessful', 'victim' of a patriarchal system, and the woman who set a precedent for the later refusal of women to the legal profession.

The reality is somewhat different, for Bertha Cave was not a victim. Her challenge to the legal establishment was extraordinary given that, at the time of her application to join Gray's Inn, women had very limited legal rights. Women could not join the professions; they could not vote until the 1918 Representation of the People Act; they were subjected to coverture upon marriage, which meant that their legal rights were suspended upon marriage, and as a legal entity the wife was incorporated into that of her husband. It was not until the Law Reform (Married Women and Tortfeasors) Act 1935 that married women could own property in the same way as men and single women. Divorce between men and women was only equalized with the Matrimonial Causes Act 1923, as was custody of children with the Guardianship of Infants Act 1925. Women raped by their husbands could only hope to secure a conviction in 1991. Cave's application was therefore audacious; she navigated her limited legal agency and used methods such as the application and appeal system of Gray's Inn to make her voice heard, to argue that women should be permitted to practise law. No woman had ever made such a direct challenge in England before, although Margaret Hall had in Scotland.[49]

We have no evidence of why she made this bold challenge; we only know the facts. Born in 1881 in Sevenoaks, Kent, the census of that year reveals that Cave's parents were living in Brasted, Kent as servants to William Tipping MP (1816–97).[50] Her father was the son of a labourer, and his occupation was recorded as a 'butler/servant', meaning that he was at the top of that serving class. Bertha's mother is not recorded as having any occupation. By 1901, the census records Cave as living in Croydon, south London, with her mother (the 'head of the household'), a brother and two lodgers. Her father was not registered there, but a later newspaper report of a civil trial revealed that her father had given his address to the Court as the family address in Croydon.[51] We can assume from that detail that her parents were not separated, but rather living separately for work. Newspaper articles written in 1903 about Cave's attempt to join the Bar gave no indication as to her background, unlike Ivy Williams (the first woman to be called to the Bar in May 1922), who was often described as a solicitor's daughter.[52]

It is also not known how Cave came to be suitably qualified to challenge the law, or what support she had. Nonetheless, on 3 March 1903, she applied to Gray's Inn to be admitted as a student member.[53] She wrote the following on her application, from which we have our first glimpse of her voice:

I am aware that my application is most unusual and no doubt without precedent, but trust that the Masters of the bench will give it their serious consideration and I should, in the event of a favourable reply, be pleased to conform to any special rules they may think fit to impose.[54]

Her application was considered during a meeting of the Benchers at Gray's Inn on 13 March and was supported by Master Rose and seconded by Master Macaskie.[55] However, the decision was adjourned and referred for further consideration to a Pension Committee.[56]

This governance committee, sat on 24 April 1903 and considered whether it had the power to admit women as students.[57] It does not appear that this had happened before, as other women were rejected outright, such as Edith Metcalfe, who made a similar application in 1903.[58] Considering the regulations on details of dress and exercise, according to their ordinary and natural sense, the Pension Committee decided that the regulations indicated that males, and males alone, were admissible as students in relation to Cave's application. They concluded that when the regulations were read—in light of the uniform and uninterrupted usage which had so long followed upon them—they appeared to be conclusively against the power of their Society to admit women for the purpose of being called to the Bar. They referred to various legal cases (none of them on point), and thus, despite having two supporters, Cave's application was refused.[59]

Cave then took her extraordinary and untried course of action: she appealed. This tribunal hearing was heard in the Moses Room of the House of Lords on 2 December 1903. Cave was unrepresented when she faced a formidable group of judges. She argued, 'I would urge in support of my case that although there are no rules for the admission of students, there appears to be none against'.[60]

Cave rightly pointed out that there were female lawyers in other countries; much of Europe had indeed already opened the profession to women: Romania in 1891, Finland in 1895, Sweden in 1897, France in 1900, and Norway in 1904.[61] In the United States, where women's right to practise law varied by state, Arabella Mansfield (1846–1911) had been accepted to the

Iowa Bar in 1869.[62] In Canada, although admission varied by province, Clara Brett Martin (1874–1923) was the first woman to be admitted to the Ontario Bar in 1897.[63] In New Zealand, Ethel Benjamin (1875–1943) became the first woman to practise in 1897 after legislation was enacted.[64] Likewise, in Australia, Grata Flos Greig (1880–1958) was admitted to the Bar in Victoria in 1905.[65] Cornelia Sorabji (1866–1954) had been appearing in court (at the judge's discretion) in Poona, India since 1894.[66]

Despite Cave's persistence in asking for legal authority as to why they were unable to admit her, the judges countered by demanding that she provide precedent that they could. As no woman had ever been admitted to the Bar, she could cite no such authority. When her appeal was rejected, she stated, 'I am very disappointed'.[67] Naturally, there was considerable press interest in her story. The *Dundee Evening Post* reported that the hearing lasted just five minutes. They focused largely on her appearance:

> [Cave] presented a charming appearance as she tripped through the lobby on her way to the Moses Chamber. Her lither, slight form was inhabited in a short blue walking skirt, with open coat of the same material, showing a light blue blouse underneath. Perched on her raven-locked hair was the smartest hat trimmed with black and white pom-poms. The only touch of legal austerity was a stand-up collar. Below her skirt appeared a dainty pair of very high-heeled boots. A fresh blush suffused her pretty face as she tripped along and her dark eyes flashed with determination.[68]

This is a description of an assured, fashionable, modern and determined woman. Bertha Cave's confidence is reflected in her dress, which would have appeared attractive to others. She was not of course attractive to the judges. She was a woman, and a threat to the status quo of the Bar. In one newspaper report, Cave stated that the exclusion of women from the professions had a bad effect on the general position of women.[69] She recognized and articulated that the legal profession was afraid of competition. She played on this fear in another interview when she threatened to become an 'outside lawyer'.[70] These were general law offices that provided legal skills to both solicitors and barristers. As they were outside of the legal profession, they had the advantage of being able to advertise, which barristers were not allowed to do. This contributed to the fear of external competition. Women were already appearing in this role of 'outside lawyer'.[71] Cave's confidence was remarkable, and her voice was far from that of a victim.

As with her assertion that other countries had already opened the legal profession to women, Cave was also right about the legal professions' fear of competition; many men were complaining that the profession was overcrowded.[72] In the 1860s, barristers lamented that their profession would become less prestigious if the lower classes were allowed to join.[73] They were feeling threatened, and rightly so. Changes were happening: men from the lower classes were becoming more vocal, calling for universal male suffrage and employment rights.[74] The world of politics was also shifting with a new organization in the shape of the Labour Party, founded in 1900, having grown out of the trade union movement and socialist societies.[75] Labour would overtake the Liberal Party and become the main opposition to the Conservative Party in the 1920s. The working classes were encroaching on and challenging the professional classes. The judges presiding over Cave's appeal were hiding behind a veil of supposed authority, *The Mirror of Justices*.[76] The medieval treatise, written in the fourteenth century, declared that '[T]he law will not suffer women to be attorneys, nor infants nor serfs'.[77] This prohibition excluded many later female would-be lawyers until the passing of the 1919 Act.

Further press reports noted that Cave was considering joining the Middle Temple, another of the four Inns of Court.[78] However, she was not contemplating becoming a solicitor as it was 'not desirable for women as the bar', and it lacked both 'dignity and refinement'.[79] Cave was still threatening the status quo of the Bar. No newspaper questioned her class, and in fact she gave her hobbies as middle-class pursuits, namely 'golf and hunting'.[80] However, they did question her ability to actually practise, not because of her sex, but because of her nervousness when public speaking during a debate with the suffragette Christabel Pankhurst (1880–1958) in January 1904.[81] What was the reason for her nervousness, given that she had appeared in front of the highest judges in the land? Perhaps she was intimidated by Pankhurst, or outshone by her fame?

Cave never applied to the Middle Temple, and despite her appearance as a guest of honour at a women's movement dinner hosted by the suffragist Lady Strachey (1840–1928), she soon disappeared from the women's struggle to join the legal profession.[82] She only briefly reappeared in November 1904 when she 'represented' her father in a dispute over non-payment for a bicycle.[83] Again, Cave showed courage, appearing in court dressed in 'cap and gown' and attempting to sit in the counsel's benches at the City of London Court. She is reported to have arranged her papers in the correct legal style and rose to make an application on her father's behalf, but a Mr Harry Strouts, solicitor, interposed: 'I am sorry but I feel bound to object to the Lady being heard from counsel's benches'. Gathering up her papers, Cave moved to the witness box and lost the case.

Conversion to Islam

It would be easy to dismiss Cave's conversion to Islam as a simple story of a woman's romantic behaviour: she converted to Islam in order to marry the man she loved. We lack contemporaneous evidence to discover the truth; currently, there are no archives, family papers, or published materials to help build an accurate picture. Cave never remarried and did not have children, so her papers were not cherished. However, a narrative that dismisses Cave's conversion as a means of furthering her romance would deny Cave her agency. Cave used her 'voice', albeit a very legally limited voice, in her challenge against the Gray's Inn rejection. Her behaviour was radical as she took on the Bar of England and Wales and the Establishment (the Bar was a feeder to parliament), and, even after her rejection, sat in counsel's place in court when representing her father.

By understanding her life before marriage, we can frame what a British Muslim woman might have been like in early twentieth century Britain. She could be educated, ambitious, inquiring, mould-breaking and loud; Cave was all of these things. By assuming that her conversion was purely for love essentializes her. It plays to a restrictive patriarchal narrative of women. Cave was a woman who refused to conform to patriarchy. Her conversion was before her marriage, so it was a conscious choice. That choice may have been a deeply held conviction, or only a passing interest in Islam, or perhaps another way in which she could defy the norm. We will never know the answer for certain, unless a diary or other piece of evidence becomes available in the future.

Conclusion

Women did not enter the legal profession in 1919 as a result of women's work during the First World War; they were granted entry because of the toil of the women's movement and the determination and exertions of women like Cave. Her application to Gray's Inn was daring; she was from the serving classes, but she took on the Establishment. It pushed her into an unknown and dangerously public situation. She had no control of the outcome or the support of an established family. Gray's Inn refused to admit her, she lost her appeal, and she faced public humiliation and rejection. She would have suffered enormous disappointment. The Establishment kept her in her 'place', and her lower-class position was reinforced, as was her sex disadvantage.

Likewise, Cave's conversion to Islam and marriage to an Indian also challenged convention. Her marriage disobeyed and violated racial, social and class rules imposed by the British Empire and the Establishment. Her marriage was unwelcome and, like her application to join Gray's Inn, unsupported by that dominating culture. We have seen that she would not have been welcomed by either the British or the Indians in India. She should have been able to marry through choice, irrespective of nationality or religion, just as she should have been able to work in a profession that she chose and not one dictated by her class and sex.

Cave lived a rich and varied life. She lived on three continents and experienced three different cultures. She was from the lower classes but refused to see this as a barrier to a life she wanted to lead. She stood up publicly for her beliefs. Moreover, she refused to be contained by convention and married the man she loved. After the failure of her marriage, she returned to England and trained in a career that would support her and make her independent. Cave was autonomous at a time when women were denied legal autonomy. She could not be restrained. She survived because of her resilience, tenacity and vitality. She was a woman ahead of her time and paved a way for other women to follow. She fought for the opening of the legal profession to women, the acceptance of mixed marriages, and the idea of equality for women. Cave navigated her social, legal and political position to challenge the Establishment—through her demand to open the legal profession to women and her demand to marry the man of her choice. Her life enables us to cast aside the idea of early twentieth-century Muslim women in Britain as subservient. Cave was a woman who acted on her deeply held convictions and strongly held principles, one of which was her conversion to Islam.

7

'FAIREST OF WOMEN'

THE CONVERSION TO ISLAM AND MUSLIM LIFE OF GLADYS MILTON BROOKE, DAYANG MUDA OF SARAWAK

Jamie Gilham

Introduction

Gladys Brooke (1884–1952), a British aristocrat and the Dayang Muda (wife of the heir presumptive to the Rajah of Sarawak), sensationally converted to Islam on a flight between London and Paris in 1932. Brooke's conversion made headlines around the world. She subsequently explained why she had become a Muslim in the press and on public radio and wrote articles about her faith for Islamic journals. However, Brooke disappeared from the limelight just before the Second World War and is relatively unknown today. The little that has been previously written about Gladys Brooke is generally derived from her long out-of-print memoir, *Relations and Complications*, which was published three years before she converted to Islam.[1]

This chapter takes a fresh look at Brooke's life, focusing on her conversion to Islam and experience as a female Western Muslim convert. It explains Brooke's path to Islam and examines the circumstances of and responses to her unusual conversion ceremony, which was overseen by an English Muslim, Khalid Sheldrake (1888–1947). It then considers how Brooke used her celebrity to challenge traditional Western views about Islam, documents her brief entanglement in disputes between Muslim factions in Britain between the wars, and accounts for her later life and religiosity.

'Relations and complications'

Gladys Milton Palmer was born in Reading, Berkshire in 1884. She was the only child of businessman and politician Sir Walter Palmer (1858–1910) and Lady Jean Palmer (*née* Craig, 1858–1909). Sir Walter was a director of the successful Huntley and Palmer biscuit manufacturers and a Conservative Member of Parliament. Gladys later wrote that she had been 'born with a silver spoon in my mouth' and, being an 'only child and heiress, was feted and perhaps spoilt a little wherever I went'.[2] She was raised in fashionable society in London and on the Continent and destined to marry into an equally distinguished family.

When not in London, Gladys lived with her parents in Sunninghill, a leafy village near Ascot. Margaret Brooke (1849–1936), Lady Brooke and Ranee (consort) of Sarawak, was a neighbour and friend of the Palmers. Lady Brooke was married to Charles Brooke (1829–1917), the second Rajah (ruler) of Sarawak, a colony in the island of Borneo, south-east Asia. The Brookes were given hereditary rights to Sarawak when Charles' uncle, Sir James Brooke (1803–68), was granted the title of Rajah by the Sultan of Brunei in 1841.[3] Like his uncle, the second Rajah lived in Sarawak. He was estranged from his wife, who had settled in England with their three sons and held court at Ascot. As the Ranee wrote in her memoirs, 'To my great delight my neighbours' houses harboured many charming damsels, lovely young girls who philandered and flirted—and quite right too!—with my sons'.[4] One of the girls was Gladys Palmer, who thought the Ranee 'one of the most charming women I had ever met, witty, brilliant and sympathetic'.[5] The Ranee likewise took to Gladys, who was introduced to the Brookes' second son, Bertram Willes Dayrell

Brooke (1876–1965). Gladys found Bertram to be 'a shy, silent man'.[6] He proposed to her, and they were married with a lavish London society wedding in 1904.[7]

Gladys and Bertram took a flat in London and mingled in fashionable circles. The first of their four children, Jean, was born in 1905, just before Bertram went to Australia as Aide-de-Camp to the Governor of Queensland. Gladys and Jean joined Bertram in Australia, and they all returned to England in 1907. The family settled in south London, where Gladys gave birth to two daughters, Elizabeth and Anne. What is known about Gladys' married life is mainly taken from her own published account; Bertram did not speak or write publicly about their relationship. According to Gladys, the marriage turned sour after they left Australia. She found Bertram sullen and preoccupied with distant Sarawak:

> The men of the [Brooke] family have been condemned to a willing exile, their wives to a grass-widowhood in England with but one single thought—the welfare of the country. [...] Once in the early days of our marriage I accused my husband of thinking more of Sarawak than he did of my happiness. He looked surprised. 'If it came to a choice between the good of Sarawak and your happiness, Gladys, I should have to sacrifice you,' he answered gravely. 'Any Brooke would do the same.'[8]

She added: 'It took me many months to realise just how little my husband belonged to me, how small a part in his life I had.' Gladys said that she tried to make her marriage a success, but she and Bertram were just not compatible: 'our interests ran in such different directions', and he scorned her many 'artistic friends', among them the celebrated actress Ellen Terry (1847–1928):

> His whole life and education had given him the idea that the only people of the slightest use in this world were men of action; he had scant patience with the thinkers and dreamers, hated music, could scarcely tolerate poets and thought that artists ought to be sternly relegated to their studios.[9]

In 1911–12, Gladys accompanied Bertram to Sarawak. She became pregnant with their fourth child and returned to England alone. To the delight of Bertram and his parents, who longed for a male heir, Gladys had a boy, Anthony (or Antoni), in December 1912. The arrival of a son and heir seems to have precipitated the end of the marriage, which broke down completely during the First World War. Bertram was alone in Sarawak when war was declared and then served in the British army. Gladys volunteered for the Red Cross in London but later moved out to the country. Her parents had died before the war, leaving her extremely wealthy. She bought Tan-y-Garth, a mansion with a poultry farm and sporting estate in Denbighshire, North Wales.[10] If Gladys had hoped that her husband might join her in Wales, she was disappointed. In 1917, her father-in-law, Rajah Charles, died, and Bertram's brother, Charles Vyner Brooke (1874–1963), became the third Rajah. As heir presumptive, Bertram took the title His Highness Tuan Muda ('Little Lord') of Sarawak, and Gladys became Dayang Muda ('Little Lady'). Rajah Charles Vyner and Bertram agreed that they would each spend half a year in Sarawak as head of state.

At Tan-y-Garth, Gladys entertained on a lavish scale, hosting her many artist and writer friends. She later wrote that her husband bitterly resented and objected to their children mixing with 'the highly cultured and refined people I gathered around me', and his letters 'became fewer and colder'.[11] One afternoon, Gladys went out for a walk: 'I came back to find an orange envelope lying on the tea-tray. I opened it and my stunned senses gradually took in the words: "Your husband has made the children wards of court. The Ranee has been appointed guardian"'.[12] Gladys went directly to London, where she appointed a lawyer who tried, unsuccessfully, to defend her:

> My husband had stated that he did not approve of the way in which his children were brought up, that he 'disliked the entourage of his wife's artistic friends.' He had determined to take the children from me and the law, the cold impersonal law which was made by men for men, allowed him to do it.[13]

Cruelly separated from her children, Gladys left—and later sold—Tan-y-Garth. She returned to London where, despite her estrangement from Bertram, she retained and used to her advantage the title Dayang Muda. In 1921, Gladys co-founded a short-lived film company and cast her friend, Ellen Terry, in the leading role of its first and only feature, *Potter's Clay* (1922).[14] Looking back on this period, Gladys admitted, 'In a desperate attempt to forget, I flung myself into the whirl of society, went to parties, entertained lavishly, but it brought me no happiness'.[15] Indeed, she soon 'grew weary of London' and 'decided suddenly that I would go to France'. Gladys' move to the Continent was certainly an escape from her unhappy life in England, but it was also financially expedient; the fortune she had inherited from her parents was subjected to a super tax, which she resented. In 1929, Gladys won a legal case in England that exempted her from paying the tax. Her lawyer successfully argued that, when she married, Gladys became 'a Sarawakan and not British', and, since she had subsequently moved overseas, she was no longer resident in Britain.[16]

Gladys went first to Paris and then rented a villa in Nice on the French Rivera. She lived mainly in Paris and Nice until the late 1930s. Gladys was in Nice in November 1931 when the two elder sons of the Nizam (ruler) of Hyderabad State in India were married there in a double wedding ceremony.[17] The Nizam's eldest son, Azam Jah (1907–70), was married to Durru Shehvrar (1914–2006), the only daughter of Gladys' friend in Nice, Abdulmejid II (1868–1944), the last Ottoman Caliph, who was living in exile in the city.[18] In the 1930s, the British Muslim writer and scholar Marmaduke Pickthall (1875–1936) was based in Hyderabad. The Nizam selected Pickthall and his wife Muriel to chaperone the two princes in France, and it is likely that Gladys first met the Pickthalls in Nice during the wedding celebrations, which lasted for several days.

In Paris, Gladys established herself at the centre of the lively expatriate community of avant-garde artists, writers, poets, actors and dancers. She hosted a monthly salon in her apartment, mingling with the likes of Gertrude Stein (1874–1946), Alice B. Toklas (1877–1967), and Raymond Duncan (1874–1966). This seems to have encouraged her to write, and she had a few articles, principally about Sarawak, published in the late 1920s.[19] Then, in 1928, Gladys decided to write a memoir, *Relations and Complications*.

Much of what is known about Gladys in the years immediately after she left England for France is based on her memoir and those of several young North American writers whom she met in France between 1926 and 1928. Their accounts were written retrospectively and are gossipy, and they paint a rather unflattering portrait of Gladys as a generous yet fragile soul, psychologically tormented by the circumstances of her separation from Bertram and their young children.

The first of the expatriates to meet Gladys was Kay Boyle (1902–92). In spring 1926, Boyle and her partner, the literary editor Ernest 'Michael' Walsh (1895–1926), travelled to Annot, a mountain village north-west of Nice. Gladys happened to be staying there with a cousin, an aspiring poet called Archie Craig (real name Cedric Harris).[20] Boyle recounted their meeting in a letter to her grandfather in the United States, describing Gladys as 'a handsome woman of forty […], and spontaneous and kindly and rich and generous. We have all become socially intimate and while she is conversationally rather dull and commonplace, she has an indisputably kind heart'.[21] Boyle was pregnant with Ernest Walsh's child when he died from tuberculosis in October 1926. Gladys and Archie supported Boyle, and they corresponded after they returned to Paris. According to Boyle's account, once Gladys had decided on producing a memoir, she needed help with both the writing and recalling events from her life. In the spring of 1928, Boyle accepted an invitation to ghost-write Gladys' book.[22] She found her employer an 'aphonic and lonely woman':

> The writing itself went rapidly enough once the bare facts of her life had been drawn, sentence by hesitant sentence, from this tall, blonde, passive, and strangely inarticulate Princess whose mind appeared to function in a state of shock. And this was quite possibly the case, for she who was armoured with shyness, and stubbornly generous with everything she owned, once told me with no sign of emotion that her hair had turned white overnight when her husband took her […] children from her and made them wards of court. […] It was therefore necessary to invent the story as one went along, and she herself was as entranced as it unfolded as Archie and I were.[23]

Boyle was helped by a fellow American, Robert McAlmon (1895–
1956), and two young Canadians, John 'Buffy' Glassco (1909–81)
and Graeme Taylor (1907–57).[24] Glassco, who completed the
typing of the final manuscript, claimed in his memoirs that Gladys
'ruminated all day long on the two subjects closest to her heart:
newspaper publicity and getting even with her husband'.[25]

Relations and Complications was published in London in June
1929. It was widely reviewed and later serialized in a London
tabloid newspaper. Whilst many reviewers welcomed the author's
apparent zest for life and her celebrity gossip, others frowned
upon her unabashed account of the failure of her marriage and
estrangement from Bertram Brooke.[26] If the general tone of
Relations and Complications is gossipy, however, it ends on a serious
note. In the final pages, Gladys revealed that, in May 1929, she had
converted to Roman Catholicism. She was baptized Veronica by
a priest at Saint Joseph's, an English-speaking Catholic church in
Paris. Her religious conversion was, she confided, the culmination
of a long search for spiritual enlightenment and contentment.
She said later that the search began in 'early youth' when she was
disillusioned with Protestantism; unable to find 'any moral support
from this cold religion', she looked to alternatives, including
Christian Science, Hinduism and Islam, but 'they all failed me'.[27]
Eventually, she took 'a bold step and was received into the Catholic
Church'.[28] She explained in *Relations and Complications*:

> This is a step which I have taken of my own accord and very
> deliberately. I assert this at once to stifle the usual accusations
> of 'influence' in cases of conversions. For eight months I have
> received instructions from Father Mac Darby. I went to him first;
> he did not come to me! I have absorbed all the sacred doctrines
> of the Church. I am happy that I have returned to the Faith of Our
> Fathers, to the One Universal Church founded by Christ when
> he sent forth St. Peter to Rome, to definite and authoritative
> interpretations of Christ's words, to the spiritual protection and
> jurisdiction of St. Peter's successor and Christ's Universal Vicar
> on earth.[29]

John Glassco, who was completing the manuscript of Gladys'
memoir in spring 1929, was a witness at her 'quiet and almost

perfunctory' conversion ceremony.[30] Glassco contradicted Gladys' explanation for her religious conversion: 'She had discovered it could be done in about a month and thought it would be a fine prelude to her campaign of insult and outrage against the Brookes— who were Anglican—which was to culminate in the publication of her memoirs'.[31] In subsequent press interviews, Gladys maintained that her conversion to Catholicism was carefully considered and that her reasons for converting were 'many and complicated'.[32] She said that 'heredity' might have played a role, since her maternal grandfather was a Catholic; she had also been surrounded by English Catholics who attended her mother's salon and, more recently, deeply affected by the simple conversion ceremony of a close friend (possibly Archie Craig, who also converted to Catholicism at this time) and, moreover, thinking back to her trip to Sarawak before the war, she admired the Catholic missionaries she had met there.[33] Shortly after her conversion, Gladys went to Rome with Archie. They had a private audience with Pope Pius XI (1857–1939) and received his Apostolic Blessing.[34]

Conversion to Islam

Gladys' commitment to Roman Catholicism did not last long; in February 1932, she formally converted to Islam. What led to her second religious conversion in less than three years? In 1929, when she declared her Catholicism, Gladys said that she had studied Islam and found it wanting. After her conversion to Islam, Gladys told the press that, in Sarawak, many years earlier, she had studied the life of its different religious communities, including the Muslim population, and she was:

> very much attracted to the moral side of her Muslim subjects, and for the first time realised the beauty of the teaching of Islam. She was struck by the purity, logic and simplicity of the religion, and felt that her whole heart and soul were wrapped in its teachings. The Qur'an appealed to her as being the direct words of God, delivered to the Prophet Muhammad.[35]

Without detracting from its validity, Gladys' account of her journey to Islam is typical of conversion testimonies, produced retrospectively and often undermining previous statements to help the convert rationalize and explain a change of faith.[36] Gladys added that, shortly after renouncing Catholicism, her interest in Islam was rekindled by a chance meeting with 'a famous archaeologist' at her Paris salon, who told her that he had recently seen a tunic covered with Arabic inscriptions of verses from the Qur'an that had been worn by the Prophet Muhammad. Gladys bought the tunic and paid scholars to research its history. Most Muslims in Paris and elsewhere refuted its authenticity, but Gladys was persuaded that it was genuine: 'My ownership of Mahomet's tunic naturally increased my interest in the literature of the East, and, knowing this, a friend sent me a copy of the Koran, which [...] led to my conversion to the religion of Islam'.[37] In September 1931, several months before she formally embraced Islam, Gladys defied the sceptics by displaying the tunic in her Paris apartment and invited prominent Muslims, scholars and reporters to view it.[38]

It is likely that one of the Muslim visitors to Gladys' apartment in September 1931 was Khalid Sheldrake, a British Muslim convert and missionary. Sheldrake was a key figure in Gladys' conversion to Islam. He had converted to Islam in London in around 1903, and became closely associated with the Indian Ahmadi Muslim missionary Khwaja Kamal-ud-Din (1870–1932) and the Woking Muslim Mission (WMM) he founded near London in 1912–13 (see Chapter 4).[39] In 1914, Sheldrake was a founding member and first honorary secretary of the British Muslim Society (later the Muslim Society of Great Britain, MSGB), a socio-religious organization affiliated to the WMM and led by a Kamal-ud-Din protégé, Lord Headley (1855–1935).[40] However, within a year, Sheldrake was writing on official WMM notepaper as the self-styled 'Sheikh of the British Muslims' and, following a major split within the Ahmadiyya community, he began to criticize Kamal-ud-Din and Lahori Ahmadi influence at Woking.[41] In 1915, Sheldrake was asked to leave the WMM.[42]

Sheldrake was readmitted to the WMM, but he left again in the mid-1920s after publicly discrediting it as a 'sectarian' organization.

Sheldrake established his own avowedly 'non-sectarian' Western Islamic Association (WIA) in London. He announced that the WIA would become an 'International Islamic Organisation', with affiliated branches throughout the world. Consequently, Sheldrake spent much time in the late 1920s and early 1930s trying to persuade Muslim public figures and Islamic associations worldwide to endorse the WIA, with modest success.[43] Although he had very limited funds, 'Dr Sheldrake' made several overseas trips on behalf of the WIA.[44] He visited France and, in Paris in 1931, was introduced to Gladys and her cousin, Conrad Simpson. Simpson described their first meeting with Sheldrake:

> 'We had [...] heard much about him, and quite expected to see an elderly man with a long beard, in fact we always thought of him as such. I shall never forget how thunderstruck I was when he entered the Salon of my cousin. Imagine if you can see a man from whom seemed to radiate energy and activity. Far from being elderly, I thought him far younger than I afterwards learned he really was. We sat and talked, and I was attracted very much by the frank manner in which he spoke. It was easy to see that he was not overawed by titles or splendour, but in spite of everything remained just as we now know him, a simple and straightforward man. Her Highness, my cousin, was indeed happy that evening [...]. After dinner we began to talk very seriously on religious matters, and I realised that here was one who had studied very deeply, and his very manner proved to me that he really believed and lived his own creed. As every Westerner has his own ideas concerning Islam [...] we wanted to know everything, and found ourselves wondering that we had not known all these things before. Objections to Islam were simply to him like straws in the wind, to be swept away like magic. You can understand how we talked far into the early hours of the morning. I think that he will remember that I told him, as we sat side by side on the divan, that I fully agreed with his views and that his beliefs were also mine.'[45]

Gladys was similarly impressed by the charismatic Sheldrake. Although from very different backgrounds, they were close contemporaries (Gladys was the elder by four years), and Sheldrake had also been a Catholic. Gladys was persuaded by Sheldrake's explanation of Islam—perhaps more so than Conrad Simpson, who converted to Islam six months after his cousin. Sheldrake told the press that, at their meetings in Paris and, later, London, he was able to explain to the Dayang Muda 'the teachings of Christianity and Islam in a comparative form and show the excellence and truth of Islam'.[46] Sheldrake sent Gladys issues of *The Muslim Review*, an English-language journal published by a Shi'i Indian missionary organization that endorsed the WIA. Sheldrake said in 1932 that Gladys had 'read every issue with keen interest and appreciation'.[47] Prior to her conversion to Islam, Gladys said little publicly about her growing interest in that faith or her connection with Sheldrake.

Gladys was not the first British aristocratic woman to convert to Islam in the early half of the twentieth century. But her formal conversion ceremony was unique. It occurred in February 1932, some months after she met Sheldrake, and does little to diminish the idea perpetuated by Boyle and Glassco that she craved publicity. It is also the case that Sheldrake was a publicity-seeker, wanting to both enhance his own reputation and raise the profile of the WIA.

In early February 1932, Gladys travelled to London, where she met Sheldrake. The pair agreed that Sheldrake would formally initiate Gladys' into Islam onboard an Imperial Airways plane en route from London Croydon Airport to Paris Le Bourget. A private compartment was booked, and a reporter and photographer from the London *Daily Express* were invited to witness the proceedings. Consequently, Gladys' journey to Paris was documented in a series of remarkable photographs. It began early on 18 February at Airways House in Victoria, where the passengers were weighed prior to the flight. They then travelled to south London and waited in the lounge while the aeroplane was prepared.[48] Gladys, dressed soberly in a black fur coat and black frock, posed with Sheldrake in front of the plane. Sheldrake gave Gladys a copy of an English edition of the Qur'an.[49] They then 'entered the reserved fore compartment of Silver Wings, which was to be the mid-air mosque. The compartment was shut off from that containing the ordinary cross-Channel passengers.'[50] More photographs were taken inside the cabin, and both Gladys and Sheldrake responded to questions posed by the *Express* reporter: '"Why go up in the air to change my faith?" she echoed my question. "Why, because surely we are nearer Allah up in the sky."'[51]

The conversion ceremony was also photographed, though it is likely that the event was staged prior to the shaky flight to France. The ceremony, as described by the *Express* journalist, was reported around the world:

> As we neared mid-Channel Dr. Sheldrake put on a red fez and laid the Koran on a table. [...] The doctor placed his hands over the palm of the princess' right hand while the princess, her face lighting into a smile, repeated the words from the Koran:
>
> 'I bear witness that nothing deserves to be worshipped but Allah, Allah.
>
> And I bear witness that Muhamed is the apostle of Allah, Allah.'
>
> Then Dr. Sheldrake announced: 'I give thee the name Khair-ul-Nissa, fairest of women.' At which the princess again smiled.
>
> That ended the ceremony. The doctor closed the Koran, put his hands in his pockets, and he and the princess sat down to lunch as we passed over the French lowlands by Boulogne.[52]

Sheldrake said that they were met in Paris by the city's 'leading Muslims', who welcomed Gladys 'as a new sister in Islam'.[53] The following day, they went to the Grand Mosque of Paris, and were received by its Director, Abdelkader Ben Ghabrit (1868–1954), and other prominent Muslims for Friday prayer. Sheldrake gave many interviews about Gladys' conversion and her reception in Paris, but he failed to mention that their appearance at the mosque created a stir. Sheldrake had tipped off the local press that they would be visiting the mosque, and consequently its complex was 'stormed' by around sixty journalists and photographers eager to catch sight of the celebrity convert.[54] Speaking afterwards to reporters, Ben Ghabrit said:

> I did not conceal from the Princess my feeling about the whole affair. I told her of my surprise that an announcement had been made that a reception was to take place at the mosque.
>
> We do not hold receptions here when a person, whoever he [sic] may be, is received into the faith.

It is a private affair for her, and the Press need not be called there to witness it. A mosque is not a centre for propaganda and publicity. It is a temple for meditation and prayer.[55]

Asked to comment on the matter, Gladys admitted, 'Everything went beautifully until I reached the Mosque':

We were ushered into a room, where Kadour Ben Ghabrit, head of the mosque, received us with a torrent of voluble French. [...]

After about five minutes we walked out. I consider that the attitude of Ben Ghabrit was so rude and uncalled for.

I gather that he took exception to the fact that a number of pressmen and photographers had arrived at the mosque to witness my appearance.

Well, that was not my fault, was it?

I was also given to understand that he did not like my costume—I was wearing the Royal Malay dress, which I am entitled to do—and objected for some obscure reason or other to the fact that I made my declaration of faith in an aeroplane.[56]

In Britain, the Aga Khan (1877–1957), the spiritual leader of Ismaili Muslims, congratulated Gladys: 'I hope in Islam your Highness will find a refuge for your spiritual life'.[57] The British tabloid press turned to the most prominent Muslim convert, Lord Headley, the MSGB President, for comment on the unorthodox conversion ceremony. Perhaps keen to avoid further direct conflict with Sheldrake, Headley did not mention him or his involvement in the affair. Instead, Headley 'expressed regret' that Gladys 'had chosen to embrace the Moslem faith while she was flying across the English Channel in an aeroplane'. Converting to Islam was, Headley emphasized, a solemn undertaking: 'To carry out the serious ceremony of conversion in this theatrical manner tends to rob it of much of its religious significance'.[58] He added: 'I don't want to be unkind, but I feel that her action is liable to be misconstrued as a desire for notoriety, even as a somewhat freakish departure from good taste. I am afraid that it will hurt the feelings of many Moslems all over the world'.[59]

Gladys did not publicly respond to Lord Headley's criticism, which was reported in newspapers internationally. Instead,

Sheldrake, who had returned to England, claimed to speak for her. He stated that 'the Princess was very indignant regarding Lord Headley's statement':

> The Princess wishes to state that far from hurting the feelings of Moslems all over the world she has received dozens of telegrams and letters from the leading Moslems in England and France, and cables from many other countries tendering heartiest congratulations in her having embraced the Islamic faith.[60]

Although Ben Ghabrit had also publicly criticized Gladys, Sheldrake aimed his rebuttal at Lord Headley. It is not clear whether the two men corresponded or met to discuss the issue. By 1932, Sheldrake was far removed from the WMM and MSGB and probably not on speaking terms with Headley.[61] Sheldrake made Gladys a patron of the WIA and, in an indirect swipe at the London-centric WMM and MSGB, he added that, in Britain, Gladys would visit 'many of the provincial towns where Moslem communities exist. She is planning to go to South Shields'.[62]

Muslim public life

Gladys and Sheldrake could not have predicted the amount of international publicity they received, nor of course could they control its tone. Newspaper headlines in Britain and beyond highlighted the sensational nature of Gladys' mid-flight conversion ('Ceremony at 100 M. P. H.') and, more often than not, concentrated on her gender and ethnicity: 'White Princess Joins Islam'; 'White Woman becomes a Moslem'.[63] The English-language press tended to portray Gladys as a privileged, eccentric woman and raised the concerns of influential Muslims like Ben Ghabrit and Lord Headley ('The Dayang Muda. Severely Rebuked by Moslem Leaders').[64] The media was also sceptical about Gladys' motivation for choosing Islam: 'The princess [...] spoke about her latest change in the most matter-of-fact way, and confessed that she had not even read the Koran'.[65] The latter claim was likely untrue; Gladys often contradicted herself, which did not help matters, but she was most certainly misquoted by some journalists. She was also castigated by disgruntled Christians in the correspondence pages of newspapers and magazines. For one reader of the *Catholic Leader* (Madras), 'The apostate in question is a sentimentalist in the superlative degree'.[66]

The negative press forced Gladys onto the defensive, and she held her own in the weeks and months that followed her conversion. She used her fame to good effect, giving many interviews and writing columns that further explained her decisions, addressed and contradicted some of the false or exaggerated claims and stories that had been circulated about her, and affirmed her commitment to Islam. In turn, she became, for a short time, a rare female Muslim public figure in western Europe and south-east Asia, where she was respected as Dayang Muda.

Initially, Gladys had to clarify and explain why she had abandoned Catholicism for Islam. She asserted that 'the Roman faith is altogether too austere for me. It makes no allowances for human nature, and tries even to control the thoughts of its followers'.[67] On 27 March 1932, she embraced technology by taking to the airwaves, giving a scripted talk in English for Colonial Radio Paris:

> Although I admired very much the great and beautiful work done by the Church of Rome for the sake of civilisation, there were things I found too difficult to accept. I remained Catholic for two years, making very sincere efforts to understand its difficult teaching.
>
> I always felt, however, that Christ never could have forbidden anyone to communicate directly with God, neither could the idea of kneeling in a confessional box where few people really speak the truth, ever have been ordained by Christ.[68]

She said that she began to study the religion and history of Islam:

> I was struck by the purity, logic and simplicity of this religion and felt that my whole heart and soul were wrapped in this teaching which is so human and understanding. The Koran appealed to me as being the direct words from God, delivered to the man who was the last Prophet. We know his life from beginning to end as we know the enormous amount of good that the doctrine of

145

Mahommed did to the world. Very few people know that while Europe was sunk in the most appalling darkness of the Middle Ages, the Muslim civilisation in Spain set a light to the glorious development of science, art and literature. It is due to the enlightened Kaliphs of Spain that Europe happily was able to find the way to the Renaissance. Unfortunately the evolution of the life of Muslim lands is too little known.[69]

Gladys did not acknowledge Sheldrake's role in her education about Islam. She simply noted that he had overseen the conversion ceremony and 'is well known for the self-sacrificing work he has undertaken all his life for the sake of a splendid ideal'.[70] However, her concluding comments closely echoed arguments made by Sheldrake and other British Muslims connected with the WMM between the wars—that Islam was the natural 'religion of the future':

> We all feel that the moral basis of life is sapped up by the powerful influence of atheism. Therefore our duty is to join a higher ideal of moral[ity] and ethics, to be able to withstand this depraving work. The East will bring to the Western lands the flame of faith, which we unfortunately have almost extinguished, and we have to study their beautiful teaching.[71]

Gladys ended the radio talk by explaining that she intended to visit Germany, England and, with Sheldrake, America, 'to explain the profound beauty of the teaching of the Prophet. I will take with me the marvellous sacred relic [tunic], which I will show to all who have asked to see this unique souvenir of the great Prophet'.[72] In a final push for publicity, Gladys—or perhaps Sheldrake, or both of them—told the press that, in March 1932, she would return to England for the first time since her conversion: escorted by armed detectives, Gladys would bring the Arab tunic—allegedly 'the world's most valuable garment', reputedly worth £500,000—so that it could be 'exhibited in a large hall in the West End', where Muslims from far and wide were expected to gather around it.[73]

In fact, Gladys did not return to England until late April 1932. She later said that she had not discussed her decision to convert to Islam with any of her family; it is likely that both her conversion

146

and the manner in which she publicly renounced Christianity led to a rift with some of them and delayed her return. Speaking of the consequences of her conversion to Islam in early March, she was quoted in the press as saying: 'I have counted the cost. I know it will mean bitter criticism, and possible alienation, from my family. I believe I shall be the first member of a ruling white house to profess the Moslem faith, but I know I shall never regret it'.[74] The Brooke family avoided commenting publicly on the matter, though, when pressed by a journalist in April, Gladys' sister-in-law Sylvia, Ranee of Sarawak (1885–1971), remarked sarcastically: 'I'd rather not say very much about it, but when [the adventurer] Dick Halliburton arrived at Sarawak, I flew 60 miles with him in his seaplane and I was not converted to Islam whilst doing it and neither did I have a camera man with me!'[75]

When Gladys returned to England, the journalists assembled at Croydon Airport noticed that none of her relations were waiting to meet her. Gladys apparently said: 'I am greatly grieved that not one single member of my family has come to greet me'.[76] Instead, she was welcomed by a group of Muslims, including Sheldrake. Despite her earlier claim, Gladys was neither escorted by armed detectives nor was she carrying the Arab tunic, which had, in the intervening weeks, been further discredited by scholars. Gladys did not publicly mention the tunic again.

Gladys continued to defy her critics. For example, at the beginning of May, she went to Wales because she had agreed to crown the 'May Queen' of Rhyl, a Miss Rene Edwards. Gladys upset the organizers just before the event by announcing that, besides presenting a copy of the Bible, which was customary at such events, she would also give the May Queen a copy of the Qur'an. Gladys briefed a local reporter:

> 'It is very amusing,' she said, as she placed an Egyptian cigarette in a long jade holder 'for the grave-faced men to point out to Miss Edwards that she might be corrupted by receiving a copy of the Koran.'
>
> 'I am a Moslem now. It has required great courage to change my religious faith. All the same, I shall give a copy of the Koran to the May Queen and shall autograph it as a memento of the occasion.'

'I shall also give Miss Edwards some Persian jewellery. I wonder if the grave-faced men of Rhyl will be equally shocked by that.'[77]

Undaunted, Gladys presented a miniature Qur'an 'the size of a postage stamp' to Miss Edwards.[78]

Back in London, Gladys gave a reception 'for her Moslem friends' at the prestigious Park Lane Hotel, Piccadilly.[79] It was reported that 'The princess sat on a gilded throne and greeted everyone personally'.[80] She then toured the south coast with Sheldrake, ending the trip at Selsey in West Sussex, where they were hosted by Sir Abdullah Archibald Hamilton (1876–1939), who had converted to Islam in 1923.[81] Gladys then returned to France, where she took every opportunity to recount the story of her journey to Islam. A letter to her cousin Conrad Simpson that repeated her Colonial Radio talk was circulated to the press and published in Britain, India and elsewhere.[82]

Between August and November 1932, Gladys penned a column entitled 'It's the Truth' for the English newspaper, *The People*. The column described rather sensational incidents from Gladys' life, largely extracted from *Relations and Complications*.[83] However, in the first instalment, Gladys explained why she had chosen Islam and refuted the claim that she had not read the Qur'an prior to her conversion:

> It happened quite casually. A friend of mine lent me one day, knowing my fondness for the literature of the East, an English copy of the Koran. I read it through several times and gradually, almost without knowing it, I felt its beauty and simplicity sink into my mind.
>
> I determined to make serious researches into the teachings of Mahomet. I procured every book I could hear of on the subject: I consulted Muslim scholars.
>
> What I learned convinced me that here I had found the religion which seemed to me the most perfect, or perhaps I ought rather to say the religion which suited best my individual ideas.[84]

Gladys indirectly addressed Lord Headley's criticism about her conversion ceremony: 'The idea came to me that I would like the simple ceremony to be performed in the air away from earthly territory, closer to the sky where, since the beginning of time man has always pictured his heaven', admitting that 'It was a foolish fancy perhaps, but a perfectly sincere one, and as I always travel between London and Paris by air, it presented no difficulties'.[85]

Gladys seemed to blame Sheldrake for turning the conversion ceremony into a publicity event. Arriving at Croydon, 'I was not so pleased to see the little crowd of curious spectators gathered round the plane, for somehow or other the story had leaked out and the morning papers had been full of "the flying convert to Islam"'.[86] This retelling of the story does not ring true given that Gladys posed for press photographs at Airways House before leaving central London for the airport. Gladys revealed that, at the airport, she experienced what today would be termed Islamophobia: 'Some of the opinions I heard expressed were unpleasantly frank [... such as] "A religion only fit for blacks"'.[87] Gladys' experience and her reaction echoed that of many other Britons, female and male, who converted to Islam between the wars: 'For the first time I felt a sense of isolation. So that was what many English people would think of me. I was going to alienate myself from my own countrymen'.[88]

At the end of the article, Gladys addressed for the first time the status of women in Islam and Muslim societies. She revealed that her visit with Sheldrake to the Grand Mosque of Paris was the first time she had entered a mosque; she was surprised that she had to take off her shoes and, as a woman, pray behind the men. Gladys did not attempt to explain or justify the latter. Instead, she asserted:

> It is curious how the idea prevails that the Muslim woman has both in religion and everyday life a place inferior to that of men. It is absolutely untrue, for, as a matter of fact, the woman of the East has certain rights and privileges which the English wife might well envy.
>
> The foremost of these is, of course, that her own quarters in the household [the harem] are sacred to her. Under no circumstances can her husband enter her room without her permission, and were he to insist on doing so this fact would in itself be considered sufficient grounds for separation. [...]

The rules which govern a Muslim household are more or less of a patriarchal character. The head of the household is obliged to maintain not only his wives and daughters, but any other unmarried females in the family, no matter how great their number.

It would be impossible to find a 'surplus woman' in any Muslim family, for she would be supported by her nearest male relative, and would have as much right to her place in his harem, even though he might be only her second or third cousin, as his wife would.[89]

Not content with writing for the popular press, in 1932 Gladys founded a monthly review called *Informations Islamiques*, intended to provide 'a true account of the evolution and of the life of Muslim lands'.[90] Published in Paris, the journal was edited by her friend, Yousouff Maghrebi. Its first issues were warmly welcomed by Marmaduke Pickthall in *Islamic Culture*, a prestigious journal that he edited from Hyderabad. Pickthall wrote that he admired the aim of *Informations Islamiques* to 'bring together the news of every Muslim country and of the Muslim communities inhabiting non-Muslim countries, to furnish first-hand information as to current problems, and co-ordinate the purpose of the various progressive movements which are now dispersed'.[91]

Informations Islamiques was discontinued after only a few issues, but Gladys also wrote articles and letters about Islam for a number of English-language Islamic journals. Between 1932 and 1934, she wrote for *Real Islam* (Singapore), *The Aligarh Magazine* (India) and *The Muslim Review* of Lucknow, which continued to endorse Sheldrake's WIA.[92] Her articles emphasized that rational Islam was the religion best suited to respond to and provide a moral and practical framework for the modern world: 'To-day, when the whole world is threatened by the menace of total destruction, when humanity is suffering from economic and moral crises, let us take the Book given by God and follow the rules, which He gave us'.[93]

Despite Sheldrake's disdain for the Lahore Ahmadiyya's influence at Woking, at the time of her conversion, Gladys was featured—presumably with her consent—on the cover of the

Lahore Ahmadi quarterly magazine, *The Muslim Revival*, which was edited by the Ahmadi leader, Maulana Muhammad Ali (1874–1951).[94] She also contributed articles to *The Muslim Revival* and another Lahore Ahmadi magazine, *The Light*, in 1932 and 1933.[95]

In January 1933, *The Light* reported that Gladys had attended the recent MSGB annual celebration of the Prophet's birthday in London. The event was hosted by, among others, Lord Headley, and attracted around 250 Muslims, most of them connected with the WMM.[96] The following issue of *The Light* contained an angry letter from Conrad Simpson, who had become Sheldrake's aide and was travelling with him on a fund-raising tour of India and south-east Asia. Simpson chastised the editor of *The Light* for discussing the Dayang Muda without crediting Sheldrake's role in her conversion to Islam. He added that he was pained to read an article in the same issue of the magazine that announced the return to India of Maulana Aftab-ud-Din Ahmad (1901–56). The latter had been assistant imam (Muslim religious leader) at Woking (1931–2) and had squabbled with Sheldrake. Daring to write on behalf of Gladys, Simpson added, 'I know that my cousin would never for a moment countenance praise of a person who deliberately attacks one who has sacrificed everything for Islam'.[97]

Sheldrake subsequently apologized to the editor of *The Light* for Simpson's letter, which he said was written whilst they were in separate cities: 'I have to forgive him for he is young, and new to Islamic traditions'.[98] However, the damage was done; Gladys, who was now on good terms with members of the WMM and MSGB, including Lord Headley, was evidently furious that Simpson/Sheldrake claimed to speak for her and criticize a trusted figure in the Lahore Ahmadiyya Movement. In early March 1933, Simpson wrote to his cousin from India, asking why she had stopped writing to him and Sheldrake. He said that he had written to *The Light* after it had reported her going to London 'to attend the Woking business' because:

> These people want to make out that your own work in Paris is simply part of the Woking and Berlin Ahmadi Movement. It is damnable, they try to make out that everything in the West is done by the followers of Mirza Ghulam Ahmad, the so-called

'Promised Messiah' of the Punjaub [*sic*]. I have stated clearly, (as also has Doctor [Sheldrake] in his speeches) that you pay yourself for everything, and that you are not an Ahmadi.[99]

Simpson asked Gladys to help him promote Sheldrake's fund-raising tour of India. Tactlessly, he offered to sell the Arab tunic 'as an "antique"', adding 'It is obvious out here that everyone knows that Muhammad had no "tunic" when he died'.[100] The letter ended thus:

I have a wonderful scheme for making money when we return [to England], and we shall have no outlay, but be able to rake in thousands. It all depends on whether you keep your name from being associated with these Ahmadi people in Woking and Berlin, otherwise we should have to do the thing ourselves, and leave you out, but we want you in, and want your name to be kept clear of troubles.[101]

Simpson's letter added fuel to the fire; in May 1933, Gladys publicly disassociated herself from Sheldrake, Simpson and the WIA. She complained to the editor of *The Light* that she had received 'so many letters' from Sheldrake and Simpson asking her to 'explain some information given by them to the Indian Press with reference to myself that I wish to state that I am in no way connected with the tour of these gentlemen and have not entrusted them with any mission whatsoever'.[102] Further, 'I am in no way concerned with the statements of Dr. Sheldrake and Mr. Simpson and I wish to notify the Press that I accept no responsibility for any information circulated about myself, unless such information has been expressly authorised by me'.[103] Gladys sent a similar letter to the India Office in London, and copies to the editors of several journals, including *The Light*, for publication. She asked that the India Office intervene to ensure that Sheldrake and Simpson stopped using her name in connection with their activities.[104] This seems to have put an end to the matter. In June 1933, Sheldrake and Simpson reached Sarawak, where the local press enquired about their relationship with the Dayang Muda; Sheldrake affirmed that she had 'absolutely nothing to do with our tour, and also, we have nothing to do with a Muslim organisation run by her in Paris'.[105] The incident clearly rankled Sheldrake. As late as October 1933, he wrote to Gladys via the correspondence pages of *The Light*, stating that he was 'very surprised' to read her statement and thought it 'absurd' that she had reported him to the India Office: 'I am sorry that, for reasons best known to her since my departure for the East, she has evidently been upset by someone or something. [...] Very reluctantly I have come to the conclusion that further correspondence would be seemingly useless'.[106]

Sheldrake and Simpson had little to fear from Gladys' connection with the WMM or MSGB. She seldom returned to England and had few interactions with Muslims in Britain after 1932. Based in France and no longer associated with the WIA, she was quite free from the divisions between Ahmadis that affected Muslim communities in Britain and elsewhere between the wars. At the end of 1933, she contributed a short article, 'The Path of God', to Pickthall's *Islamic Culture*.[107] It is not clear if she was invited by Pickthall to write the article or whether she submitted it for his consideration. The article is not well written, and the fact that Pickthall published it is a testament to his admiration for or liking of Gladys. In the article, Gladys opaquely philosophized about the universe, humanity and the quest for a harmonious and fruitful life: 'Humanity must progress according to a plan fixed by God and known by Him only. It must progress painfully towards a state which grows gradually nearer perfection until it becomes, as the Scripture says, the Kingdom of God'.[108]

It was certainly an achievement to be published in Pickthall's prestigious journal but—for reasons unknown—one that Gladys did not build upon. In fact, she was little heard of between late 1933 and 1936, when a second article, 'The Unity of God', a convoluted account of the development of spiritual monotheism, also appeared in *Islamic Culture*.[109] The article showed that, contrary to popular belief, Gladys was versed in the history of the Abrahamic religions, especially of Islam, and knew the Qur'an well.

In a rare press interview given in London in December 1936, Gladys confirmed her commitment to Islam. She said that her conversion had been 'a great success', but admitted that 'I do not follow all the Moslem customs'.[110] This indicates that, like

Sheldrake and other British Muslim converts of the period, Gladys took a pragmatic approach to practicing her religion. Recognizing Islam to be a rational and tolerant faith, Gladys and other British Muslims found ways to reconcile the demands of Islamic rituals with their daily lives without necessarily diminishing their fundamental beliefs or religiosity.[111]

Later years

By the time war began in Europe in 1939, Gladys' celebrity had waned. She never returned to live in Britain permanently and, in the late 1930s, divided her time between Paris, the French Riviera and Greece. She left France for Greece just before war was declared. When Italy invaded Greece in autumn 1940, Gladys tried but failed to secure a passage to Australia and instead went to India. She took rooms in the Ritz Hotel in Bombay and stayed there until she was reunited with her son Anthony in India in 1946.[112] Two years earlier, Bertram Brooke had relinquished his claim as heir to the Rajah title in favour of Anthony. However, in 1946, Rajah Charles Vyner Brooke decided to cede Sarawak to the British government as a crown colony. Encouraged by Gladys, Anthony first opposed the plan from London and then, from 1947, campaigned to revoke the cession from the home he shared with his mother in Singapore.[113]

For a few years in the late 1940s, Gladys was a fixture of the Singapore colonial social scene and featured fleetingly in the local society gossip columns, much as she had done when she lived in London in the 1920s. She also threw herself into the anti-cession campaign, arguing that the Rajah had 'decided to abandon the country which he held in sacred trust'.[114] She returned to Sarawak several times and continued to speak against the cession until 1951, when her son Anthony admitted defeat and renounced his claim as heir to the Sarawak crown.[115] Anthony left Singapore, and Gladys, who was in poor health, moved to Ceylon (Sri Lanka). She died in Colombo in June 1952.[116]

Although she had largely removed herself from Muslim public life in the late 1930s, Gladys remained committed to the faith she had embraced twenty years before her death. Her last will and testament, written in February 1952, confirmed that she was 'commonly known as Khair ul Nissa Gladys Sarawak', indicating that she retained her Muslim name. It also stated that she had completed the manuscript of a second memoir called *Rome to Mecca*, but its whereabouts are currently unknown, and it is presumed lost or destroyed. The will stipulated that Gladys' body should be 'immediately embalmed' and 'buried at Kuching in Sarawak in the manner prescribed for those of the Moslem faith and I direct my Trustees to pay the Imam who conducts the burial of my body the sum of One hundred pounds'.[117] Since she died in Ceylon, Gladys' body was buried in a Muslim burial ground at Colombo.[118] In the final clause in her will, Gladys declared:

> I SHALL be watching you all my children from another World and I shall want you to be happy as I shall be myself and my last wish therefore is that the Trustees shall immediately on my decease hand to my said son Antoni the sum of One hundred pounds [...] so that he may pay the expenses to enable you (if possible) to congregate for a champagne lunch or dinner followed by a theatre with those of your friends and those of mine whom you think would like to share this last behest[,] it being my especial wish that you will all dress in white or gay colours in order that you should not depress me by looking like a lot of crows for everyone is sent to this world with a return ticket and must some day leave it[,] and this I shall have done and so au revoir and God bless you all.[119]

The British press considered it rather ironic that the Dayang Muda 'was buried as a Moslem but retained enough of the Christian spirit to leave £100 for a funeral champagne party'.[120]

Conclusion

Untangling and documenting Gladys Brooke's adult life offers a rare insight into what it meant to be a female Western Muslim convert of high social status, albeit one who lived mainly outside of Britain, between the wars. It also shines new light on aspects of Islam in Britain—primarily London and south-east England—in that period, including relations between Muslims and differences of opinion among them. The writers who knew Gladys around the time she settled in France have shaped our understanding of her personality and biography and do not paint a flattering portrait of her. The circumstances of Gladys' formal conversion to Islam and episodes that punctuate her first years as a Muslim do little to dampen her reputation as a publicity-seeker. This is not helped by her brief but formative relationship with Khalid Sheldrake, who exploited Gladys' conversion and his role in her journey to Islam for his own ends. If she was not taken seriously by the English-language press, it was partly because she was a wealthy woman of independent means and partly because she made some poor decisions, most of which were taken in association with Sheldrake. But Gladys was not a victim of Sheldrake's self-aggrandizement; in fact, she had more agency than he did. Conversely, Gladys' gender, financial status, class and colonial privilege made her a celebrity, and this was respected by Muslim editors, especially in South Asia, including Maulana Muhammad Ali and Marmaduke Pickthall, who gave her a voice in their Islamic journals.

Though Gladys was not a great writer, she shared her beliefs and views about modern Islam to non-Muslims and Muslims. She tended to focus on what she knew from her reading and discussions with other Muslims about Islam's spiritual and moral benefit to humanity, rather than complex debates about gender and the position of women in Islam and Muslim societies, of which she had little first-hand knowledge; indeed, as we have seen, when she dipped into the latter, she perpetuated a rather idealized view of the perfect equality between the sexes in Muslim majority societies. Gladys' public writing about Islam and Muslims seems to have cemented her faith and commitment to it long after her celebrity had waned and she was living out of the public eye.

SECTION 4

MUSLIM WOMEN IN BRITAIN
SOJOURNERS, SETTLERS, LEGACY-MAKERS

8

'WE WERE NOT ANYTHING LIKE
WHAT THEY IMAGINED!'

MUSLIM WOMEN TRAVELLERS FROM
SOUTH ASIA TO BRITAIN, 1890s TO 1930s

Siobhan Lambert-Hurley and Daniel Majchrowicz

Introduction

Shortly after the First World War, Safia Jabir Ali (1893–1962) travelled alone from Bombay to London by steamship and rail. Her husband, Jabir Ali (1887–1974), who was a merchant based in Rangoon (now Yangon) in Burma (Myanmar), had progressed to Europe ahead of her with a new business partner. While abroad, the latter died suddenly of a heart attack. This unfortunate turn of events seems to have occasioned Safia's own journey to join her husband. The couple reunited in the imperial capital, where they stayed for six weeks before touring various towns and cities across England, Scotland and Germany. Jabir's investment in wolfram mining and hardware resulted in an atypical European itinerary for this educated, 'well-to-do' couple, which included industrial cities and ports that Safia explored alone while her husband worked. Upon her return to India, she gave a speech in English to a local ladies' club detailing what had left the 'best, most vivid impression' at each location. No matter where she went, she explained, she was surprised by 'the ignorance even educated people showed towards India'. This appeared odd to her. They seemed, she recalled, to believe she would be 'scared to death' to move about freely: 'They are under the impression that Indian-ladies, generally lie on durwans [divans] in gorgeous apparel, waited on by women, [dreaming] away their days surrounded by wealth and luxury! I had to tell them that [...] we were not anything like what they imagined!'[1]

Hers was not a singular experience. A wealth of evidence from travel writing by Muslim women visitors from South Asia to Britain in the high and late colonial period suggests that Orientalist fantasies structured British perceptions of their lives—as though women from the subcontinent were only accessible through English literature. In fact, Indian Muslim women had been making this journey for at least three centuries. Many of the earliest had arrived as female servants and nursemaids, or *ayahs*, while others accompanied British or European husbands who had served in colonial India.[2] The majority of these earlier travellers—often illiterate and sometimes living in precarious circumstances—did not leave written accounts of their experiences. An autobiographical record only begins in the late nineteenth century, when more elite Muslim women travellers like Safia Jabir Ali started writing letters, keeping diaries and giving speeches. Initially circulated privately, these accounts were increasingly published in magazine articles or travel books. At least until the middle of the twentieth century, most writing by these women appeared in Urdu and, to a lesser extent, in English.[3]

This literature is badly preserved and almost completely unstudied despite a deep tradition of travel writing in modern Muslim South Asia. From the 1870s, the genre exploded in popularity across a range of Indian languages and literatures.[4] With just a single exception, none of the earliest published literature was by Muslim women.[5] It took a few more decades for several overlapping impulses to converge in a way that allowed them to contribute more. Decisive shifts included faster, cheaper travel facilitated by steam, reduced economic barriers to accessing print culture, increased schooling and higher women's literacy. Thanks to these changes, travel accounts by Indian Muslim women began to circulate publicly from the 1890s and, by the 1930s, they were relatively common. Most often, this literature discussed pilgrimage travel both within and outside South Asia.[6] A smaller set dealt with European travel. These writings focused on Britain, and more precisely England, which constituted the primary destination of most itineraries, with women generally making only shorter side trips to neighbouring countries. In this chapter, we draw on twelve such travel narratives written between the 1890s and the late 1930s. We read these texts for what they tell us about women's experiences in late colonial Britain, and also for what they reveal about what their authors wanted their Indian readers to know about life in Britain—in other words, how they represented everyday life in a distant country that had such a sizeable influence on Indian life.

The authors discussed here were necessarily elite or upper middle class, for other groups would have lacked the literacy to record and preserve accounts of their journeys or the wealth to travel to Britain independently. Despite this, these authors came from varied social and geographic backgrounds. Four of them, including Safia Jabir Ali, belonged to the wealthy Tyabji clan within Bombay's minority Sulaimani Bohra community. Another two, of royal pedigree, came from Bhopal in central India. This princely locality was associated with the production of women's autobiographical and travel writing linked to four generations of female Muslim rule.[7] Several more were connected to other princely states, including Hyderabad in the south and Janjira on the west coast. The remainder hailed from territories ruled directly by the British colonial government from Bombay to Bengal, though particularly the north's United Provinces, where they descended from or belonged to estate-owning families. Many also had connections to India's new professional classes engaged in civil service, law, medicine and education. Despite this variance of location and status, it is significant that all the authors were associated in one way or another with reform movements—for example, Islamic modernism—that emerged in colonial India to strengthen the Muslim community through social and religious change.[8] Perhaps as a result, most of these authors viewed travel to Britain as a learning opportunity. For some, that involved study at a British university (Oxford, London, Leeds) or teacher training college (Maria Grey Teaching College, for example), while, for others, travel itself was a means of education. All these women had the financial wherewithal to travel to England, were highly literate (a rare distinction for Indian women at the time), and had the leisure to write.

Their travelogues were generally written for Indians and primarily, but not exclusively, for women. This target audience is sometimes made explicit and is at other times revealed through references to readers as 'my sisters'. Among the striking commonalities to emerge from the corpus of Indian Muslim women's travelogues is a focus on everyday life, family and the home. The accounts are saturated with astute observations on the quotidian in Britain and en route: How did they interact with one another and conduct their society? What kinds of clothes did they wear? How did they raise their children? How did they treat Indian visitors? These observations were almost inevitably compared with Indian practice. Such comparisons might help Indians decide which British practices they should adopt and which they should reject. Against unfamiliar backdrops, female authors thus constructed an image of themselves that, whether intentionally or otherwise, gives insight into their ideas of self, community, culture, service, foreignness and familiarity.

To capture these complex reflections, this chapter is organized around some of these travel authors' own considerations and preoccupations, with sections on travelling companions, veiling and seclusion, dress and children.[9] These themes, prominent in the travelogues themselves, introduce the everyday life of Indian Muslim woman travellers in Britain. More than that, though, they reveal the diversity of Indian responses to life and travel in Britain. While many of the authors had similar experiences, their responses were not uniform, nor were their manners of presenting them to an Indian audience. It must be emphasized, too, that these visits and accounts were not purely anthropological. For these women, Britain offered the opportunity not only to observe, but to experiment. The rules of Indian social life could be bent or suspended while abroad. New ideas about cooking, dress and social interaction that Indian Muslim women encountered in Britain could be tested out relatively risk-free. In short, Muslim women's engagement with Britain was deep and critical; they sought to examine their own beliefs and practices in light of their experiences abroad.

Travelling companions

In their narratives, most early-twentieth century Muslim women travellers from India addressed the question of with whom they travelled and thus the permissibility of their journeys. For some, this was a social issue: 'noble' women travelling alone were not always well-received. For others, it was a religious matter, with some interpretations of Islamic law requiring women to travel in the company of a close male relative, or *mahram*. Accordingly, nearly all our authors related how they were accompanied to Britain by fathers, husbands, brothers or sons.

The earliest author discussed here, Amina Tyabji (1866–1942), travelled to Britain as part of a princely entourage from the state of Baroda in 1893–4. Her role was as companion to the ruler's royal consort, the Maharani of Baroda, a position to which she was well-suited thanks to her excellent command of English. On this trip, she was accompanied by her husband, Abbas, who had been employed in Baroda's judicial service after eleven years of British education; he in turn advised the Maharaja.[10] Another author, Nazli Begum (1874–1968), similarly acted as a princely escort on a royal tour of Britain, continental Europe and the Middle East in 1908. She travelled with her husband, Sidi Ahmad Khan Sidi Ibrahim Khan, the Nawab of Janjira.[11] Also in the party were her sister Atiya, her brother Ali Asghar, two state officials, a doctor and servants.[12] Two other, larger delegations from an Indian principality, in 1911 and 1925–6, were led by a woman ruler, Nawab Sultan Jahan Begum of Bhopal (1858–1930)—but even as a widow she was accompanied by at least one son. Her youngest, Hamidullah, also acted as *mahram* to his wife Maimoona Sultan (1900–82), who was still a child of eleven on the first visit but a mother of three daughters by the second.[13]

Other Muslim women travelled in more modest circumstances, usually alone with their husbands, perhaps with their children in tow. Exemplifying the companionate ideal core to reformist imaginings of Muslim marriage in this period was Sughra Humayun Mirza (1884–1958), who travelled through Europe with her husband in 1924. In her *Safarnamah-i Yurop*, she presented her husband as not just a *mahram*, but an equal partner. The pair appear to be in perfect harmony as they decide where to travel and what to see.[14] Begum In'am Habibullah (1883–1975) visited Britain with her husband and young daughter Tazeen in the early 1920s too, but, as we will see in the final section below, her focus was more on her three sons at boarding school whom she met after four years of being apart.[15] Other women travelled to Britain with a male relative but then moved about independently once *in situ*. Begum Sarbuland Jang (d. 1956), for instance, generally spent the evenings with her husband during their visit to London in 1910 but roamed freely during the day.[16] More remarkable was Iqbalunnisa Hussain (1897–1954), who came to Britain with her eldest son (having left five other children in Mysore) in 1933. While he prepared for the Indian Civil Service exams in London, she studied education at the University of Leeds, where she took a room in a university hall.[17] Atiya Fyzee (1877–1967) also lived in a boarding house for female students while at Maria Grey Training College in London in 1906–7, but at a lesser remove from her *mahram*, a brother who lived across the city.[18] These examples disclose that, while women typically travelled 'with' *mahrams*, there was broad interpretation as to how far apart they might drift away from them, and for how long.

There were also exceptions. Some women reported travelling entirely alone or at least without male accompaniment, even holding that it was sufficient for them to be accompanied to the station or the seaport by a *mahram*.[19] Safia Jabir Ali crossed from Bombay and went sightseeing solo while her husband attended to business. Another useful example is Muhammadi Begum (1911–

90), who travelled to Britain from Hyderabad with her husband Syed Jamil Husain shortly after their marriage in 1934. Both studied at the University of Oxford, but different programmes meant different schedules, and she often found herself alone for whole days, comforted only by letters from home and her private diary. As she wrote despondently in the latter, quoting a couplet from the Indian poet Ghalib:

> These days, I must spend my time shut up alone in a small room whose door is always closed. Jamil is very busy. He is always going to the library. There is no tradition of going to meet one another or corresponding with one another here. All there is here is this: 'Should you fall ill, there will be none to care for you. And should you die, there will be none to mourn you'.[20]

Other sections of Muhammadi Begum's diary and autograph book suggest that she actually kept a wide social circle, even meeting prominent figures of the time, including writers H.G. Wells (1866–1946) and George Bernard Shaw (1856–1950), as well as the barrister and politician Muhammad Ali Jinnah (1876–1948).[21] But, when 'agitated' by homesickness, her answer was to walk alone in the park until the caretaker closed the gates at dusk.[22]

Later, in September 1935, Muhammadi Begum recalled travelling back from Germany by train and boat with only her infant son Anwer, having left Jamil behind in Bonn:

> I was to travel alone today [...] Jamil, concerned that I was traveling alone, left no stone unturned to ensure he arranged absolutely everything. He even gave me a piece of paper on which he had written instructions for the journey. 'Eat your food on the train, have your tea on the steamer. Have dinner on the train from Dover to London'. And so on. 'Take such-and-such a taxi. The trains from Paddington to London leave at these times. You should take this one'. I understood it all, but it is not always easy to travel alone. Especially with an infant. Yet it was I who had insisted that Jamil stay here for longer so that he might spend more time getting to know the country.[23]

The brief summary here points to the complexities of her solo journey with babe in arms, involving a long train ride through

Germany and Belgium; a steamship from Ostend to Dover with passport control and customs on both ends; another train journey from England's south coast to London; a taxi from one London train station to another; and a final train from Paddington Station to Oxford. Arriving at 2am, the exhausted Muhammadi Begum was unable to find a taxi home and ended up sleeping in the waiting room with her baby and luggage until morning.[24] Clearly, then, religious precepts defining a woman's travelling companions were open to interpretation, if not disavowal, when faced with personal commitments and the vagaries of circumstance on a trip to Britain. The elements are engaged prominently in these travellers' accounts.

Veiling

Another common point of discussion, and one that shaped how Muslim women travellers saw Britain and how they were seen in Britain, was the impact of veiling practices, or purdah. A revealing example here is provided by Maimoona Sultan who, as seen in the previous section, travelled to Britain for the first time as a child in 1911 with a princely delegation headed by her mother-in-law Sultan Jahan Begum, the ruling Nawab of Bhopal. Part of the 'zenana party'—a term used to reflect that many of her fellow travellers were in purdah—Maimoona spent the entire trip in curtained travel compartments, secluded hotel rooms or rented accommodation where even outdoor gardens were 'screened from public view'.[25] These purdah arrangements were largely for her and her sister-in-law, Shaharyar. Her mother-in-law, for instance, did not abide by the same rules, but instead went about her public business wearing a body-enveloping burqa. As Sultan Jahan explained to Queen Alexandra (1844–1925) no less, unlike her daughters-in-law, she was a head of state with differing rules and needs. Sultan Jahan's granddaughter, Birjis, though nearly the same age as Maimoona, also went out regularly to attend various events around London. The key difference was probably the girls' marital status: Maimoona was married; Birjis was not. Maimoona thus had to rely on family members or, at times, information gleaned from newspapers, for knowledge of London. This situation meant that many descriptions in her travelogue were filtered through second-hand narration, rather than the result of her own direct observation.

Maimoona had more than one opportunity to visit London, however, and on subsequent trips in the 1920s and 1930s, she saw more of the city for herself. On a trip in 1925–6, again in the company of her mother-in-law, she continued to maintain strict purdah, but did—with her husband Hamidullah's explicit approval—occasionally go out without a veil. Some years later, her daughter Abida Sultaan recounted that her mother had joined her three children on 'clandestine' visits to the cinema dressed elegantly in a sari 'without even the semblance of a burqa'.[26] When Maimoona and Hamidullah visited London again in 1928 without Sultan Jahan, she abandoned purdah entirely. The change, uncoincidentally, took place after her husband had been officially crowned as the ruler of Bhopal. Photographic evidence suggests that on her three subsequent visits to Britain in the 1930s, Maimoona opted to wear only a light headscarf. Her daughters were pictured with fashionable hats or bare-headed.[27]

Maimoona's experience is thus indicative of the broad range of practices and possibilities in terms of presentation and conduct that Indian Muslim women could adopt in Britain. The decision often varied depending on where one was travelling to or whom one wished to meet as well as the circumstances of the meeting. We also see how these practices changed over time, a shift that was often on full display as the travel authors explained their decisions to readers, each in their own way. Of the authors considered in this chapter, an increasing number chose not to practice purdah at all, particularly from the 1920s onward. The women of the Tyabji clan, who were renowned in India as some of the first elite Muslim women to abandon purdah, provided the earliest examples. Hence, Amina Tyabji narrated her experience of sightseeing on the streets of London, Paris and Rome as early as the 1890s.[28] Atiya Fyzee still emphasized her modest apparel, however, when writing to her family and for a primarily Muslim female audience in India over a decade later, noting how, when going out, she always wore a 'gauze cloth' over her head and a Turkish-style cloak around her body: 'Everything is covered except my face'.[29] Contemporary photographs suggest that, at the very least, she wore a long-sleeved and high-necked blouse under her sari and covered her head with the loose end of the fabric, or *pallu*.[30] She also reported on the virtuous conduct of 'upper-class' British girls at her London college, whom she praised for their simple and tasteful dresses in discreet Edwardian style.[31]

Others did not abandon the veil entirely, but wrote that they considered being abroad a sort of 'vacation' from purdah: veils were removed once they were out of sight of their own home societies, whether while at sea or upon arrival in Europe. A paradigmatic example is Nazli Begum of Janjira. As the wife of an Indian ruler, she practiced a strict form of purdah—despite being from the liberal Tyabji clan—to avoid becoming a 'target of censure'. Abroad, though, in Paris as in London, she mixed freely without any such concerns. Curious about this transition, Britons whom she met engaged her in conversation about whether she found it 'strange' to appear in mixed company and also if she would 'go back' into purdah upon her return to India.[32] Begum In'am Habibullah (1883–1975) also experimented with living outside purdah while in Britain in the early 1920s, only to decide that she would abandon it upon her return to India. She was shunned and even banned from many homes for her choice, but it also likely facilitated her ability to contest elections from which she was elected as a member of the Legislative Assembly of the United Provinces in 1936.[33] Women who diverged from their usual practices while abroad often highlighted in their writing that the experience was variously unnerving, thrilling or even terrifying.

Dress

Indian Muslim women travellers faced further sartorial questions beyond veiling. They also had to determine what sort of everyday dress they would wear while in Britain. Men faced a simpler set of calculations. There was little judgement if they wore Western clothing, and many, at least upper-class men, even felt a strong expectation to wear 'cuff and collar', with perhaps exceptions for religious holidays.[34] Qazi 'Abd al-Ghaffar, for instance, enjoyed 'strutting about in clothes stitched on Bond Street through the markets of London'.[35] It was only in the 1930s that, inflamed with anti-colonial fervour, a trip to London inspired him to abandon Western clothing forever. This decision was largely a political statement, not due to social compulsion.[36] Indian Muslim women, though, faced quite a different calculus. In India, Partha Chatterjee has argued that women's bodies were treated as markers of culture and identity. Personal preferences and idiosyncrasies aside, the nationalist logic on the preservation of 'Indian culture' meant that women were highly discouraged from wearing Western clothes, even in Britain.[37]

The contentiousness of dress and identity come to the fore in a host of Indian travel writing by men and women as they assessed one another's decisions, sometimes derisively. The topic was hotly debated. Muhammadi Begum, studying at Oxford in the 1930s, provided a concise introduction to the topic:

> As a rule, [male] students from Hindustan adopt the English way of dressing as soon as they arrive. This practice is, however, unheard of among women who prefer to dress native style, wrapped in a sari. So, what should be the proper attire for men as long as they are in this country? Should they dress Hindustani style or adopt Western garb? In my opinion, they ought to wear what feels comfortable. Why should they feel awkward making a public appearance in a native outfit?[38]

This final line is telling in that it points to a certain discomfort with British reactions to Indian dress. Indeed, the debate over what Indians should wear extended even to the British themselves. They might ask, as did Muhammadi Begum's tutor,

> why we Hindustanis chose to give up wearing our native dress just because we were living on foreign soil. This is what he said: 'You would find us odd if we followed a certain line of reasoning and came out Hindustani style in public just as your adoption of English style could give rise to similar feelings in us'.[39]

Atiya Fyzee's vicious account of an Indian woman who had taken to wearing 'badly tailored and tasteless, gaudy English clothes'—

complete with wig, fake jewels, artificial beauty marks and a painted face—suggests her agreement: 'Why Indians make a spectacle of themselves in this way I don't know'.[40]

Nearly all the travellers considered in this chapter chose to wear the same clothing in Britain that they wore at home. Underscoring her stance in the previous quotation, Atiya Fyzee stated unequivocally, 'I have continued wearing my Indian clothes and do not intend to ever give them up'.[41] This was some type of sari draped over a blouse of full or half sleeves, rather than the *salwar kameez* (trousers and long shirt/tunic) that would become the norm for many Muslim women from South Asia later on. Clearly, this type of attire was not suited to the British climate. Travellers thus made strategic additions to their ensembles, including woollen sweaters, gloves, various types of cloaks and close toed shoes.[42] Clothing constituted a recurring theme for travellers visiting in winter. Cold, rainy weather made the process of dressing and walking about a challenge: 'Begin with a coat, then add gloves, clutch a handbag and hold onto an umbrella, added nuisance, if you ask me'.[43] Eventually, even those who most staunchly adhered to wearing purely Indian outfits were forced to give up. As Muhammadi Begum noted in her diary in March of 1935:

> I noticed Miss Sarabhai, wrapped up in a coat that came down to her knees, give a little shiver, and stride past. Her appearance so warmly dressed meant that she had finally accepted the vagaries of the weather. I had seen her on a number of occasions in the past dressed most unsuitably for the weather, not even wearing socks!'[44]

The chill of an English summer could induce a similar response. At a rainy Henley Regatta in June 1907, Atiya Fyzee felt so 'sick due to the cold' that she was obliged to don a heavy cloak.[45]

As suggested above, these accounts suggest that Indian Muslim women's dress drew immediate and constant attention. The public response varied from glee, to curiosity, to disgust, with a timid interest seemingly the most common, at least in the case of the relatively elite women discussed here. Here again, Muhammadi

Begum provides insight. She and her husband kept a wide range of friends, many of whom were fascinated by their clothing while at Oxford. One of her friends, Suzanne, 'very much wanted to try on Indian clothes':

> She has been asking me when I would dress her up in one of my saris, and I promised to do it today. So I dressed her up in my *karchobi* sari and *kurta*. My bangles didn't fit her. Instead, I had her wear the loose brass bangles that Mrs. Aishi had sent me. I also gave her Jamil's shoes to wear. Charles put on Jamil's gold-embroidered wedding *shervani*. It was dark by then, but we took pictures anyway. [...] Suzanne wore my clothes until it was time to leave.[46]

By her telling, a substantial proportion of London's women were fascinated by the clothing they saw their Indian visitors wear: 'Everyone here crazy about Hindustani clothes. Ever since the [Silver] Jubilee [of George V] in London [in 1935] this has become the latest fashion trend'.[47] This vogue apparently led to losses, as her friends borrowed her saris and then, because they were unable to keep them properly draped, ultimately returned them 'in tatters'.[48] Nearly every traveller to Britain had similar experiences. Atiya Fyzee, for instance, wrote in 1906 that

> The lady editor and a woman photographer-artist from the Lady's Pictorial met me. [...] They were both amazed by the artistry and suitability of my clothes. Until now they had ungainly thoughts regarding Indians. If they meet an Indian who does not meet their stereotypical views, they are totally flabbergasted. I do not know at what level.[49]

In short, when it came to what to wear in Britain on a daily basis, the experiences and expectations of South Asian Muslim women set them apart from most male travellers. However, it was not just clothing that excited interest; their mere presence alone was enough to elicit a range of responses, as exemplified by the following quote from Safia Jabir Ali: 'Talking of children, and of the curiosity they showed to us, I will tell you of how when we visited the London Zoo, children, merely to look us, would pass us and repass us, whispering and discussing us'.[50]

Children

Children appear repeatedly in Indian Muslim women's accounts of travel to Britain. In men's accounts, they make more fleeting appearances, perhaps because their children were in the charge of others, be it servants, wives or other female relatives. Women, in contrast, discuss their children almost as a rule, whether they were present or not. For many travellers, bringing their children on the long and expensive trip to Britain was impossible. In these cases, women's travelogues account for the arrangements they made for their children, or, at a minimum, describe their sorrow at leaving them behind. One Indian Muslim couple demonstrate this dichotomy neatly. Nawab Hamidullah Khan Sarbuland Jang and his wife Akhtar al-Nisa Begum Sarbuland Jang travelled to England together in 1910, each writing separate travel accounts of the journey. In the Nawab's account there is little mention of his children or the arrangements made for them. In his wife's account, on the other hand, we learn the children's names, how they were arranged for before her departure, and her pangs of separation: 'I wish I could take [my daughter] Khurshid Begum with me, but Nawab sahib would never allow it'. She also had to consider her daughter's needs: 'And then there is the impact on her education to consider. Accordingly, I have left Begum Khurshid here with my other children. My mother and sister-in-law have come to stay in our house with them'. [51]

When children were brought along, they often took a dominant role in the narrative. Begum Habibullah discussed her children at length or, alternatively, apologized that she had not 'been able to make daily entries to my journal, [because] I am busy with the children all day long'.[52] Children meant countless considerations to balance. The universal challenges of motherhood were magnified by being away from home and particularly by being in a foreign place like Britain, whose climate, social and meteorological, was not always ideal. The challenges were particularly great for women accustomed to the help of servants and family members.[53] Women had to navigate how to carry their luggage while attending to a child or carrying a baby, understand how to change a nappy in Britain's public spaces, or even know whom to trust. After the birth of her son Anwer in London in 1935, Muhammadi Begum's travel diary balanced concern for her studies at Oxford with caring for the new child. Her challenges were not only material, but also included dealing with the prejudice she encountered as an Indian, a Muslim and a mother. Her instructors at Oxford, for instance, were completely unwilling to accommodate her. On the road, she faced further struggles. A particularly difficult moment involved her journey to London from Germany alone but for her newborn:

> I scrambled into my seat on the train to London with Anwer beside me just as dinner was announced. Grabbing my handbag with one hand, and hauling the pram with the baby inside with the other, I rose immediately to find out the location of the dining car. To my dismay I learnt that it would be served at the other end of the train. It was a dilemma I had to face. I knew I did not have the energy to make a trip all the way with a baby in a pram.

The dilemma was resolved by entrusting the baby to a British couple while she went to the dining car:

> I noticed a couple with a small child who formed an agreeable family group and saw a way out of my trouble. Would it be possible for them to mind Anwer while I went to the dining car until my return? I asked. Of course they would, they said. I hurried to the dining car where I ordered soup and a plate of fish. I had just sat down to eat when an alarming thought arose in my mind. Suppose the couple had to leave the train at the next station, and decided to take the baby with them because I was not to be found? I beat a hasty retreat and rushed to the compartment to find the husband holding the baby who seemed to be enjoying the fuss made over him![54]

As this passage shows, while some Indian Muslim women did find life with a baby difficult, they also found support from strangers. It is hard to know precisely what these British interlocutors thought of Indian parenting, but these accounts give the strong sense that travelling with a child created a space for interaction that superseded questions of cultural difference.

Children often constituted the very reason women travelled to Britain. More than a few of the authors considered in this chapter went to see their children off to school, or to visit children that had long been studying and who did not have the time to travel home themselves. An exemplar here is Begum Habibullah. She travelled to Britain with her daughter, who was studying at Lucknow, to visit her three sons, who were being educated in the south of England. This was a family visit, but it had several objectives. On the one hand, Begum Habibullah wanted to ensure that her children were being looked after. At the same time, she was concerned that life in England would cause them to grow distant from their own Indian roots—not an uncommon vexation in these accounts. Begum Habibullah was particularly concerned that her children would forget how to pray, that they would not understand the Qur'an, and that they would forget how to speak Urdu well.[55] To her relief, her concerns were misplaced:

> I was happy to see that, [in fact,] the boys spoke Urdu just as well as they had when they went abroad. They told me that they had seen a fair bit of England during their time here, but that this country had not been blessed with the beauty that one encounters in Hindustan. Everything here is so uniform, they complained, that viewing it gives no pleasure. Person by person, they asked after each of their friends and relatives. They had not forgotten a single lane in all of Lucknow! By God's grace, their religious beliefs are intact, as well.[56]

Begum Habibullah ultimately spent a few months living near them during their school holidays and taking them on short trips in the countryside or to the beach.

The focus on children in these accounts is reflected not only in their authors' concerns for their own children, but in their abiding fascination with British parenting. As already mentioned, Indian Muslim women's travel was typified by a reformist conviction. These authors evinced an ongoing interest in observing the lives of others abroad to discover 'best practices' they could adopt themselves. Muhammadi Begum described her approach as follows:

> [Their] methods may be foreign to me, but worth the effort
> of finding out how the women of England are affected by new
> thinking. I do not mean to suggest that a copycat approach should
> be used where bringing up children the English way is concerned.
> But adopting what is practicable is worth looking into.[57]

For many, this meant keeping a close eye on the British mothers around them. While they found many commonalities with their European counterparts, they could be taken aback, too. Begum Habibullah, for instance, remarked on the tendency for parents to encourage their children to play in the dirt, an observation that marks a pointed inversion of colonial attitudes regarding savagery and civilization:

> There are lots of small children here. Some of them swung on the
> swings, while others walked about the beach barefoot. Where we
> live, playing in the dirt and walking barefoot are considered bad
> habits. But here, children are built to be strong and sturdy. Just
> as a child is to be given food, water, and a place to sleep, it is also
> considered necessary for them to play in this way. This is why the
> children here are so strong and healthy.[58]

Despite her surprise, Begum Habibullah did not condemn the practice, but instead tried to locate its possible benefit and open-mindedly allowed her daughter to follow suit. Other parenting approaches were still more astonishing, even distressing. Muhammadi Begum took particular objection to British approaches to children's health. She was shocked at the British tendency to give children 'fresh air' on frigid mornings, and to put them down to sleep by open windows. She was also concerned by what they ate and how they were given medicine, concerns spurred particularly by her extended observations of a child named 'Toddles':

> For a one-year-old child, I have noticed he eats whatever he can
> get hold of, from apples to bread to sweets to papadoms [thin
> crisp bread] to potatoes to cauliflower to his own special baby
> food! When I asked about his cough, I was told children ought
> not to be given medicine unless the doctor says so. I understand
> the reason, but I am appalled at the casual approach towards what
> children should eat.[59]

She concluded her ruminations with a gesture of consolation: 'I have no desire to criticise anyone. My purpose is to observe and record my own views and see how these views change over time'.[60] Most other Indian Muslim women authors would agree. Somewhat in contrast with British travel writing on India, they were largely open-minded and generous. They did not adopt all that they saw, but they expressed a genuine and studied curiosity in these alternative ways of living.

Conclusion

In this chapter, we focus on travel writing as a rare source from which to extrapolate South Asian Muslim women's experiences of and reflection on travel to Britain in the 'age of empire'. Of course, the accounts examined in this chapter are not simple reflections of Indian Muslim women's experiences in Britain. They are, rather, consciously crafted texts written for an audience curious not only about Britain and the British, but also about what it meant to visit or live there as an Indian, as a Muslim and as a colonial subject. Most original readers of the materials interrogated here would never make such a trip themselves. These accounts were thus a rare opportunity to see Britain through the lens of Muslim women who shared their cultural practices. Authors focused on those matters that they thought would be most interesting to their readers and, above all, on those questions that spoke to debates at home about everyday practices, particularly as they related to women. We thus find in these accounts a wealth of observations about questions related to how to travel, what to wear, how to maintain one's children and how to present oneself abroad.

As the opening vignette suggests, travel between colonized India and imperial Britain, particularly for the relatively elite women discussed here, revealed a complex dynamic of foreignness and familiarity. Most of these women spoke English, some quite well, and had already familiarized themselves with British practices in India—or at least the practices that British visitors to India presented before them. Thus, while Safia Jabir Ali suggests that Indian women like her knew the British quite well, these travellers were also astonished again and again, sometimes by the small details they had not encountered before, but also by the discrepancies between British life in India and that in Britain. This fascination with cultural practice and difference is reflected in these accounts' emphasis on Britain's human geography. By far, these travel accounts focused on everyday human interactions over the natural or technological wonders that were more dominant in Muslim men's accounts.

This emphasis on human geography brings to the fore the complexities and challenges of travelling from India as colonial subjects to the heart of the empire, a land where Indians were only occasionally fully welcome. Yet, there are many instances in these travelogues that underline a shared humanity that clearly transcended the stark racial and religious barriers then inscribed in British society, such as when kindly individuals helped these travellers to manage their children. Even without children, these travellers were able to facilitate new connections and build friendships. Atiya Fyzee, for instance, described the many close friends she made and met while studying in Britain at the height of the Edwardian era.[61] Even those women who staunchly embraced the division between 'East' and 'West', or between colonizer and colonized, nevertheless found that these boundaries blurred in their individual reactions. These moments recall Leela Gandhi's invocation of 'affective communities'—cross-cultural collaborations and political networks forged through friendships between Indian nationalists and European dissidents—that emerged even at the peak of British colonialism.[62]

These latter experiences may seem at odds with the large body of scholarship that has highlighted the racial abuse and ostracism many male students encountered in Britain.[63] The distinction suggests that racialized attitudes towards Indians in late colonial Britain were inflected by gender, or at least, that their expression was dampened in the case of elite women. Scholarship has shown that Indian men—regardless of their religion—were often perceived to be, or treated as, sexual, economic or political threats. In the case of well-to-do women though, those concerns do not seem to have come forward as directly. Women were subject more to curiosity than otherwise. Safia Jabir Ali described, for example, an instance in which unknown children approached her at a tramway station in Scotland to gift her flowers. At London Zoo, other children walked by just to have a closer look, but did not otherwise disturb her. She later reported, clearly amused, that she had become 'a part of the zoo for them!'[64] The tiny number of Indian women in Britain, particularly elite Muslim women, meant that they did not appear to be a threat up to the late 1930s at least, but instead constituted an exotic presence that was largely not unwelcome.

It should be emphasized, though, that this treatment was starkly different than that meted out by colonialists in India itself. Furthermore, racism and intolerance were never fully absent for Muslim women in Britain. Begum Habibullah noted feeling distinctly uncomfortable dining with her Indian friends at a restaurant because the people sitting at a nearby table gawked at them incessantly, such that she could not focus on the occasion itself. She remarked that, when confronted with Indians, these diners had clearly felt they did not need to follow proper etiquette— which should have mitigated against staring openly at strangers.[65] Muhammadi Begum, too, felt forlorn at times. Though she had a vast range of friends, as we have noted already, she ultimately concluded, 'It is true, after all, the West is the West and the East is the East!'[66] In a similar fashion, many Indian Muslim travel writers, after spending time in Britain, ultimately decided that 'Western' society was not as grand or inimitable as it had first appeared. Sultan Jahan Begum left Indian shores in 1911 with the invocation: 'May those sailors live long who are trying to take us all from the island of ignorance to the land of knowledge and refinement'.[67] But she returned to India a sharp critic of the 'freedom' of European dress and lifestyle.[68] Unsurprisingly, her young daughter-in-law Maimoona Sultan made similar observations, worrying that Indian Muslims were turning away from their own religious and cultural practices in favour of a more British style.[69] Begum Habibullah, as we have seen, even travelled to England to ensure that this fate would not befall her children.

'WE WERE NOT ANYTHING LIKE WHAT THEY IMAGINED!'

Reflecting on her travels abroad, Begum Sarbuland Jang concluded:

> The very blind freedom that was destroying Hindustan had already plundered the tranquillity and true repose of the West. This blind freedom and foreign culture has made their lives appear outwardly to be very attractive and pleasant indeed; but their internal life is not so pleasant at all, rather, it seems to be devoid of any spiritual contentment.[70]

Perhaps not all travellers would have agreed with this point. Nazli Begum of Janjira, in fact, opened her own travelogue with the following words: 'When I compare Europe and Asia I become less in my own eyes. Sadly, Asia has become the way Europe was a thousand or twelve hundred years ago'. All, though, would have been sympathetic with the reformist impulse underpinning both quotations. As we see here and throughout this chapter, Indian Muslim women travellers to Britain in this period were above all interested in weighing up life abroad with that at home. Every author had her own reactions to Britain, but all were driven to comparison because of the long history intertwining the two countries and a colonial discourse that suggested Indians look to Britain for guidance. The Britons they met were undoubtedly inspired by the 'othering' impulse at the heart of an imperial project as well—and yet, as Safia Jabir Ali and others realized, there was little to underpin it when the Muslim woman of the British imagination was so different to their reality. Only through travel and exchange could preconceptions be undone.

9

NOOR INAYAT KHAN

A BRITISH MUSLIM HERO?

Pir Zia Inayat Khan

Introduction

The Allied agent Noor Inayat Khan (1914–44) was awarded the George Cross in 1949, five years after her execution at the infamous Dachau concentration camp in Germany. Her friend, Jean Overton Fuller, traced her life and wartime career in a biography published in 1952.[1] It was not until the publication of Shrabani Basu's biography of Noor in 2006, however, that her story meaningfully entered the public imagination of Great Britain.[2] As a result of Basu's persistent advocacy and the resonance of Noor's example, a statue of Noor now stands in Gordon Square in London; a Blue Plaque has been affixed to the London house in which she stayed as a child; and a Royal Mail postal stamp bears her image. Hailed as a 'British Muslim hero', Noor is now frequently invoked as a symbol of national coherence in an age of racial and religious pluralism.[3] How seamlessly do the rhetorically constructed symbol and the historically founded reality mesh?

The aim of this chapter is to explore the complex and nuanced manner in which Noor inhabited the contested categories of

Britishness, Muslimness and heroism. Particular advantage will be taken of unpublished recollections and insights from Noor's cousin, Shaikh-ul-Mashaik Mahmood khan (b. 1927), who spent time with Noor on numerous occasions in France and Holland before the war and remains a unique witness to her personality and its formative circumstances and milieu.[4] Drawing on Mahmood khan's testimony and other sources, it will be shown that Noor's allegiance to Britain was of a pre- and post-nationalist character, that she embraced a vision of Islam that was notably universal in scope, and that her heroic sensibility found its most natural and immediate expression in literature.[5]

Noor, a short biography

Before turning to the details of Noor's life and their implications, an initial portrait of Noor's character is in order, and Mahmood khan's recollections aptly meet the need:

> Dainty, refined, beautiful, and modestly withdrawn, she was simultaneously a smart Parisienne, a talented musical and academic student, and a contemporaneously-attuned romanticist writer. High-voiced, of delicate expression and behaviour, and of deep sensitivity, she had as well an abiding sense of insecurity and disorientation due to the loss of the father who had been her and her siblings' universe. Even so, future promise radiated all over her. To all appearances she was one of those destined to aid in restoring civilization and humanitarian values after the war, rather than becoming a sacrifice to it. What then actuated her to gaze into, rather than beyond, that devastating disaster? How does anyone come to be as she was—out of what silent dimensions does such a phenomenon proceed?[6]

Noor has often been described as a 'princess'.[7] Her father Inayat khan (1882–1927) came from a distinguished Indian family. By paternal descent, he was a *yüzkhan*, the scion of a noble (*sultani*) Oğuz Turkmen (*ashraf-i atrak*) lineage of horde-lords and shamans. Noor's biographers Fuller, Basu and Arthur Magida, however, emphasize her ancestral connection to Tipu Sultan (1751–99), the south Indian Muslim ruler who fell in battle against British forces

in 1799.[8] Tipu Sultan's direct descendants were exiled to Calcutta
following his defeat, but his maternal uncle's family remained in
Mysore and bore the title of 'Tipu Sahib'. A lady of this house,
Qasim Bi, married the prominent musician Mawlabakhsh, who
was elevated to princely rank (*rajkufu*), and Inayat khan was the
first son of their second daughter. Mahmood khan concludes:

> Given the original significance of the title sultan as applied to
> both men and women of noble descent from the Seljuks to the
> Mughals, moving downwards in time there is nothing to prevent,
> and much to commend, applying the corresponding designation
> of princess to Noor.[9]

Raised in Baroda, Inayat khan grew to become an accomplished
singer, exponent of the vina and musicologist.[10] In Hyderabad,
he underwent Sufi training.[11] This was done at the hand of the
Akbarian scholar and preceptor Sayyid Abu Hashim Madani (d.
c.1907).[12] In 1910, he travelled to the United States with his
brother Maheboob khan and cousin Mohammed Ali khan. As 'The
Royal Musicians of Hindustan', Inayat khan and his companions
pioneered the introduction of classical Indian music to the West.[13]
In New York, Inayat khan lectured at the Sanskrit College founded
by Pierre Bernard (1875–1955), an early American proponent of
yoga, and a rapport developed between Inayat khan and Bernard's
half-sister and ward Ora Ray Baker (1892–1949). Inayat khan left
for England in 1912, and Ora Ray followed him a year later; the
two were married in London, whereupon Ora Ray took on the
name Ameena Begum.

Further travels took Inayat khan and his family to France,
and then to Russia, where the Royal Musicians met with an
enthusiastic reception. Pirzadi Noor-un-nisa Inayat Khan was
born in Moscow on 1 January 1914. The outbreak of the First
World War compelled the travellers to return to London, where
they would remain until the end of the war. During this period,
at the urging of his students, Inayat khan founded the first order
of Sufism ever to be established west of the Balkans. Meanwhile,
three additional children were born: Vilayat, Hidayat and Khair-
un-nisa.

As travel became possible again with the end of the war, Inayat khan's Sufi work underwent rapid expansion. The family moved to France, and Inayat khan commenced a series of international lecture tours. A disciple presented Inayat khan's family with a stately home in Suresnes, on the outskirts of Paris. Each summer, Sufi adherents converged in Suresnes for a three-month Summer School. Mahmood khan explains the transformation of Inayat khan from a musicologist and recitalist into an active Sufi exponent in this way:

> In his early travels in the West, Hazrat Inayat khan intended to present Indian classical music as a supreme paradigm, artistically, aesthetically, and spiritually. It soon turned out that, outside academic circles, people were more interested in the spiritual component of his expertise rather than the musical one, seeking to become his disciples in Indian Sufism instead of in music. The result was a huge output of lectures and teachings on contemplative philosophy and mysticism.[14]

In 1926, Inayat khan revisited India. He was not to return to Europe; he fell ill and died in Delhi in February 1927. Ora Ray sank into depression and withdrew into seclusion, leaving the management of the household to Noor, now a teenager. The following year, the family travelled to India to pay their respects at Inayat khan's grave. Noor speculated that her father may not have actually died and was probably living as an ascetic. This line of thought gave rise to her mystical drama *Aède of the Ocean and Land*.[15]

Back in France, following the completion of her secondary schooling, Noor studied Child Psychology at the Sorbonne, Music at the École Normale de Musique de Paris and Hindi at the École des Langues Orientales Vivantes. Fondly recalling the stories her father had told her as a child, and pondering his philosophy of childhood education, she resolved to become a writer of children's stories. The Sufi disciple and popular illustrator Henriette Willebeek Le Mair (Baroness van Tuyll, 1889–1966) encouraged her to retell a selection of Buddhist tales, and the result was *Twenty Jataka Tales*, illustrated by Willebeek Le Mair and published in 1939 by George G. Harrap in the United Kingdom and David

McKay in the United States. Noor was making plans to found a children's literary newspaper when the Second World War broke out, changing everything.

Noor and her siblings were repulsed not only by the aggressive territorial ambitions of the Nazi regime in Germany, but also and especially by its ideology of white supremacy and antisemitism. Looking back, Noor's brother Vilayat wrote:

> We had to decide either to stay and knuckle under the ignominious regime or join forces that were heroically resisting the evil tide. [...] In our service to the Message of unity we had been preaching respect of all religions, and races, the divinity in man. Now came the test: were these just words or were we going to stand up with our lives for that which we pledged ourselves to.[16]

Amidst falling bombs, Ora Ray, Noor, Vilayat and Khair-un-nisa retreated to England to volunteer their services to the war effort. Noor joined the Women's Auxiliary Air Force (WAAF) and was trained in wireless telegraphy. Eventually, Noor's fluency in French brought her to the attention of the Special Operations Executive (SOE), the clandestine organization created by British Prime Minister Winston Churchill to undermine the enemy by means of espionage and sabotage as well as collaboration with the French Resistance. Welcoming recruitment, Noor underwent training in intelligence and paramilitary skills at Beaulieu in Hampshire.

Noor's training was still incomplete when, on the night of 16– 17 June 1943, she was flown covertly into France with the mission of transmitting vital information to London at regular intervals via wireless radio. Within a week of her arrival, all of the leading operatives of the Prosper Circuit of the SOE were captured, and by the middle of August, Noor was the sole radio operator in Paris. For months, she continued transmitting and evading capture, but when an acquaintance betrayed her, she was arrested and taken to the Gestapo headquarters at Avenue Foch for interrogation. Her refusal to cooperate, together with two attempts at escape, led to her being branded a 'highly dangerous prisoner' and consigned to prison in Pforzheim, Germany. She remained in solitary confinement at Pforzheim, chained to a wall, until 12 September

1944, when she was transferred to Dachau, savagely beaten in the night, and executed by pistol in the morning.

Was Noor British?

Inayat khan was a British Protected Person and Ora Ray was American, but their four children were British citizens from birth. Noor's official nationality is therefore a simple matter; but was she British in a fuller sense of the word, inclusive of a conscious identification with the culture and destiny of Great Britain?

Ora Ray's ancestors were of largely British stock. Her family oral history emphasizes origins in Scotland. In her memoirs, Noor's sister Khair-un-nisa reports a wartime exchange between the two (in fact, the sisters' last conversation), demonstrating Noor's active interest in her Scottish heritage:

> I asked Noor what she was doing in the yeomanry (British volunteer cavalry force). 'When the war is over', she replied, 'I shall be wearing the family tartan on horseback.' I asked her what color that was. 'Lavender' was her reply.[17]

While stationed in Edinburgh for training, Noor expressed the desire to deepen her acquaintance with the folklore of the Celtic North. She wrote in a notebook:

> And more, being stationed in Scotland by some lucky chance, my one longing is to be acquainted with the tales the grandmothers tell the laddies at night. The [illegible] of Edinburgh seems to hold endless legends. I want to dive deep into the spirit of old Scotland and relate this to children as best I can.[18]

The same set of notes evinces Noor's fascination with the Arthurian corpus and the larger 'Matter of Britain' to which it belonged:

> No-one can deny that the legends which originate from Arthur's round table personify the spirit of Britain in all its democracy, in all its nobility. There is an integrity about these, an unbeaten steadfastness and a constant bearing in mind of the aim. The medieval heroes were [illegible] knights, immensely brave but more adventurous, in a way, getting into trouble more easily.

Going forwards [illegible] losing [illegible] but winning in the end
at the cost of mighty sacrifice. And such they are and such they
shall always be.[19]

It needs emphasizing, however, that Noor's folkloric interests
were by no means exclusively parochial to Britain. Growing
up in France, the French legends of Roland and Jean d'Arc had
riveted her imagination.[20] Poland's plight under Nazi rule drew
her attention to Polish lore and its self-determinist leanings.
Other tales she retold were of Scandinavian, Russian, Chinese and
Indian provenance.[21]

Whereas Noor's maternal connections with Britain were
ancestral, her paternal connections with the nation were colonial.
India had been under the direct rule of Britain since 1858 and
would remain so until 1947, three years after Noor's death. The
house of Mawlabakhsh accepted the British presence in India
as something like a force of nature and was apt to follow Saiyid
Ahmad Khan's (1817–98) example in appreciating the 'New Light'
of Western modernity and science introduced by the British while
endeavouring to reconcile it to time-honoured Islamic traditions.
Mahmood khan explains:

In relation to the British, it may be recalled that before the advent
of late-nineteenth-century nationalism, feelings and views were
very different. The brothers grew up in an anything but anti-
British world. Despite the horrors of the Rebellion of 1857, the
British still were one player among many as there had been from
the Aryan invasions onwards, with the Muslims most recently
in charge. Moreover, for those living in the Princely States, the
[British] Viceroy's regime might provide a useful counterbalance
where rulers were too self-willed, like Baroda's Malhar Rao,
whereas a good one might filter the many useful items of British
rule whilst avoiding unwanted elements as in diet or such. [...]
Still the British were the political component that happened to
have come out on top, and provided huge new benefits as well.[22]

Though London was not the first destination of Inayat khan's
world tour, it nonetheless recommended itself as a logical haven
during the war years. Why then, as non-Francophones with few

connections on the Continent, did he and his family abandon England in favour of France at the end of the war? Inayat khan provides the answer in his memoirs when he speaks of a sea change in the prevailing English attitude toward Indians and Muslims in reaction to the Gandhian Non-Cooperation Movement in India coupled with the rising support of Indian Muslims for the Ottoman Empire following the defeat of British forces at Gallipoli: 'Everything Oriental was regarded with suspicion [...] and it had a paralysing influence upon my efforts'.[23]

For Noor, the simultaneity of the Nazi threat to Europe and the surging momentum of the Indian independence movement in 1942 forced her to examine her competing loyalties. She found that, while she supported Indian self-rule, the road to independence required discretion in light of the urgency of Hitler's menace. She aspired to make a difference herself if she could. Jean Overton Fuller offers valuable testimony of her thinking:

> We used to talk about Indian affairs. The imprisonment of Gandhi, Nehru, and other Indian leaders in August had made a deep impression on her, and she began to feel the shadow of imprisonment falling across her own future if she should go out there after the war. Yet though she believed in Independence, and was prepared if need be one day to fight for it, she was not wholly at one with the action Gandhi had taken. She did not think the Indians should use pressure to force the British out at a time when they were embarrassed by the need to fight an external war.
>
> She had a point of view, which was in keeping with her way of thought concerning the value of renunciation. If India were willing to sink her claims whilst Britain herself was at a disadvantage, and support her without stint, it would create such confidence that after the war Independence would automatically be given. Although impatient at Abingdon, she thought that her being in Air Force blue might have some value if people saw that an Indian was serving with them.
>
> I can see her now, standing before the mantelpiece, as she said, 'I wish some Indians would win high military distinctions in this war. If one or two could do something in the Allied service which was very brave and which everybody admired it would help to make a bridge between English people and the Indians.'[24]

To sum up, the British component of Noor's identity had hybrid roots, ancestral and colonial. Though born in Russia, Noor spent her formative childhood years in London and found it natural to return to England during the war, if only as a launching point for paramilitary action in France. She supported the self-determination of Britain's colonies but envisioned an amicable political separation.

Was Noor Muslim?

The establishment of Inayat khan's and his brothers' families in Europe before and during the First World War put them in a somewhat unusual position vis-a-vis other Muslim Europeans. They did not belong to the long-established groups of Muslims subsisting on the fringes of European society for centuries, including Polish-Lithuanian Tatars, Balkan Bosnians, Albanians, Pomaks, Greek-speaking Cretans and Andalusian morisqui. But neither were they part of the later mass migrations commencing at the end of the Second World War. They were, in this regard, a rule unto themselves, and their method of negotiating Islamic, Indian and Western conventions was distinctly *sui generis*. Mahmood khan outlines their stance as follows:

> Secularization, learned in India already, then advocated in Britain, matched well with the Sufi ideal of the unity of mystical realization through whichever channel, while in their private lives still providing for liberal Muslim religious awareness, Indian culture and aptitudes, and aristocratic attitudes and values.[25]

Inayat khan identified Sufism as a 'religious philosophy', a phrase that locates the Sufi worldview at the intersection of tradition-borne revelation and personal truth-seeking. In his classic work *Islam*, the leading modernist scholar Fazlur Rahman (1919–88) used the comparable term 'philosophic religion' to characterize the intellectual legacies of the Sufi philosophers Shihab ad-Din Yahya Suhrawardi (d. 1191) and Muhyi ad-Din Ibn 'Arabi (d. 1240), known to posterity as the schools of Illumination (*ishraq*) and the Unity of Being (*wahdat al-wujud*) respectively.[26] Implicit in these speculative trajectories was an acknowledgement of the relativity of exoteric norms and, equally, an affirmation of the possibility of accessing spiritual knowledge directly from the Unseen. Shahab Ahmed has underscored the implications of Rahman's insights in the following terms:

> Rahman's fundamental, and insufficiently recognized, historical point is that the Sufi and philosophical claim to a Real-Truth (*haqiqa*) that lay above and beyond the truth of the Revealed Law (*shari'a*) was not a bit of intellectual or esotericist *marginalia*, but was effectively the whole manifesto of a wide-ranging social and cultural phenomenon that Rahman has called 'a religion not only within religion but above religion.' We might profitably characterize this 'religion not only within religion but above religion' as the *Sufi-philosophical (or philosophical-Sufi) amalgam.*[27]

The intra- and supra-religious phenomenon Rahman is describing here is succinctly invoked by Suhrawardi in the introduction to his magnum opus *The Wisdom of Illumination* (*Hikmat al-ishraq*):

> In every seeking soul there is a portion, be it small or great, of the light of God. Everyone who strives has intuition, be it perfect or imperfect. Knowledge did not end with one people, so that the doors of heaven are shut behind them and the rest of the world is denied the possibility of obtaining more. [...] The most evil age is the one in which the carpet of striving has been rolled up, in which the movement of thought is interrupted, the door of revelations bolted, the path of visions blocked.[28]

The assertion that sacred truth can be found in all religions and eras, and is an essential property of the human soul, echoes through Inayat khan's discourses. He decisively amalgamates this key tenet of philosophical universalism with the historically Islamic tradition of Sufism when he says, 'Sufism, divine wisdom, is for all, and is not limited to a certain people. It has existed from the first day of creation, and will continue to spread and to exist until the end of the world'.[29]

Inayat khan's Indian Sufi predecessors had made similar statements. Upon seeing a Hindu perform his devotions, Nizam ad-Din Awliya' (d. 1325) remarked, 'for every people there is a religious path and a direction for prayer' (alluding to Qur'an 2:148).[30] Sharaf ad-Din Manayri (d. 1381) identified Adam as the first Sufi.[31] Shaykh 'Abd ar-Rahman Chishti (d. 1683) composed a Sufi commentary on the Bhagavad Gita.[32] Hindus were routinely enrolled in the Chishti Order without the requirement of converting to Islam. In the Naqshbandi-Mujaddidi Order, Hindu disciples went on to become Sufi masters in their own right.[33] Accommodations of these kinds continued into the twentieth century, when Hasan Nizami (d. 1955), in his introduction to Hinduism, defined yoga as 'the science of Sufism and dervishhood'.[34] Noor inherited her father's Islam as well as his philosophical universalism. Concerning a biography of Muhammad that she was reading, she wrote, 'I do not believe that there could exist a more beautiful book on life'.[35] She studied the Qur'an and recorded her observations on its second and longest *sura*, Baqara.[36] But her spiritual studies were not limited to the Qur'an and her father's volumes. She also studied and made notes on the Mahabharata, the Hebrew Bible and the Gospels.

The wide scope of Noor's religious interests and sympathies is demonstrated by a series of classes she gave for the children of Sufi disciples in Suresnes before the war. One week, she made her students memorize a stanza from Alfred de Vigny's poem 'Moïse', while another week, the subject was Gautama the Buddha. This diversity of focus was no departure from Islam as Inayat khan understood it, since he held, in accord with Qur'an 3:84, that, 'a Sufi considers all prophets and sages, not as many individuals, but as the one embodiment of God's pure consciousness, or the manifestation of divine wisdom, appearing on earth for the awakening of man from his sleep of ignorance, in different names and forms'.[37]

If Sufism did not always provide the vocabulary of Noor's writings, it nonetheless supplied their grammar, so to speak. Her play *Aède of the Ocean and Land* is a case in point. *Aède* re-narrates Homer's Odyssey with a surprising twist: Odysseus' homeward journey becomes the story of the soul, a tale that ends not with domestic bliss in Ithaca, but rather with the endless horizon of the spiritual itinerary of the Sufi. The play consists of seven acts, and seven is the number of valleys, or mystical stations, in Farid ad-Din 'Attar's celebrated Sufi poem *The Conference of the Birds* (*Mantiq at-tayr*), a work that Inayat khan likely introduced to Noor.[38] The resonance of 'Attar's seven valleys—the quest (*talab*), love (*'ishq*), knowledge (*ma'rifat*), detachment (*istighna*), unity (*tawhid*), bewilderment (*hayrat*) and poverty and nothingness (*faqr o fana'*)—is palpably evident in the spiritual transformation of *Aède's dramatis personae*.[39] In the end, as in so many of Noor's writings, sacrifice proves the central theme.

The preponderance of Sufi writers and preceptors known to history have been men, though notable exceptions exist.[40] For his part, Inayat khan promoted women to the highest levels of responsibility and authority in his Esoteric School, where they outnumbered men. He wrote: 'I see as clear as daylight that the hour is coming when women will lead humanity to a higher evolution'.[41] There was, accordingly, no impediment to Noor's agency as an interpreter and representative of her father's Sufi tradition.

Was Noor a hero?

The governments of France and Britain officially acknowledged Noor's wartime heroism by awarding her the Croix de Guerre (1946) and George Cross (1949) respectively. The British citation observed: 'Assistant Section Officer Inayat Khan displayed the most conspicuous courage, both moral and physical, over a period of more than twelve months'.[42] The job of wireless radio operator was the most dangerous of SOE missions, and life expectancy was no more than six weeks. Noor not only accepted the assignment despite the odds, but declined the SOE's invitation to return to London when the demise of the Prosper Circuit put her in extraordinary peril. As the last link in Paris, she insisted she had to continue. Shifting from place to place and employing disguise to evade her relentless pursuers while continuously relaying critical information over the space of three months, she performed a service to the Allied cause that her recruiter Vera Atkins would later describe as 'magnificent'.[43] Afterwards, as a prisoner at the Gestapo station at Avenue Foch, she twice attempted daring escapes. The George Cross citation notes these attempts, and also recognizes that, both in France and in Germany, Noor refused to give her captors any information regarding her work, or that of her colleagues. Her last word as she knelt to be shot, having been tortured through the night ('she did not cry or say anything'), was reportedly one of defiant hope: 'Liberté'.[44]

The argument is occasionally made that Noor's heroism was marred by a mistake that, allegedly, cost the lives of fellow agents. The case is built on the fact that she kept her codes in a notebook, against SOE policy. As Shrabani Basu has shown, however, Noor believed that she was following the required protocol by 'filing her messages', a misunderstanding that points to a gap in her training:

> London had indeed said that all agents were to be very careful about filing their messages. They had, however, meant the use of the term 'filing' in a journalistic sense (as in sending a story). Noor had taken it literally as 'filing' in the bureaucratic sense and preserved the messages neatly and in order. This simple mix-up could have been avoided if agents had been told in clear terms to destroy all their messages after they had been sent.[45]

After Noor's capture, her radio set was used by the Nazis to impersonate her and in this way entrap SOE agents. The captured radio sets of previous agents had been used similarly.[46] While her captors had the codes from her notebook, they were unable to make Noor reveal her bluff security check. The absence of the bluff check in the false transmissions should have alerted the SOE listening station to the fact that the set was now in the hands of the enemy.[47] It cannot therefore be reasonably argued that Noor was responsible for the deaths of fellow agents.

It should be clear that the military valour popularly attributed to Noor rests on a sound historical basis. What requires further attention, however, is the manner in which Noor's celebrated wartime actions derived directly from the chivalric worldview she inherited from her father and methodically articulated and developed in her writings. Thomas Carlyle wrote in 1840, 'The Hero as *Man of Letters* [...] is altogether a product of these new ages; and so long as the wondrous art of *Writing* [...] subsists, he may be expected to continue, as one of the main forms of Heroism for all future ages'.[48] From this perspective, Noor may be evaluated as a hero of the pen as well as of the sword. As Lara R. Curtis shows in her recent book, *Writing Resistance and the Question of Gender*, this is a distinction Noor shares with fellow female allies of the Resistance Charlotte Delbo and Germaine Tillion.[49]

Recalling the bedtime stories her father had told her, Noor approached literature first and foremost as a source of moral and spiritual edification for the growing mind of a child. The stories she retold in her *Twenty Jataka Tales* do not only entertain; more fundamentally, they inculcate ethical values of universal significance. Beyond these retellings, only one of Noor's stories was published in her lifetime ('*Ce qu'on entend quelquefois dans le bois*', published in the Parisian newspaper *Le Figaro*). The recent publication of her hitherto unpublished works, however, makes a panoramic view of her oeuvre now possible. Reading her stories, essays and notes side-by-side brings into clear relief two constant preoccupations: the revalorization of imagination as a spiritual faculty and the pursuit of the good through self-sacrifice.[50]

Noor's brief essay 'Life is a Fair Trade' is a veritable manifesto of mystical self-sacrifice based on the Qur'an and her father's teachings. She writes, 'The greatest joy, the highest and most inconceivable, is achieved by the price of the experience of nonexistence and the sole existence of God. This joy is attained step-by-step on the path, by every sacrifice, every service, every offer, by restraining from judging, and by forgiving.'[51] Mahmood khan traces the sacrificial theme in Noor's life and work to the patrician traditions of her family:

> The agriculturally-based, feudal, aristocratic structure of society of India ended only in 1947, and then with revolutionary abruptness. Inayat khan and his brothers therefore emerged from a social value system entirely different from that of the contemporary West. The age-long culture of the gentleman, echoes of which still survived in the West as well, involved an ethical education in the code known as *futuwwa* or *jawanmardi*, which is to say chivalry in its various secular, spiritual, physical, and psychological dimensions. Nor was this a general theory only:

Mahashaik Bahadur khan, Inayat khan's paternal grandfather, was a knight-errant in the traditional sense, ultimately perishing in his attachment to valiant honour. Inayat khan, with all his poetic values, still fully shared in his grandfather's ancestral chivalric code of courage and generosity: 'Sufism is not pacifism.' In no uncertain terms, he condemned idealists' refusal to participate in their country's wars: 'War is good at the time of war, peace is good at the time of peace.' His father—whose motto, 'sadagi, khandanagi', was glossed in English as 'unpretentious aristocracy'—left an imprint on Inayat khan that is clearly reflected in the latter's Iron, Copper, Silver, and Golden Rules. These more private, disciplinary aspects of Inayatian Sufism cannot but have conditioned and attuned Noor's entire view of human existence, a dharma that was to forever serve as the hallmark of her lineage identity.[52]

When the war broke out, Noor's first instinct was to confront Nazism by means of stories. The Nazis had appropriated the folkloric legacy of the Grimm Brothers and were actively employing fairy tales as a tool of racist propaganda.[53] Noor envisioned a counter-strategy whereby folkloric stories would be used to show the interconnectedness of human cultures and the moral imperative of kindness. Jean Overton Fuller describes her friend's intentions in this way:

> Noor became furiously upset when she read of the persecution of the Jews or heard of the bullying of helpless people by the SS. Yet she asked herself what she could do in a social sense. She did not want to take part in a propaganda of hate against the German people—her own principles prevented it—and it seemed to her that she had a gift for interesting children, and could supply them through the medium of stories with moral spiritual food, her part might be to work for those who were growing up.[54]

Noor managed to write several stories during her WAAF and SOE training, including 'The White Eagles of Poland' and 'Princess Wanda', a pair of heroic tales celebrating Poland's proud history of independence. The eponymous eagles of 'The White Eagles of Poland' ostensibly explain the origin of the Polish flag, but Noor may have also intended them as a symbolic tribute to the hundred and fifty Polish airmen that flew in the Battle of Britain. The story concludes with a reference to the defeated state of the nation, together with the confident prediction that 'Poland shall live again forevermore'.

Like 'The Monkey Bridge', 'The Fairy and the Hare' and 'The Great Elephant' in *Twenty Jataka Tales*—stories that Reiko Ohnuma classifies as 'super-*jatakas*'—'Princess Wanda' is a tale of patriotic gallantry that foreshadows Noor's own self-sacrifice.[55] Wanda chooses to drown herself in the Vistula river rather than submit to the German prince Rytygier's demands for her hand and, with it, dominion over Poland. Lady F. C. Anstruther published her own retelling of the tale in 1945. The plot is identical in the two tellings, but whereas Anstruther describes 'typical Germans' as cruel and rapacious, Noor portrays the people of Germany as victims of their oppressive king. It may be inferred that Noor was inclined to differentiate between the Nazi regime and the population of Germany at large. Noor wields persuasive narrative power in her laconic but trenchant treatment of Wanda's selfless and elegant death ('like a pure white swan') and the elemental immortality she thereby attains ('the Vistula still repeats her words as it flows'). For Lara Curtis, 'Wanda at last assumes an exalted patriotic grandeur that takes her well beyond the folkloric milieu in which she originated. Noor has transcended that tradition by transforming Wanda into a civilizing heroine of mythic proportions'.[56]

In retrospect, many of Noor's stories appear strikingly oracular in their anticipation of the author's ultimate self-sacrifice. As Inayat khan said, 'Thought draws the line of fate'.[57] Noor's literary productions established the chivalric pattern on which she would model her wartime choices. Perhaps the most portentously autobiographical of her stories is 'Snow-Drop'. Written in one of Noor's wireless training notebooks and likely inspired by Igor Stravinsky's opera *Perséphone* (1934), 'Snow-Drop' describes the life, execution and resurrection of a fairy known only as 'Great Sun's little daughter', or 'Little Daughter'.[58] The heroine's abductors are given the names Frost-Bite, Fog-Gloom and North Wind, calling to mind 'Pluto, Hell, and Winter's king' from *Perséphone*, but also, eerily, the fatal 'Night and Fog' (*Nacht und Nebel*) programme suffered by Noor as an imprisoned enemy of the Third Reich. Little Daughter's fate is cruel, but at last she triumphantly, albeit inconspicuously, returns to life in a new form, as a snowdrop or galanthus flower, and 'the big big world was happy once again'. For Sandra Lillydahl, editor of the story collection *King Akbar's Daughter*, Little Daughter's reappearance as a flower seems to unconsciously forecast the burgeoning of her legacy in the twenty-first century.[59]

Conclusion

Lee R. Edwards wrote that the hero 'is the result of a collaboration, entered into for the sake of human progress, between the hero's self and some surrounding social group or audience'.[60] Noor was the passionate curator of a literary Valhalla of valiant animals, fairies, knights and princesses. Now her own biography is material in the hands of contemporary rhapsodists of the heroic. If the popular memorialization of her life does not always match her historical actuality with precision, such is the nature of the constant rhetorical negotiation that lends heroism such a compelling social meaning. In this way, to borrow Carlyle's timeless words, hero-worship 'enters deeply [...] into the secrets of Mankind's ways and vitalest interests in this world'.[61]

AFTERWORD

Sariya Cheruvallil-Contractor and Jamie Gilham

Muslim women in Britain and elsewhere in the West face much negative media coverage and public scrutiny. Former Prime Minister Boris Johnson famously compared Muslim women in *burqas* with 'letter boxes'.[1] In 2016, when then-Prime Minister David Cameron was launching a new scheme to teach immigrants (including Europeans) English, the policy-speak and media coverage pejoratively emphasized Muslim women in Britain as being unable to speak English.[2] We are intensely aware of the significant social, cultural, political and economic contributions of Muslims to British society, past and present. And while the stories of some women are beginning to be heard, much more needs to be done to recognize Muslim women's agency in shaping the diverse and multicultural Britain that we call home.

This is where, we hope, *Muslim Women in Britain, 1850–1950* will make a contribution. It issues a historical corrective that places Muslim women at the centre of the earliest British communities. By recognizing these women as writers, leaders, educators, citizens and visitors, it sets the scene for a new kind of lens through which to view British Muslim women. It clarifies these women's roles, not as mute spectators of history as it passed by, but as active agents of change who helped make history. It reveals these women's agency. It illuminates for all of us that these women were part of the same history of nation-building

199

that we participate in. This book also shows us these women's vulnerabilities. They were mothers, sisters and partners, who had jobs and caring responsibilities. Some, like Gladys Brooke, came from the highest echelons of British society. Others, like Fatima Cates in the Victorian period and Olive Salaman in the last century, were from working-class backgrounds. They were Muslim, female and British, characteristics that had very different flavours but which they nevertheless shared in common.

When we have told these women's stories in public forums, we have seen how inspiring they can be for women and men, young and old, Muslim or not. These stories inspire us too. Our hope is that this volume will lead to further exploration of the roles, lives, and experiences of Muslim women in Britain, and encourage more nuanced recognition of their contributions in shaping Islam as we know and experience it in Britain today. We also hope that, by showcasing these historical stories of Muslim women who lived in Britain, this book will contribute to understandings about what exactly it means to be British.

NOTES

INTRODUCTION

1. Cedric Larson, 'The British Ministry of Information', *Public Opinion Quarterly*, vol. 5, no. 3 (1941), pp. 412–31.
2. See Brian Best, *Reporting the Second World War*, Barnsley: Pen and Sword Books, 2015, Ch. 5.
3. See Mixed Museum Website, https://exhibition.mixedmuseum. org.uk/museum/timeline/1943-muslim-community-everyday-life-in-butetown-cardiff-wales-19432, last accessed 12 January 2023.
4. Imperial War Museum Website, https://www.iwm.org.uk/collections/item/object/205200257, last accessed 12 December 2022.
5. See Fred Halliday, *Arabs in Exile: Yemeni Migrants in Urban Britain*, London: I. B. Tauris, 1992; Mohammad Siddique Seddon, *The Last of the Lascars: Yemeni Muslims in Britain, 1836–2012*, Markfield: Kube, 2014.
6. For example, Ian McLaine, *Ministry of Morale: Home Front Morale and the Ministry of Information in World War II*, London: Routledge, 1971; Simon Eliot and Marc Wiggam (eds), *Allied Communication to the Public During the Second World War: National and Transnational Networks*, London: Bloomsbury, 2020.
7. Books include Humayun Ansari, *'The Infidel Within': Muslims in Britain since 1800*, London: Hurst, 2004/2018; Ron Geaves, *Islam in Victorian Britain: The Life and Times of Abdullah Quilliam*, Markfield: Kube, 2010; Seddon, *The Last of the Lascars*; Jamie Gilham, *Loyal Enemies: British Converts to Islam, 1850–1950*, London: Hurst, 2014; Jamie Gilham and Ron Geaves (eds), *Victorian Muslim: Abdullah*

Quilliam and Islam in the West, London: Hurst, 2017; Ron Geaves, *Islam and Britain: Muslim Mission in an Age of Empire*, London: Bloomsbury, 2018; Martin Pugh, *Britain and Islam: A History from 622 to the Present Day*, New Haven and London: Yale University Press, 2019; Jamie Gilham, *The British Muslim Convert Lord Headley, 1855–1935*, London: Bloomsbury, 2020.

8. Sariya Cheruvallil-Contractor, 'Women in Britain's First Mosques: Hidden from History, but Not without Influence', *Religions*, vol. 11, no. 2 (2020), pp. 1–12.

9. See, for example, Richard I. Lawless, *From Ta'izz to Tyneside: An Arab Community in the North-East of England during the Early Twentieth Century*, Exeter: Exeter University Press, 1995.

10. See, for example, Ansari, 'The Infidel Within', part I; Gilham, *Loyal Enemies*; Cheruvallil-Contractor, 'Women in Britain's First Mosques'.

11. On Nawab Sultan Jahan, see Siobhan Lambert-Hurley, *Muslim Women, Reform and Princely Patronage: Nawab Sultan Jahan Begam of Bhopal*, London: Routledge, 2007.

12. For example, Jean Overton-Fuller, *Madeleine: The Story of Noor Inayat Khan*, London: Victor Gollancz, 1952; Shrabani Basu, *Spy Princess*, Stroud: The History Press, 2006; Arthur Magida, *Code Name Madeleine*, New York: W. W. Norton and Company, 2020.

13. Kimberlé Williams Crenshaw, 'Mapping the Margins: Intersectionality, Identity Politics, and Violence against Women of Color', *Stanford Law Review*, vol. 43, no. 6 (1991), pp. 1241–99; Avtar Brah and Ann Phoenix, '"Ain't I a Woman?" Revisiting Intersectionality', *Journal of International Women's Studies*, vol. 5, no. 3 (2004), pp. 75–86.

14. Lady Evelyn Cobbold, *Pilgrimage to Mecca*, London: John Murray, 1934.

15. Jamie Gilham, 'Cobbold, Lady Evelyn', in *Oxford Dictionary of National Biography*, suppl., ed. Lawrence Goldman, Oxford: Oxford University Press, 2007 and online: https://doi.org/10.1093/ref:odnb/95642, last accessed 4 December 2022.

16. In addition to Cobbold's biography in the *Oxford Dictionary of National Biography* (2007), see William Facey, 'Mayfair to Makkah', *Saudi Aramco World*, vol. 59, no. 5 (2008), pp. 18–23; William Facey and Miranda Taylor, 'Introduction: From Mayfair to Mecca—The Life of Lady Evelyn Cobbold', in Lady Evelyn Cobbold *Pilgrimage to Mecca*, new edn, London: Arabian Publishing, 2008, pp. 1–80. Items

from Cobbold's archive were included in the British Museum's 'Hajj: Journey to the Heart of Islam' exhibition (2012) and illustrated in the accompanying catalogue by Venetia Porter (ed), *Hajj: Journey to the Heart of Islam,* London: British Museum Press, 2012. On Cobbold's Hajj, see also Marcia Hermansen, 'Roads to Mecca: Conversion Narratives of European and Euro-American Muslims', *The Muslim World*, vol. 89, no. 1 (1999), pp. 56–89; John Slight, 'Pilgrimage to Mecca by British Converts to Islam in the Interwar Period', in Ingvild Flaskerud and Richard J. Natvig (eds), *Muslim Pilgrimage in Europe*, Abingdon: Routledge, 2018, pp. 70–82.

17. June Purvis, 'Using Primary Sources When Researching Women's History from a Feminist Perspective', *Women's History Review*, vol. 1, no. 2 (1992), pp. 273–306; June Purvis (ed), *Women's History: Britain, 1850–1945. An Introduction*, Abingdon: Routledge, 1995.

18. Meredith McGuire, *Lived Religion: Faith and Practice in Everyday Life*, Oxford: Oxford University Press, 2014; Nancy T. Ammerman, *Sacred Stories, Spiritual Tribes: Finding Religion in Everyday Life*, Oxford: Oxford University Press, 2013.

19. English Heritage Website, https://www.english-heritage.org.uk/visit/blue-plaques/propose-a-plaque/, last accessed 12 January 2023.

20. The plaques are installed at 4 Taviton Street, Bloomsbury and 26 King Edward's Road, Hackney respectively.

1. UNEQUAL HISTORY

1. Sophie Gilliat-Ray and Jody Mellor, 'Bilād al-Welsh (Land of the Welsh): Muslims in Cardiff, South Wales: Past, Present and Future', *The Muslim World*, vol. 100, no. 4 (2010), pp. 452–75.

2. Patricia Aithie, *The Burning Ashes of Times: from Steamer Point to Tiger Bay*, Bridgend: Seren, 2005.

3. Fred Halliday, *Arabs in Exile: Yemeni Migrants in Urban Britain*, London: I. B. Tauris, 1992.

4. Gilliat-Ray and Mellor, 'Bilād al-Welsh'.

5. Ron Geaves, *Islam in Victorian Britain: The Life and Times of Abdullah Quilliam*, Markfield: Kube, 2010; Jamie Gilham, *Loyal Enemies: British Converts to Islam, 1850–1950*, London: Hurst, 2014.

6. Mohammad Siddique Seddon, *The Last of the Lascars: Yemeni Muslims in Britain, 1836–2012*, Markfield: Kube, 2014.

7. June Purvis, 'Using Primary Sources When Researching Women's History from a Feminist Perspective', *Women's History Review*, vol. 1, no. 2 (1992), pp. 273–306.

8. Halliday, *Arabs*.
9. Gilliat-Ray and Mellor, 'Bilād al-Welsh', p. 470.
10. Humayun Ansari (ed), *The Making of the East London Mosque, 1910–1951,* Cambridge: Cambridge University Press, 2011, p. 99.
11. Cited in Gilliat-Ray and Mellor, 'Bilād al-Welsh'.
12. Ceri-Anne Fidler, 'The Impact of Migration upon Family Life and Gender Relations: The Case of South Asian Seafarers, c.1900–50', *Women's History Review*, vol. 24, no. 3 (2015), pp. 410–28.
13. Quoted in Halliday, *Arabs*, p. 48.
14. Seddon, *The Last of the Lascars*; Gilliat-Ray and Mellor, 'Bilād al-Welsh'.
15. Halliday, *Arabs*.
16. BBC, *Tamed and Shabby Tiger*, 1968.
17. National Archives of Wales (hereafter NAW), MD808, Interview with Olive Salaman and Betty Campbell by Selwyn Roddren and Monique Ennis, 2004.
18. NAW, MD789, Interview with Olive Salaman by Monique Ennis, 2006.
19. NAW, MD790, Group interview with Olive Salaman, Selwyn Roddren, Betty Campbell, Monique Ennis, and Sian Roddren, undated (c. 2000s).
20. Gilliat-Ray and Mellor, 'Bilād al-Welsh'.
21. Ibid.
22. Halliday, *Arabs*.
23. Mass Observation, *Tiger Bay* (1941), p. 2.
24. Halliday, *Arabs*.
25. BBC, *Tamed and Shabby Tiger,* 1968
26. Halliday, *Arabs*.
27. Mass Observation, *Tiger Bay*, p. 15.
28. BBC, *Tamed and Shabby Tiger*.
29. Wales Online (2005), https://www.walesonline.co.uk/news/wales-news/film-makers-capture-life-cardiff-2390433, last accessed 12 January 2023.
30. Ross Cameron, '"The Most Colourful Extravaganza in the World": Images of Tiger Bay, 1845–1970', *Patterns of Prejudice*, vo. 31, no. 2 (1997), pp. 59–90, quote at p. 75.
31. Wales Online (2005).
32. NAW, MD789, Interview with Olive Salaman.
33. BBC, *Tamed and Shabby Tiger*.
34. NAW, MD789, Interview with Olive Salaman.

35. BBC, *Tamed and Shabby Tiger*.
36. NAW, MD789, Interview with Olive Salaman.
37. John Bowen, *Why the French Don't Like Headscarves: Islam, State and the Public Space*, Princeton: Princeton University Press, 2008.
38. Halliday, *Arabs*.
39. BBC, *Tamed and Shabby Tiger*.
40. BBC, *Mixed Britannia*, 2011, https://www.bbc.co.uk/programmes/b015skx4, last accessed 25 January 2023.
41. Ibid.
42. Muslims in Britain, UK Mosque Statistics/Masjid Statistics (2017), http://www.muslimsinbritain.org/resources/masjid_report.pdf, last accessed 29 November 2019.
43. Line Nyhagen, 'Mosques as Gendered Spaces: The Complexity of Women's Compliance with, and Resistance to, Dominant Gender Norms, and the Importance of Male Allies', *Religions*, vol. 10, no. 5 (2019), p. 321.
44. BBC, *Tamed and Shabby Tiger*.
45. NAW, MD808.
46. NAW, MD808, Interview with Olive Salaman and Betty Campbell.
47. Ibid.
48. The 1941 Mass Observation report confirms that the Scandinavian Sailor's Home was destroyed in enemy action, and also confirms the existence of a Norwegian Sailors Home and Church (p. 14). It is not clear which building Olive was referring to. It is also possible that she was confused between the two.
49. NAW, MD808, Interview with Olive Salaman and Betty Campbell.
50. Ibid.
51. Ibid.
52. Ibid.
53. Ibid.
54. NAW, MD789, Interview with Olive Salaman.
55. NAW, MD808.
56. Ibid.
57. NAW, MD789, Interview with Olive Salaman.
58. Ibid.
59. Gilliat-Ray and Mellor, 'Bilād al-Welsh'.
60. NAW, MD808.
61. Ibid.
62. Ibid.
63. Ibid.

64. BBC, *Mixed Britannia*.
65. NAW, MD808.
66. Ibid.
67. NAW, MD789, Interview with Olive Salaman.
68. Halliday, *Arabs*.
69. Ibid.
70. Ibid.
71. Ibid.
72. *The Daily Herald*, 24 May 1955, n.p.
73. Halliday, *Arabs*.
74. NAW, MD789.
75. Ibid.
76. Ibid.
77. Wales Online (2005).
78. BBC, *Mixed Britannia*.
79. Lady Evelyn Cobbold, *Pilgrimage to Mecca*, London: John Murray, 1934.
80. NAW, MD789.

2. FATIMA ELIZABETH CATES

1. General Register Office (England) [hereafter GRO], Birth Certificate of Frances Elizabeth Murray, 5 January 1865.
2. Census of England and Wales 1871 (Birkenhead, Ecclesiastic District of Holy Trinity).
3. GRO, Marriage Certificate of Peter Cottam and Agnes Murray, 15 June 1873.
4. GRO, Death Certificate of John Murray, 13 May 1870.
5. *The Times*, 28 August 1866, p.8.
6. *The Crescent* [hereafter *TC*], vol. 16, no. 408 (1900), p. 298.
7. *The Star*, 16 December 1890, p. 4; *The Manchester Examiner*, 10 December 1890, p. 8.
8. Abdullah Quilliam Society, 'Cairo Speech 1928', http://www.abdullahquilliam.org/cairo-speech-1928/, last accessed 28 November 2022. For the speech itself, see William H. Quilliam, *Fanatics and Fanaticism: A Lecture*, Liverpool: T. Dobb and Company, 1890.
9. Ibid.
10. Ibid.
11. Ibid.
12. Fatima E. Cates, 'How I Became a Mahommedan', *The Allahabad Review*, 11 September 1891, p. 142.

13. Ibid.

14. Ibid.

15. *The Star*, 16 December 1890, p. 4; *The Manchester Examiner*, 10 December 1890, p. 8.

16. 'I declare that there is no god but God and I declare that Muhammad is His Messenger'.

17. *TC*, vol. 2, no. 29 (1893), p. 229.

18. GRO, Marriage Certificate of Hubert Henry Cates and Frances Elizabeth Murray, 28 February 1889.

19. Cates, 'How I Became a Mahommedan', p. 144.

20. James Monro, *Moslems in Liverpool*, Calcutta: Methodist Publishing House, 1901, p. 41.

21. Ibid., p. 26.

22. Ibid., p. 16.

23. *TC*, vol. 2, no. 29 (1893), p. 229.

24. *TC*, vol. 1, no. 5 (1893) p. 38.

25. *TC*, vol. 6, no. 135 (1895) p. 116.

26. *TC*, vol. 8, no. 190 (1896) p. 987.

27. *The Glasgow Herald*, 1 November 1890, p. 7.

28. *Liverpool Mercury*, 27 April 1891, p. 6.

29. *Liverpool Mercury*, 10 April 1891, p. 6.

30. Fatima E. Cates, 'The Marriage Question', *Liverpool Mercury*, 17 April 1891, p. 5.

31. Anon [Fatima E. Cates], 'On the Folly of Heeding Scandal', *TC*, vol. 16, no. 409 (1900), pp. 307–10.

32. *TC*, vol. 15, no. 384 (1900) p. 332.

33. Monro, *Moslems in Liverpool*, p. 13.

34. Fatima E. Cates, 'A Moslimah's Prayer', *The Allahabad Review*, 11 September 1891, p. 114; Anon, *A Collection of Hymns Suitable for use at the Meetings of the English Speaking Moslem Congregations*, Liverpool: T. Dobb and Company, 1892, p. 40.

35. See Chapter 4 of this volume, which focuses on Shahjahan Begum's daughter and successor, Nawab Sultan Jahan.

36. Fatima E. Cates, 'Khajida', *TC*, vol. 2, no. 36 (1893), p. 288.

37. *TC*, vol. 16, no. 408 (1900), p. 299.

38. Allen Horstman, *Victorian Divorce*, New York: St Martin's Press, 1985, p. 20.

39. Ibid., p. 78.

40. The National Archives, London, Public Records, Divorce Court File: 14745, Appellant: Frances Elizabeth Cates / Respondent: Hubert Henry Cates, p. 2.

41. Ibid., p. 3.
42. Ibid., p. 4.
43. Ibid. The other persons resident in the house were Fatima's sister Clara (Haleema) Murray [Cottam]; two Muslim Indian students who were boarding there—Ahmad Mohammad and Syed Abdul Haleem, who later married Clara (Haleema); and a servant, Margaret Eaton. See Census of England and Wales 1891 (West Derby, Liverpool).
44. The National Archives, Public Records, Divorce Court File: 14745, p. 5.
45. Ibid., pp. 5–6.
46. *Al-Ustadh*, 4 April 1893, pp. 766–8, translated by A. Abouhawas, 'An Early Arab View of Liverpool's Muslims', https://www.everydaymuslim.org/blog/an-early-arab-view-of-liverpools-muslims/, last accessed 10 October 2022.
47. *Reis and Rayyet*, 10 December 1892, p. 567; *TC,* vol. 1, no. 17 (1893), p. 132.
48. *TC*, vol. 5, no. 107 (1895), p. 34; date of death recorded as 2 January 1895 in *TC*, vol. 5, no. 108 (1895), p. 42.
49. *TC*, vol. 5, no. 108 (1895), p. 42.
50. GRO, Birth Certificate of Hubert Haleem Quilliam, 19 May 1896.
51. Ibid.
52. *TC*, vol. 16, no. 408 (1900), p. 299.
53. Ibid.
54. PRO, Will of William Henry Quilliam of Liverpool, 23 August 1932.
55. Yusuf Samih Asmay, *Islam in Victorian Liverpool: An Ottoman Account of Britain's First Mosque Community*, translated, edited and introduction by Yahya Birt, Riordan Macnamara and Münire Zeyneb Maksudoğlu, Swansea: Claritas Books, 2021, p. 92.
56. Census of England and Wales 1881 (Birkenhead).
57. *TC*, vol. 16, no. 407 (1900), p. 281.
58. *TC*, vol. 16, no. 408 (1900), p. 299.
59. *Daily Despatch* (Manchester), 1 November 1900, p. 7.
60. *TC*, vol. 16, no. 408 (1900), p. 299.
61. Ibid.
62. Ibid., p. 301.
63. Ibid., pp. 299–300.
64. *TC*, vol. 17, no. 432 (1901), p. 260.
65. *TC*, vol. 16, no. 408 (1900), p. 300.

66. Ibid.
67. Ibid., p. 301.
68. Quoted in *Liverpool Echo*, https://www.liverpoolecho.co.uk/news/liverpool-news/inspiring-story-pioneering-woman-buried-24149520, last accessed 1 December 2022.
69. Philip Lewis and Sadek Hamid, *British Muslims: New Directions in Islamic Thought, Creativity and Activism*, Edinburgh: Edinburgh University, 2018, p. 66. For more information on the *madrasa*, see www.fatimaelizabethphrontistery.co.uk, last accessed 1 December 2022.
70. See *Liverpool Echo*, https://www.liverpoolecho.co.uk/news/liverpool-news/inspiring-story-pioneering-woman-buried-24149520, last accessed 1 December 2022.

3.   DYNAMISM AND DISCONTENT

1. On Abdullah Quilliam and the LMI, see Ron Geaves, *Islam in Victorian Britain: The Life and Times of Abdullah Quilliam*, Markfield; Kube, 2010; Jamie Gilham, *Loyal Enemies: British Converts to Islam, 1850–1950*, New York: Oxford University Press, 2014, pp. 51–121; Jamie Gilham and Ron Geaves (eds), *Victorian Muslim: Abdullah Quilliam and Islam in the West*, London: Hurst, 2017.
2. Abdullah Quilliam Society Facebook Page, 17 January 2019, https://www.facebook.com/AbdullahQuilliamSociety/posts/2334800216754367, last accessed 12 October 2022.
3. Exceptions include Diane Robinson-Dunn, '"Fairer to the Ladies" and of Benefit to the Nation: Abdullah Quilliam on Reforming British Society by Islamising Gender Relationships', in Gilham and Geaves, *Victorian Muslim*, pp. 57–78; Sariya Cheruvallil-Contractor, 'Women in Britain's First Muslim Mosques: Hidden from History, but Not Without Influence', *Religions*, vol. 11, no. 2 (2020), pp. 1–12.
4. Umar Abd-Allah, *A Muslim in Victorian America: The Life of Alexander Russell Webb*, Oxford: Oxford University Press, 2006; Patrick Bowen, *A History of Conversion to Islam in the United States, Volume 1: White American Muslims before 1975*, Leiden: Brill, 2015, pp. 88–114, 139–59.
5. Fatima E. Cates, 'How I Became a Mahommedan', *The Allahabad Review,* September 1891, pp. 142–4.
6. *The Glasgow Herald*, 1 November 1890, p. 7.
7. *The Crescent* [hereafter *TC*], 7 November 1900, pp. 298–9.

8. Anonymous, *al-Ustadh*, vol. 33 (4 April 1893), pp. 766–8; Abdurahman Abouhawas, 'An Early Arab View of Liverpool's Muslims,' Everyday Muslim, https://www.everydaymuslim.org/blog/an-early-arab-view-of-liverpools-muslims/, last accessed 7 April 2022.

9. On the concept of 'Ottoman image management and damage control', see Selim Deringil, *The Well-Protected Domains: Ideology and the Legitimation of Power in the Ottoman Empire 1876–1909*, London, I. B. Tauris, 2011, pp. 135–49. On Ottoman relations with Quilliam and the LMI, see Matthew A. Sharp, '"On Behalf of the Sultan": The Late Ottoman State and the Cultivation of British and American Converts to Islam', PhD Diss., University of Pennsylvania, 2020, pp. 34–139.

10. For Lütfi Bey's longest and most detailed report, see Başbakanlık Osmanlı Arşivi/Ottoman Archives of the Prime Ministry [hereafter BOA], Y.PRK.EŞA 13/88, 7 July 1891.

11. BOA, HR.SFR.3 446/50, 14 June 1895.

12. BOA, HR.SFR.3 384/44, 28 September 1891.

13. BOA, HR.SFR.3 446/50, 14 June 1895.

14. M. A. Sherif, 'A Forgotten Memorial from Abdullah and Mariam Quilliam to the Ottoman Sheik-ul-Islam', *The Islamic Review Special Edition* (2018), pp. 34–5. There is a major discrepancy between the date given in Quilliam's appeal to the Ottoman Shaykh-ul-Islam in 1900 and a report suggesting Lütfi Bey attended the *nikah* sometime between 1891 and 1893.

15. Fatima Cates, 'To the Editors of the Liverpool Mercury', *Liverpool Mercury*, 16 April 1891, p. 6.

16. For example, the British Foreign Office investigated Quilliam over the legality of the marriages; see Gilham, *Loyal Enemies*, p. 73.

17. BOA, HR.SRF.3 446/50, 18 June 1895. The *shahada* is the Islamic testimony of faith and the first of the five 'pillars' of Islam: 'I declare that there is no god but God and I declare that Muhammad is His Messenger'.

18. Nafeesah M. T. Keep, 'The Shahzada in Liverpool', *TC*, 10 July 1895, pp. 26–9.

19. See passport applications in National Archives and Records Administration [hereafter NARA], Washington D.C., Roll #: 238; Volume #238, 1 December 1880—28 February 1881, and Roll #505, volume #505, 18 April 1898—30 April 1898. I believe she was from West Liberty in Logan County, Ohio because Anthony Klamroth, presumably her father, resided in Logan County in 1840.

20. *The Sun*, 25 June 1887, p. 4; *Rutland Daily Herald*, 17 January 1888, p. 1.

21. *The Courier-Journal*, 31 December 1899, p. 15.

22. On Webb and the Ottoman state along with Keep, see Sharp, "'On Behalf of the Sultan'", pp. 140–90.

23. BOA, HR.SYS 63/45, 18 July 1894.

24. On the rivalry, see Brent S. Singleton, 'Brothers At Odds: Rival Islamic Movements in Late Nineteenth Century New York City', *Journal of Muslim Minority Affairs*, vol. 23, no. 3 (2007), pp. 473–86.

25. Missouri Historical Society, St. Louis, Missouri, John A. Lant Papers [hereafter JALP], Abdullah Quilliam to John A. Lant, 26 September 1894.

26. Nafeesah Keep, 'An American Woman's Views of Islam', *TC*, 20 February 1895, pp. 58–63.

27. For example, Nafeesah Keep, 'The Position of Women under Islamic Law', *The Islamic World*, March 1895, pp. 342–51; Keep's lecture on 'Muslim Morals', in 'Editorial Notes', *TC*, 1 May 1895, pp. 137–8.

28. Yahya Birt, Riordan Macnamara and Münire Zeyneb Maksudoğlu, 'Introduction' in Yusuf Samih Asmay, *Islam in Victorian Liverpool: An Ottoman Account of Britain's First Mosque Community*, translated, edited and introduction by Yahya Birt, Riordan Macnamara and Münire Zeyneb Maksudoğlu, Swansea: Claritas Books, 2021, p. 8.

29. Cheruvallil-Contractor, 'Women in Britain's first Muslim Mosques', p. 8.

30. JALP, Quilliam to Lant, 21 February 1895.

31. Robinson-Dunn, "'Fairer to the Ladies'", p. 57.

32. Cemil Aydin, *The Idea of the Muslim World: A Global Intellectual History*, Cambridge, MA: Harvard University Press, 2017, pp. 73–4.

33. Keep, 'An American Woman's Views of Islam', p. 60.

34. Keep, 'The Position of Women under Islamic Law', p. 351.

35. Little is currently known about Terése Vielé. For an example of her rhetoric against Armenians and their complaints against Abdulhamid II and the Ottoman state, see 'The Armenian Agitation', *TC*, 2 January 1895, p. 7.

36. *TC*, 22 May 1895, p. 164.

37. Ibid., p. 165.

38. Keep, 'The Shahzada in Liverpool', p. 29.

39. *TC*, 22 May 1895, p. 162.

40. BOA, Y.A.HUS 355/83, Nafeesah Keep to Abdulhamid II, 3 August 1895. See reproduced letter in Asmay, *Islam in Victorian Liverpool*, pp. 119–21.

41. BOA,Y.A.HUS 335/83, 3 August 1895.

42. Ibid.

43. Ibid.

44. Ibid.

45. BOA, HR.SFR.3 446/50, 9 September 1895.

46. BOA, HR.SFR.3 446/50, 12 September 1895.

47. Yusuf Samih Asmay, *Liverpool Müslümanlığı*, Cairo: El-Müeyyed Matbaası, 1313/1896, republished in an English translation as Asmay, *Islam in Victorian Liverpool*.

48. Ibid., pp. 74, 76.

49. Ibid., pp. 84–5.

50. Ibid., p. 101.

51. See Humayun Ansari, 'Maulana Barkatullah Bhopali's Transnationalism: Pan-Islamism, Colonialism, and Radical Politics', in *Transnational Islam in Interwar Europe* in Götz Nordbruch and Umar Ryad (eds), New York: Palgrave Macmillan, 2014, pp. 181–209; Samee Siddiqui, 'Coupled Internationalism: Charting Muhammad Barkatullah's Anti-Colonialism and Pan-Islamism', *ReOrient*, vol. 5, no. 1 (2020), pp. 25–46.

52. Asmay, *Islam in Victorian Liverpool*, p. 88.

53. Ibid., pp. 88–9.

54. Ibid., p. 99.

55. Ibid., pp. 97–100. On the brothel allegation, see Birt et al., 'Introduction' in ibid., pp. 19–25.

56. On the Keep-Asmay connection see ibid., pp. 28–31.

57. Asmay, *Islam in Victorian Liverpool*, pp. 67–8.

58. Ibid., p. 66.

59. Ibid., p. 113.

60. I have in mind Barakatullah, the sometime LMI vice-president Rafiüddin Ahmed (1865–1954) and Mustafa Khalil, a Syrian teacher at the LMI's Liverpool Muslim College who later wrote to an Arabic newspaper against Quilliam. Their departures and the LMI's amnesia about them require further study.

61. *TC*, 21 August 1895, p. 116.

62. *TC*, 1 July 1896, p. 842.

63. The best example was Mustafa Khalil, a member of the LMI and volunteer from Syria, who wrote to the Arabic Islamic newspaper in Beirut, *Thamarat al-Funun*, and then later to the Ottoman embassy in London; see Sharp, '"On Behalf of the Sultan"', pp. 77–8 and 214–16.

64. *TC*, 5 August 1896, pp. 918–9.
65. *TC*, 23 June 1897, p. 387.
66. Asmay, *Islam in Victorian Liverpool*, p. 113.
67. See almost identical articles in: *The Sun*, 31 December 1899, p. 7; *The Courier-Journal*, 31 December 1899, p. 15; *Sunday Herald*, 31 December 1899, p. 30; *The Philadelphia Inquirer*, 14 January 1900, p. 4; *Utica*, 11 February 1900, n.p.
68. UK and Ireland, Outward Passenger Lists, 1890–1960. See passport applications in NARA, Roll #505, Volume #505, 18 April 1898—30 April 1898. Thanks to Riordan Macnamara for helping to locate these documents.
69. 'Al-Muslimūn fī Lundrā', *Thamarāt al-Funūn*, no. 1197 (12 September 1898), p. 4.
70. *The Sun*, 31 December 1899, p. 7.
71. As it stands, she was likely the first American woman to publicly convert to Islam.
72. *The Mirror*, 19 December 1925, p. 2.
73. *TC*, 20 December 1899, p. 387.

4. SULTAN JAHAN AND THE WOKING MUSLIM MISSION

1. Kamal-ud-Din's account was recalled by Kazi Abdul Haq, 'The Mosque at Woking: A Miniature of Mecca in the Days of the Pilgrimage', *The Islamic Review* [hereafter *IR*], vol. 18, no. 7 (1930), pp. 242–4.
2. On the early history of the Woking mosque, see Jamie Gilham, 'Professor G. W. Leitner in England: The Oriental Institute, Woking Mosque, Islam and Relations with Muslims, 1884–1899', *Islam and Christian-Muslim Relations*, vol. 32, no. 1 (2021), pp. 1–24.
3. Haq, 'The Mosque at Woking', p. 242.
4. [Sultan Jahan Begum], *An Account of My Life (Gohur-I-Ikbal)*, trans. C.H. Payne, London: John Murray, 1912; [Sultan Jahan Begum], *Hayat-i-qudsi: Life of the Nawab Gauhar Begum alias the Nawab Begum Qudsia of Bhopal*, trans. W. S. Davis, London: Kegan Paul, 1918. Hereafter, these publications are referred to in these notes as *Account* and *Qudsia* respectively.
5. In the beginning of her biography of Qudsia, Sultan Jahan explains that she has studied and written about the history of her ancestors so that she might profit by their example. In addition, Qudsia served as a 'role model' for not only three succeeding generations of female rulers but also Muslim women in India more generally.

See Shaharyar M. Khan, *The Begums of Bhopal: A Dynasty of Women Rulers in Raj India*, London: I. B. Tauris, 2000, p. 89.

6. Ibid., pp. 68, 71–3, 87–9.

7. Ibid., pp. 98–9, 102, 107–8.

8. See ibid. Chapters six and seven focus on Shahjehan and Sultan Jahan respectively, pp. 119–87. Also see Claudia Preckel, *Begums of Bhopal*, New Delhi: Roli Books, 2000.

9. Adil Hussain Khan notes that Shahjehan was the 'principal benefactor' in the publication of Ghulam Ahmad's book, which first appeared in Qadian, India in 1880: Adil Hussain Khan, *From Sufism to Ahmadiyya: A Muslim Minority Movement in South Asia*, Bloomington: Indiana University Press, 2015, p. 35. Kamal-ud-Din had contemplated converting to Christianity, but decided not to, crediting his steadfast commitment to Islam to his teacher Ghulam Ahmad. In addition, Kamal-ud-Din explained his eventual decision to move to England and found the WMM as a way of atoning for almost having renounced the faith of his birth: see Anon, 'Hazrat Khwaja Kamal-ud-Din', *The Hope Bulletin*, vol. 7, no. 9. (2013), pp. 12–22.

10. Sultan Jahan funded the publication of Kamal-ud-Din's book on Muhammad, *The Ideal Prophet*, and invited him to speak in Bhopal as well. See Siobhan Lambert-Hurley, 'Out of India: The Journeys of the Begam of Bhopal, 1901–1930' in Tony Ballantyne and Antoinette Burton (eds), *Bodies in Contact: Rethinking Colonial Encounters in World History*, Durham, NC: Duke University Press, 2005, quotation on p. 300; Siobhan Lambert-Hurley, *Muslim Women, Reform and Princely Patronage: Nawab Sultan Jahan Begam of Bhopal*, New York: Routledge, 2007, p. 57.

11. *IR*, vol. 13, no. 12 (1925), pp. 409–14, 414–5, quotation on p. 415. Film footage of this visit is available online: British Pathé, https://www.youtube.com/watch?v=82f0hWbQrf8&t=8s, last accessed 5 September 2022.

12. *Qudsia*, pp.16, 102, 108–9, 120–2, 141.

13. *Account*, pp. 5, 8–14. She was the first ruler to have the laws of Bhopal codified.

14. *Account*, pp. 6–7, quotation on p. 16.

15. *Qudsia*, pp. 97–103. Each of these names can be transliterated a number of ways. I have retained the spellings used by Sultan Jahan.

16. *Qudsia*, pp. 102–3.

17. *Account*, pp. 3–4, 10.

18. Women who observe purdah, or female seclusion.
19. *Qudsia*, pp. 99, 6. After having weathered the Maratha onslaught, Bhopal asserted its independence and became the second most important Muslim state in India after Hyderabad: see Khan, *The Begums*, pp. 73, 56–8.
20. *Account*, p. 363. Here the term 'ancestors' most likely refers to the Pathan, or Pashtun, warriors from Afghanistan from whom the Begums of Bhopal descended.
21. *IR*, vol. 2, no.1 (1914), p. 4.
22. *Qudsia*, p. 115.
23. *Account*, p. 120.
24. Sultan Jahan explains this in *Account*, p. 41.
25. Ibid., pp. 40, 43.
26. Ibid., 371.
27. Khan, *The Begums*, p. 158.
28. Leila Ahmed, *Women and Gender in Islam: Historical Roots of a Modern Debate,* New Haven and London: Yale University Press, 1992; Beth Baron, *The Women's Awakening in Egypt: Culture, Society, and the Press*, New Haven and London: Yale University Press, 1994.
29. Sultan Jahan began her book on the *hijab* by stating that female seclusion was 'one of the most important and serious questions that have been engaging the thought and attention of the Islamic world for the last thirty or forty years': H. H. The Ruler of Bhopal, *Al Hijab: Or, Why Purdah is Necessary,* Calcutta: Thacker and Sprink, 1922.
30. *Qudsia*, p. 104.
31. The term 'acrobatic' is from Ruler of Bhopal, *Al Hijab*, p. 109. For a modern scholarly discussion of the meaning and use of the curtain or *hijab* in the early days of Islam, see Fatima Mernissi, *The Veil and the Male Elite: A Feminist Interpretation of Women's Rights in Islam,* Cambridge, MA: Perseus, 1991, pp. 85–101.
32. Sultan Jahan relates her practice of conducting meetings from behind a screen in *Account*, p. 268. The reference to Ayesha is from Ruler of Bhopal, *Al Hijab*, p. 144. She discusses travels through her territories in *Account,* pp. 275-81, and on p. 278 relates how she always met with local women, which was enjoyable and supplied her with valuable information and insights. Khan notes that she patiently listened to the problems of the women in the rural villages: Khan, *The Begums*, p. 171.

215

33. Lambert-Hurley, *MuslimWomen*, pp. 4–5, 111, 116. For a discussion of Sultan Jahan's efforts to promote female emancipation, see Khan, *The Begums*, pp. 154–87, 180, 224. Other organizations with which Sultan Jahan was involved include the All-India Muslim Ladies Conference, All-India Ladies Association, the National Council of Women in India and the All Indian Women's Conference: see Lambert-Hurley, *Muslim Women*, p. 145. See also Tuhina Islam, 'Social and Educational Reforms of Nawab Sultan Jahan Begum', *The International Journal of Humanities and Social Sciences*, vol. 2, no. 4 (2014), pp. 47–52.

34. *IR*, vol. 2, no. 4 (1914), pp. 159–60; Lambert-Hurley, *Muslim Women*, p. 60.

35. *IR*, vol. 6, nos. 10—11 (1918), pp. 361–6, quotations on pp. 362 and 364–5.

36. Ibid., pp. 388–9.

37. In 1913, Kamal-ud-Din wrote that he had converted two men and two women: Ron Geaves, *Islam and Britain: Muslim Mission in an Age of Empire,* London: Bloomsbury, 2018, p. 104. In 1914, there were four converts, all women; in 1916 there were fourteen converts with seven men and seven women: Jamie Gilham, *Loyal Enemies: British Converts to Islam, 1850–1950*, New York: Oxford University Press, 2014, p. 147. A 1913 photograph at the Shah Jahan Mosque shows Kamal-ud-Din with 21 converts: Geaves, *Islam and Britain,* p. 110. Some or all in the picture may have come to Islam before the establishment of the WMM.

38. Letter from Ebrahim to Mrs. Khader Jung reprinted in *The Review of Religions*, vol. 12, no. 12 (1913), pp. 519–21. Also see Geaves, *Islam and Britain*, p. 103 and Gilham, *Loyal*, p. 128.

39. Ebrahim's speech entitled 'Your Highness, Ladies, and Sisters in Islam' is reproduced in *IR*, vol. 4, no. 3 (1916), p.107. While the exact date of the speech is not given, it had to have occurred sometime between the end of 1914, when she first arrived in India, and the date of publication.

40. Sultan Jahan includes a chapter on her pilgrimage to Mecca in *Account*, pp. 338–52; see [Sultan Jahan Begum], *The Story of a Pilgrimage to Hijaz*, Calcutta: Thacker, Spink and Company, 1909 and 1913.

41. Khan, *The Begums*, p. 104.

42. Gilham, *Loyal*, p. 193.

43. *IR*, vol. 6, nos. 10 and 11 (1918), pp. 361–2.

44. Geaves, *Islam and Britain*, p. 109.

45. Photograph reproduced in ibid., p. 110.

46. In addition to its place of publication, certain passages indicate that Eastern women were her intended audience. For example, the warning to readers that their husbands might try to introduce Western freedom to them: *Al Hijab*, p. 103. In addition to India, she also refers to Egypt and 'Turkey' as places where Muslims have been influenced by Western ideas. *Hijab* is a headscarf.

47. Marmaduke Pickthall, who eventually would become one of the most outspoken British Muslim converts, wrote of how Lady Evelyn Cobbold tried to persuade him to embrace Islam in Claridge's restaurant in London in 1914, even calling upon two Muslim waiters to act as witnesses: cited in Gilham, *Loyal*, p. 153. Cobbold was not a regular attendee at the WMM, but remained in contact with Kamal-ud-Din until his death.

48. Lady Evelyn Cobbold, *Wayfarers in the Libyan Desert*, London: Humphreys, 1912; Marmaduke Pickthall, *Veiled Women*, London: Eveleigh Nash, 1913.

49. Cobbold, *Wayfarers*, p. 67; the quotation from Pickthall's novel is in Gilham, *Loyal*, p. 193.

50. Gilham notes that over the course of twenty years the harem went from being a prison to a sanctuary in Cobbold's eyes: Gilham, *Loyal* pp. 194–5, footnote 86.

51. Lambert-Hurley discusses Sultan Jahan's decision to abandon purdah at the end of her life and how by doing so she served as an intermediary between an older and younger generation of Muslim female leaders and reformers: Lambert-Hurley, *Muslim Women*, pp. 121–2. Maimoona travelled to England with her mother-in-law in both 1911 and 1925, and Abida, Sajida and Rabia accompanied her in 1925 (see Chapter 8 of this volume). As Khan explains, Maimoona was taught English and French as well as Urdu and Persian. She learned needlework, cooking and silk embroidery but also the skills associated with the 'feudal machismo' of the Bhopal aristocracy, such as riding and shooting. She was educated in the Qur'an and *hadith* (report of the traditions of the Prophet Muhammad), but also understood Western culture and etiquette and could converse 'easily and graciously' with Englishwomen. Sultan Jahan raised her granddaughters in the same manner. Khan, *The Begums*, pp. 170, 184.

52. *IR*, vol. 2, no. 9 (1914), pp. 447–9.

53. This process has been explored in the French context by Mary Louise Roberts, *Civilization without Sexes: Reconstructing Gender in Postwar France, 1917–1927,* Chicago: University of Chicago Press, 1994.

54. *IR*, vol. 6, no. 4 (1918), pp. 190–1. By 1918, the people of Britain, like so many others in Europe and the world, had grown sick and tired of the war and desired peace. The losses had been devastating, and the initial enthusiasm of the early years had given way to grief, anger and despair. This transformation is captured in Vera Brittain, *Testament of Youth*, London: Victor Gollancz, 1933.

55. Ruler of Bhopal, *Al Hijab*, 3. The exact quotation is: 'A great portion of my life has been spent in thinking over the important and grave problems touching the welfare of my own sex; and the most interesting and important among them are the education and seclusion of women.'

56. Her changing attitudes can be seen in the greater freedom she gave her daughter-in-law and grand-daughters to sightsee and enjoy London during their 1925 trip as compared to her belief in the need to confine Maimoona to the hotel room in 1911: Lambert-Hurley, *Muslim Women*, p. 120.

57. *IR*, vol. 6, nos. 10—11 (1918), pp. 392–6.

58. On gender debates in the Muslim world, see Baron, *The Women's Awakening*; Ahmed, *Women and Gender*.

59. [Sultan Jahan Begum], *Muslim Home. Part I, A Present to the Married Couple,* Calcutta: Thacker, Spink and Company, 1916, pp. 18–20. Mention is made of distributing *Muslim Home* at Woking in *IR*, vol. 5, no. 11 (1917), pp. 447–8; *Account*, p. 371; Waltraud Ernst and Biswamoy Pati (eds), *India's Princely States: People, Princes and Colonialism,* London: Routledge, 2007, p. 144. Occasional echoes of Abdullah Quilliam's (1856–1932) arguments in support of polygyny as preferable to the bleak alternatives facing unwed mothers in Victorian England, which he made as leader of the Muslim community in late nineteenth-century Liverpool, made their way into WMM discourses, perhaps because he gravitated towards the Woking community later in life: see Diane Robinson-Dunn, '"Fairer to the Ladies" and of Benefit to the Nation: Abdullah Quilliam on Reforming British Society by Islamising Gender Relationships', in Jamie Gilham and Ron Geaves (eds), *Victorian Muslim: Abdullah Quilliam and Islam in the West*, New York: Oxford University Press, 2017, pp. 57–78.

60. [Sultan Jahan Begum], *Muslim Home*, pp. 20–1; Her Highness the Ruler of Bhopal, 'Polygamy', *IR*, vol. 4, no. 5 (1916), p. 211.
61. *IR*, vol. 5, no. 10 (1917), pp. 436, 440.
62. Over the course of the war, both the British people and government became increasingly aware of the dangers of infant mortality to the nation. Concern for the overall health and wellbeing of the next generation inspired a series of reforms, culminating in the Child Welfare Act of 1918: Rex Pope, *War and Society in Britain 1899– 1948*, New York: Routledge, 1991, pp. 26–7, 58.
63. Here Kidwai reproduces an excerpt from *The Herald*, in *IR,* vol. 5, no. 10 (1917), p. 443.
64. The circular was in the form of a letter entitled 'White Wives of Brown Men' by Sir John Rees, MP. That and Kamal-ud-Din's responses, documented in *IR*, are cited in Eric Germain, 'The First Muslim Missions on a European Scale: Ahmadi-Lahori Networks in the Inter-war Period', in Nathalie Clayer and Eric Germain (eds), *Islam in Inter–war Europe*, New York: Columbia University Press, 2008, pp. 89–127, especially pp. 115–6. Also see *TheWaimate Advertiser*, vol. 16, no. 26 (1913), p. 4.
65. *IR*, vol. 1, no. 2 (1913), pp. 75–8, quotations on p. 78.
66. While Sultan Jahan opposed the women's suffrage movement, as Lambert-Hurley explains in *Muslim Women*, pp. 167–75, her position was not publicized through WMM materials. Nor was it discussed in her writings published in London for an English-speaking readership.
67. *IR*, vol. 1, no. 2 (1913), p. 78.
68. *IR*, vol. 5, no. 8 (1917), pp. 343–8, quotations on pp. 343 and 348. Pickthall formally declared his conversion to Islam in 1917.
69. For in-depth discussion of these dominant discourses, see Diane Robinson-Dunn, *The Harem, Slavery, and British Imperial Culture: Anglo-Muslim Relations in the Late Nineteenth Century*, Manchester: Manchester University Press, 2006.
70. This position is presented in Violet Ebrahim, 'A Message from the West to the East', *IR*, vol. 4, no. 3 (1916), p. 108 and Sheikh Kidwai, 'Women under Islam', *IR*, vol. 6, nos. 10—11 (1918), p. 388.
71. [Sultan Jahan Begum], *Muslim Home*, pp. ii–iii, 27–34, 42; Her Highness the Begum of Bhopal, 'A Muslim's Obligations to his Kinsmen', *IR*, vol. 4, no. 2 (1916), pp. 51–5; Her Highness the Begum of Bhopal, 'The Relative Position of Man and Woman in Islam', *IR*, vol. 4, no. 7 (1916), pp. 300–5.
72. *IR*, vol. 3, no. 7 (1915), pp. 357–9. Also see *IR*, vol. 5, no. 8 (1917), pp. 329–33 and vol. 6, nos. 8—9 (1918), pp. 337–42. Kidwai

addresses the matter of divorce specifically in *IR*, vol. 5, no. 11 (1917), pp. 469–84.

73. *IR,* vol. 3, no. 7 (1915), pp. 293–4 and vol. 4, no. 1 (1916), pp. 14–17.

74. Gilham, *Loyal*, pp. 146, 193.

75. [Sultan Jahan Begum], *Muslim Home*, pp. ii, 2–3.

76. *IR*, vol. 1, no. 5 (1913), p. 185.

77. 'An Ideal Husband' is followed by 'The Testimony of Khadijah' in *IR*, vol. 1, no. 5 (1913), pp. 188–90. In addition, discussion of the respect due to women in Islam can be found in, for example, *IR*, vol. 3, no. 10 (1915), pp. 526–8 and Shaikh Kidwai's series of articles entitled 'Woman under Islam' that appeared during the first half of 1917: *IR*, vol. 5, nos. 2—3 (1917), pp. 125–8; vol. 5, no. 4 (1917), pp. 156–61; and vol. 5, no. 5 (1917), pp. 204–8.

78. [Sultan Jahan Begum], *Muslim Home*, p. 40. Sheikh Kidwai notes that one fourth of Muslim juristic traditions derived from her: *IR*, vol. 6, nos. 10–11 (1918), p. 388.

79. Coventry Patmore's (1823–96) poem 'Angel in the House' was first published in London in 1856–62. The influence of that ideal would continue to grow over the years, with Virginia Woolf (1882–1941) famously describing her struggle to kill that 'phantom' in her speech on 'Professions for Women' delivered to the National Society for Women's Service in 1931, published in Virginia Woolf, *The Death of the Moth and Other Essays*, New York and London: Harcourt, 1942, pp. 235–42.

80. [Sultan Jahan Begum], *Muslim Home*, p. ii; *IR*, vol. 1, no. 5 (1913), p. 186.

81. [Sultan Jahan Begum], *Muslim Home*, pp. 5–6. These ideas also are presented in 'The Relative Position of Men and Women in Islam', *IR*, vol. 4, no. 7 (1916), pp. 300–5.

82. *IR*, vol. 6, nos. 10—11 (1918), p. 366.

83. See discussion of domestic life in England during the late nineteenth and early twentieth centuries and its relationship to representations of femininity and middle-class respectability in Lenore Davidoff, *World's Between: Historical Perspectives on Gender and Class*, New York: Routledge, 1995. Still relevant, although focusing on the previous period, is the seminal book by Lenore Davidoff and Catherine Hall, *Family Fortunes: Men and Women of the English Middle Class, 1780–1850*, Chicago: University of Chicago Press, 1987.

84. Pickthall even commented on the elasticity of Islam with regard to gender and other issues, explaining how the religion is dynamic, not static, and thus capable of comprehending the 'needs of every age and every people': cited in Gilham, *Loyal*, p. 194.

85. Women's rights advocates also called for the repeal of the Contagious Disease Acts and legal reform, particularly with regard to issues of divorce, child custody and domestic violence. See, for example, Martha Vicinus (ed), *A Widening Sphere: Changing Roles of Victorian Women*, 1977, New York: Routledge, 2013; Judith Walkowitz, *Prostitution and Victorian Society:Women, Class and the State*, Cambridge: Cambridge University Press, 1980; June Purvis and Sandra Stanley Holton (eds), *Votes for Women*, London and New York: Routledge, 2000; Andrew Rosen, *Rise Up,Women! The Militant Campaign of the Women's Social and Political Union 1903–1914*, London: Routledge, 2013; Philippa Levine, *Victorian Feminism 1850–1900*, Gainesville: University Press of Florida, 2018.

86. For a thought-provoking analysis on the dynamic relationship between war, modernism and culture in early twentieth-century Europe, including Britain, see Modris Eksteins, *Rites of Spring: The Great War and the Birth of the Modern Age,* New York: Houghton Mifflin, 1989.

5.   'FATMA *HANIM* OF THE ENGLISH CONVERTS'

1. There are some references to Fatma *Hanım* (Mrs Fatma)—Fatma, or Fatima, being the name Hannah adopted after converting to Islam—in Turkish sources, although these sources are largely inaccurate. Commentators in Turkey have tended to focus more on the life of one of her sons, Ahmet Robenson (original name, Peel Harold Robinson), who became a sporting legend in the Ottoman Empire. However, Hannah Rodda has featured as a case study in two recent PhD theses. For an overview of Ahmet Robenson's life, see Gareth M. Winrow, 'Who was Ahmet Robenson?', *Journal of Anglo-Turkish Relations*, vol. 1, no. 2 (2020), p. 5, https://dergipark.org.tr/tr/download/article-file/1154386, last accessed 14 October. 2022. For an account of Hannah's life which is full of errors, see Ali Sami Alkış, *Çanakkale'de Şehit Düşen Futbolcular:Yedi Kandilli Avize*, Istanbul:YarımdaYayınları, 2008, pp. 53–64. For more on Hannah, see Ayşe Ebru Akcasu, 'Non-Ottomans of Hamidian Istanbul: Exiles and Expatriates', PhD Diss., University of London, 2017; Matthew A. Sharp, '"On Behalf of the Sultan": The Late Ottoman State and

the Cultivation of British and American Converts to Islam', PhD Diss., University of Pennsylvania, 2020.

2. In this chapter, after her conversion to Islam, Hannah Rodda (Robinson) is referred to as Fatma.

3. For further information about Hannah's early life see, Gareth Winrow, *Whispers Across Continents: In Search of the Robinsons*, Stroud: Amberley, 2019, pp. 92–9, 102–12.

4. Email communication from Kristi Newton to the author, 30 March 2020.

5. For further details of the life of Gertrude Eisenmann, see Winrow, *Whispers Across Continents*, pp. 133–53.

6. Ibid., pp. 37–8, 45–6, 88.

7. Alkış, *Çanakkale'de Şehit Düşen Futbolcular*, pp. 53–64. This story has been presented in the form of a comic strip for children in Turkey: Osman Arslan, *Galatasaray'lı Hasnun Galip ve Robensonlar'ın Çanakkale Destanı*, Istanbul: Mavi Medya Yayıncılık, 2007.

8. Sara Korle, 'Ahmet Robenson'u New York'ta buldum!', *Hayat*, no. 26 (24 June 1965), p. 9.

9. *The Crescent* [hereafter *TC*], 11 May 1898, p. 299.

10. *Pall Mall Gazette*, 27 November 1891, p. 6.

11. The National Archives [hereafter TNA], London, Foreign Office Papers, FO195/1743, no. 157, Mrs Robinson to the Office of the Prime Minister, 20 June 1892.

12. *Sussex Agricultural Express*, 31 October 1891, p. 2.

13. TNA, FO195/1747, no. 280, Additional letter of Mrs Robinson, 10 September 1892.

14. David Fromkin, 'The Great Game in Asia', *Foreign Affairs*, vol. 58, no. 4 (1980), pp. 936–51.

15. TNA, FO 195/1747, no. 280, First letter of Mrs Robinson, 10 September 1892.

16. Başbakanlık Osmanlı Arşivi [hereafter BOA], The Ottoman Archives of the Prime Minister's Office, Istanbul, I. DH. 1264/99346, Letter from the Yildiz Palace Secretariat, 4 February 1892.

17. BOA, HR. TO. 65/46, Ottoman Embassy in London to the Ottoman Ministry of Foreign Affairs, 27 November 1891.

18. *Liverpool Mercury*, 20 April 1891, p. 6.

19. TNA, General Registry Office Papers, RG/48/310, The Quilliam Case (1905): Moslem Marriage in Mosque, 15 June 1905.

20. Diane Robinson-Dunn, '"Fairer to the Ladies" and of Benefit to the Nation: Abdullah Quilliam on Reforming British Society by

Islamising Gender Relationships', in Jamie Gilham and Ron Geaves (eds), *Victorian Muslim: Abdullah Quilliam and Islam in the West*, London: Hurst, 2017, pp. 74–6.

21. *Cambridge Independent Press*, 4 December 1891, p. 6.
22. Humayun Ansari, '*The Infidel Within': Muslims in Britain since 1800*, London: Hurst, 2004, p. 77.
23. *Dublin Evening Telegraph*, 30 November 1891, p. 2.
24. Yusuf Samih Asmay, *Islam in Victorian Liverpool: An Ottoman Account of Britain's First Mosque Community*, translated, edited and introduction by Yahya Birt, Riordan Macnamara and Münire Zeyneb Maksudoğlu, Swansea: Claritas Books, 2021, p. 99.
25. Anon, 'Profile—Abdullah Quilliam: An Anglo-Muslim who Defended Islam in the UK', Anadolu Agency, https://www.aa.com.tr/en/life/profile-abdullah-quilliam-an-anglo-muslim-who-defended-islam-in-uk/1799868, last accessed 17 October 2022.
26. Celil Bozkurt, '1. Dünya Savaşı'nda Filistin Suriye Cephesi'nde Nili Casusluk Örgütünün Faaliyetleri', *Atatürk Araştırma Merkezi Dergisi*, vol. 30, no. 88 (2014), p. 108.
27. Akcasu, 'Non-Ottomans of Hamidian Istanbul', p. 158.
28. See Winrow, 'Who was Ahmet Robenson?', p. 5.
29. Jamie Gilham, 'Abdullah Quilliam, First and Last "Sheikh-ul-Islam of the British Isles"', in Gilham and Geaves (eds), *Victorian Muslim*, p. 98.
30. *The Times*, 20 December 1890, p. 12.
31. Gilham, 'Abdullah Quilliam', p. 98; Ron Geaves, *Islam in Victorian Britain: The Life and Times of Abdullah Quilliam*, Markfield: Kube, 2010, pp. 71–2, 223.
32. Sharp, '"On Behalf of the Sultan"', p. 128.
33. BOA, HR.TO. 65/46, 27 November 1891.
34. BOA, I. DH. 1264/99346, 4 February 1892.
35. TNA, FO 195/1747, no. 280, Additional letter of Mrs Robinson, 10 September 1892.
36. TNA, FO 800/32/37 and FO 800/32/38, Correspondence between Arminius Vambery and the British Foreign Office September—October 1892; TNA, FO 78/4416 no. 280, Memo by Mr Adam Bloch, Dragoman, 5 September 1892.
37. TNA, FO 787/4416, no. 280, 5 September 1892.
38. I am grateful to Mehmet Yüce, who pieced together this information from various documents in the Ottoman Archives.

39. BOA, HR.TO. 00537 00027.002 and 00537 00027.003, Letter of Fatma *Hanım* to the Grand Vizier, 13 June 1892.
40. A. Ebru Akcasu, 'Migrants to Citizens: An Evaluation of the Expansionist Features of Hamidian Ottomanism', *Die Welt des Islams*, vol. 56, nos. 3–4 (2016), pp. 411–2.
41. TNA, FO 195/1743, no.157, 20 June 1892.
42. TNA, FO 195/1747, no. 280, First letter of Mrs Robinson, 10 September 1892.
43. Ibid.
44. TNA, FO 78/4416, no. 280, Foreign Office Memo, 16 September 1892.
45. TNA, FO 78/4416, no. 280, Letter of Ambassador Francis Clare Ford, 10 September 1892.
46. Winrow, *Whispers Across Continents*, p. 99.
47. TNA, FO 78/4416, no. 280, Foreign Office Memo, 16 September 1892.
48. Selim Deringil, *Conversion and Apostasy in the Late Ottoman Empire*, Cambridge: Cambridge University Press, 2012, pp. 157–8.
49. Akcasu, 'Non-Ottomans of Hamidian Istanbul', pp. 158–9.
50. TNA, FO 195/1747, no. 280, Additional letter of Mrs Robinson, 10 September 1892.
51. BOA, BEO 000125. 009371.002, Fatma *Hanım* to the Grand Vizier, 28 January 1893. I am grateful to Matthew Sharp for drawing my attention to this document. Quilliam's original letter of reference is not included in this document.
52. BOA, BEO 000019 001374 002001, Petition of Fatma *Hanım* to the Ottoman Ministry of Interior, 20 June 1892.
53. BOA, BEO 000019 001374 003001, Petition of Fatma *Hanım*, 19 June 1892.
54. Winrow, *Whispers Across Continents*, pp. 125–6.
55. Information provided in email communication to the author from Mehmet Yüce, 31 January 2019.
56. *TC*, 11 May 1898, p. 299.
57. *TC*, 25 May 1898, p. 331.
58. On Quilliam's departure, see Geaves, *Islam in Victorian Britain*, Ch. 8.
59. TNA, FO 383/345, Mrs M. M. Thompson to Ahmed Robinson Bey, 6 November 1917.
60. *Peel City Guardian*, 28 November 1908, p. 5.
61. *TC*, 10 April 1907, p. 1069.

62. Author's interview with Gülperi Ceylan, 31 May 2021.
63. See Winrow, *Whispers Across Continents*, p. 193.

6. 'NO ROOM AT THE INN'

1. The author would like to thank the following people for their help with research for this chapter: Andrew Mussell, Archivist at Gray's Inn; Humayun 'Hank' Khan, descendant of Colonel Altof; Gary Phillips, Solicitor, Sills and Betteridge Solicitors.
2. Membership of an Inn of Court was the precursor to a career at the Bar; without such membership, a person could not be 'called to the Bar' and therefore could not appear in court or represent clients. See Richard L. Abel, *The Making of the English Legal Profession, 1800–1988*, Washington, DC: Beard Books, 1998, p. 37.
3. The most famous of which was Christabel Pankhurst: see June Purvis, *Christabel Pankhurst: A Biography*, Abingdon: Routledge, 2018, p. 51.
4. Abel, *The Making of the English Legal Profession*, p. 75.
5. For example, women could not legally vote due to the finding in *Chorlton v Lings* 4 CP 374 (1868).
6. Lincoln's Inn Register of Admission, vol. 2 (1800–93), p. 409. Altof is recorded as 'Iltaf Ali'.
7. Lincoln's Inn Register of Admission, vol. 3 (1894–1956), p. 35. Altof is recorded as 'Altof Ali'.
8. *The Times*, 25 June 1903, p. 15. Altof is recorded as 'Ali Altof'.
9. *The Times*, 3 December, 1903, p. 10.
10. Anon, 'The Light of the World', *Pan-Islamic Press*, vol. 2, no. 1 (1906), p. 105. The article suggests that Altof, and possibly Cave, were members of the Pan-Islamic Society in London, which focused on issues that affected the Muslim world. See also the report in *Islamic Review and Muslim India*, vol. 2, no. 1 (1914), p. 32.
11. Altof family information, supported by photographic evidence.
12. Jamie Gilham, 'Professor G. W. Leitner in England: The Oriental Institute, Woking Mosque, Islam and Relations with Muslims, 1884–1899', *Islam and Christian–Muslim Relations*, vol. 32, no. 1 (2021), pp. 1–24.
13. *Islamic Review and Muslim India*, vol. 2, no. 1 (1914), p. 32.
14. The 1870 Naturalisation Act legislated that British women who married foreign men lost their British nationality on marriage. This became a feminist campaign, as men did not lose their nationality on marriage to a foreign woman. The law was finally changed in 1948 with the British Nationality Act.

15. For a detailed discussion, see Jane Garrity, *Step-Daughters of England: British Women Modernists and the National Imaginary*, Manchester: Manchester University Press, 2003, pp. 46–8.

16. For more context, see M. P. Baldwin, 'Subject to Empire: Married Women and the British Nationality and Status of Aliens Act', *The Journal of British Studies*, vol. 40, no. 4 (2001), pp. 522–56; Garrity, *Step-Daughters*, p. 47.

17. Helen Irving, *Citizenship, Alienage and the Modern Constitutional State: A Gendered History*, Cambridge: Cambridge University Press, 2016, p. 45.

18. For example, the 1870 Married Women's Property Act allowed women to keep their income but not their property upon marriage; the 1873 Custody of Infants Act only allowed women custody of their children under the age of sixteen: see Judith Bourne and Caroline Derry, *Gender and the Law*, Abingdon: Routledge, 2018, pp. 43–63.

19. For example, the parents of feminist Barbara Leigh Smith Bodichon (1827–91) refused to marry because of women's inequality in marriage: see Pam Hirsch, 'Bodichon, Barbara Leigh Smith', in *Oxford Dictionary of National Biography*, https://www.oxforddnb.com/view/10.1093/ref:odnb/9780198614128.001.0001/odnb–9780198614128-e-2755, last accessed 25 August 2022.

20. See Chamion Caballero and Peter J. Aspinall, *Mixed Race Britain in the Twentieth Century*, Basingstoke: Palgrave Macmillan, 2018, p. 1.

21. Rebecca Probert, *Tying the Knot: The Formation of Marriage, 1836–2020*, Cambridge: Cambridge University Press, 2021, p. 163.

22. Ibid.

23. Pamela Cox, *Gender, Justice and Welfare in Britain, 1900–1950*, Basingstoke: Palgrave Macmillan, 2002, p. 142.

24. The typical age gap was between four and five years in the early twentieth century, but much older husbands did not cause concern within society: see Jay Winter, 'Demography', in John Horne (ed), *A Companion to World War I*, Oxford: Wiley-Blackwell, 2010, p. 259.

25. Private Collection, Altof Papers, undated documents, c. 1905.

26. See Hilary Perraton, *A History of Foreign Students in Britain*, Basingstoke: Palgrave Macmillan, 2014, p. 51.

27. For example, Henry Sylvester Williams, a black man, was practising at the Bar in England in the early 1900s: Dudley J. Thompson and Margaret Cezair-Thompson, *From Kingston to Kenya: The Making of a Pan-Africanist Lawyer*, Dover, MA: Majority Press, 1993, p. 45.

28. Perraton, *A History of Foreign Students in Britain*, p. 50.
29. Ibid., p. 52.
30. Ibid., p. 57.
31. Ibid., p. 50.
32. Shompa Lahiri, *Indians in Britain: Anglo-Indian Encounters, Race and Identity, 1880–1930*, Abingdon: Routledge, 2013, p. 4.
33. Kumari Jayawardena, *The White Woman's Other Burden: Western Women and South Asia During British Rule*, London: Routledge, 2014.
34. Caroline Keen, *Princely India and the British: Political Development and the Operation of Empire*, I. B. Tauris, 2012.
35. Jordanna Bailkin, *The Afterlife of Empire*, Berkeley, CA: University of California Press, 2012, p. 139.
36. Ronald Hyam, *Empire and Sexuality: The British Experience*, Manchester: Manchester University Press, 2017, p. 120; Kenneth Ballhatchet, *Race, Sex and Class Under the Raj: Imperial Attitudes and Policies and Their Critics, 1793–1905*, London: Weidenfeld and Nicolson, 1980, p. 6.
37. Jayawardena, *The White Woman's Other Burden*, p. 4.
38. Khushwant Singh, *Captain Amarinder Singh: The People's Maharaja. An Authorized Biography*, London: Hay House, 2017.
39. Ballhatchet, *Race, Sex and Class*, p. 8.
40. Jayawardena, *The White Woman's Other Burden*, p. 4; Anton Gill, *Ruling Passions: Sex, Race and Empire*, London: BBC Books, 1995, p. 98.
41. Margaret Strobel, *European Women and the Second British Empire*, Bloomington, IN: Indiana University Press, 1991, pp. 4–5.
42. Ibid.
43. Ibid.
44. Private Collection, Altof Papers, Bertha Cave to Altof, n.d. [c. 1912].
45. Judith Bourne, 'Cave [married name Altof], Bertha', in *Oxford Dictionary of National Biography*, https://www.oxforddnb.com/view/10.1093/odnb/9780198614128.001.0001/odnb-9780198614128-e-111931, last accessed 18 November 2022.
46. For example, when Helena Normanton applied to join the Honourable Society of the Middle Temple, one of the stated reasons for her rejection was Bertha Cave's failed appeal: Judith Bourne, *Helena Normanton and the Opening of the Bar to Women*, Hook: Waterside Press, 2016, p. 69.
47. For example, R. Blain Andrus, *Lawyer: A Brief 5,000-year History*, Chicago, IL: American Bar Association, 2009, p. 403, which mentions a newspaper report about Cave and her legal challenge.

48. Gisela Shaw and Ulrike Shultz, *Women in the World's Legal Professions*, London: Bloomsbury, 2003, p. 143; here, it is stated that Cave was wrongly admitted to Gray's Inn and then the mistake was rectified. However, there is no evidence in the Gray's Inn records to support this.

49. *Hall v Incorporated Society of Law-Agents* (1901), 3 F 1059. See also Alison Lindsay, "'This Fair Lady, in Her Laces": Margaret Howie Strang Hall, the First Woman in Scotland to Try to become a Lawyer', *Women's History Review*, vol. 29, no. 4 (2020), pp. 555–62.

50. Edward Walford, *The County Families of the United Kingdom; Or, Royal Manual of the Titled and Untitled Aristocracy of England, Wales, Scotland, and Ireland,* London: R. Hardwicke, 1860.

51. *The Times*, 12 November 1904, p. 15.

52. *The Times*, 10 May 1922, p. 7.

53. As recorded in the Gray's Inn Pension Records, 13 March 1903, p. 708.

54. Ibid.

55. A 'Master' is a 'Master of the Bench', more commonly referred to as a 'Bencher'. They were, and still are, responsible for the governance of the Inn. Masters are elected by their peers from the Inn's members who have been called to the Bar. The majority of the Inn's Benchers were King's Counsel (senior barristers or senior members of the judiciary).

56. Gray's Inn Pension Records 1903, pp. 718–20. The Pension Committee was a meeting that considered governance of the Inn and was made up of Masters of the Bench.

57. Gray's Inn Pension Records 1903, pp. 718–20.

58. Ibid., p. 720.

59. Ibid.

60. A transcript is held in the Middle Temple Archives, MT3/MEM.

61. Mary Jane Mossman, *The First Women Lawyers: A Comparative Study of Gender, Law and the Legal Professions*, Oxford: Hart, 2006.

62. See Martha May, *Women's Roles in Twentieth-Century America*, Westport, CT: Greenwood Press, 2009.

63. Christopher Moore, *The Law Society of Upper Canada and Ontario's Lawyers, 1797–1997,* Toronto: University of Toronto Press, 1997, p. 183.

64. Janet November, *In the Footsteps of Ethel Benjamin: New Zealand's First Woman Lawyer,* Wellington: Victoria University Press for the Law Foundation of New Zealand, 2009.

65. Mossman, *The First Women Lawyers,* p. 155.

66. Suparna Gooptu, *Cornelia Sorabji: India's Pioneer Woman Lawyer,* New Delhi: Oxford University Press, 2006.

67. A transcript is held in the Middle Temple Archives, MT3/MEM.
68. *Dundee Evening Post*, 4 December 1903, p. 6.
69. *Rugby Advertiser*, 26 January 1904, p. 2.
70. *Gloucestershire Echo*, 16 January 1904, p. 1.
71. See Leslie Howsam, 'Orme, Eliza (1848–1937)', in *Oxford Dictionary of National Biography*, https://www.oxforddnb.com/view/10.1093/ref:odnb/9780198614128.001.0001/odnb-9780198614128-e-37825, last accessed 18 November 2022; J. Collingwood, 'Rye, Maria Susan (1829–1903)', in *Oxford Dictionary of National Biography*, https://www.oxforddnb.com/view/10.1093/ref:odnb/9780198614128.001.0001/odnb-9780198614128-e-35896, last accessed 18 November 2022.
72. Abel, *The Making of the English Legal Profession*, p. 37.
73. Ibid.
74. See Eric J. Evans, *Parliamentary Reform in Britain, c.1770–1918*, Harlow: Longman, 2000; Ross McKibbin, *Parties and People: England 1914–1951*, Oxford: Oxford University Press, 2010.
75. Henry Pelling and Alastair J. Reid, *A Short History of the Labour Party*, Basingstoke: Macmillan, 1996.
76. William Joseph Whittaker (ed), *The Mirror of Justices*, London: B. Quaritch, 1895.
77. Ibid., p. 88.
78. *St. James's Gazette*, 15 November 1904, p. 14.
79. *The Daily News*, 8 April 1904, p. 5.
80. *The Croydon Guardian and Surrey County Gazette*, 23 January 1904, p. 5.
81. *The Sheffield Daily Telegraph*, 22 January 1904, p. 4; *St James's Gazette*, 21 January 1904, p. 10.
82. *The Daily News*, 24 December 1903, p. 12; Cave was reported as looking 'girlish'.
83. *St. James's Gazette*, 12 November 1904, p. 14.

7.   'FAIREST OF WOMEN'

1. H. H. The Dayang Muda of Sarawak, *Relations and Complications. Being the Recollections of H. H. The Dayang Muda of Sarawak*, London: John Lane, 1929.
2. Her Highness The Dayang Muda of Sarawak, 'Kubelik, my first love', *The People*, 11 September 1932, p. 5.
3. See Steven Runciman, *The White Rajahs: A History of Sarawak from 1841 to 1946*, Cambridge: Cambridge University Press, 1960;

Nigel Barley, *White Rajah: A Biography of Sir James Brooke*, London: Little, Brown, 2002.

4. The Ranee Margaret of Sarawak, *Good Morning and Good Night*, 1934; London: Century, 1984, p. 269. Three sons died in infancy.

5. Dayang Muda, 'Kubelik'.

6. Ibid.

7. *The Morning Post*, 29 June 1904, p. 7; Dayang Muda, 'Kubelik'.

8. Her Highness The Dayang Muda of Sarawak, 'The weeping empress', *The People*, 18 September 1932, p. 7.

9. Ibid.

10. *Cheshire Observer*, 29 November 1924, p. 11.

11. Her Highness The Dayang Muda of Sarawak, 'The enchanted village', *The People*, 25 September 1932, p. 7; Dayang Muda, *Relations*, p. 166.

12. Dayang Muda, 'The enchanted village'.

13. Her Highness The Dayang Muda of Sarawak, 'Money isn't everything', *The People*, 2 October 1932, p. 7.

14. *Gloucester Citizen*, 8 March 1922, p. 2.

15. Dayang Muda, 'Money'.

16. *The Straits Times* [hereafter *TST*], 3 August 1929, p. 12.

17. Her Highness The Dayang Muda of Sarawak, 'Sultan with a tin mug', *The People*, 16 October 1932, p. 7.

18. The successor of the Prophet Muhammad as the leader of the *umma*, the universal Muslim religious community.

19. For example, S. A. la Dayang Muda de Sarawak, 'Sarawak. Le pays des rajahs blancs', *La Géographie*, July/August (1928), pp. 1–16.

20. Robert McAlmon and Kay Boyle, *Being Geniuses Together, 1920–1930*, San Francisco: North Point Press, 1984, p. 187.

21. Sandra Spanier (ed), *Kay Boyle: A Twentieth-Century Life in Letters*, Urbana, IL: University of Illinois Press, 2015, p. 108.

22. McAlmon and Boyle, *Being Geniuses*, p. 219.

23. Ibid., pp. 257–8.

24. See ibid., pp. 273–4, 294–5.

25. John Glassco, *Memoirs of Montparnasse*, 1970; New York: New York Review of Books, 2007, p. 161.

26. Contrast, for example, reviews in *The Northern Whig and Belfast Post*, 20 July 1929, p. 11 and *Malaya Tribune*, 5 August 1929, p. 2.

27. The Brooke Heritage Trust Archive [hereafter BHTA], MPS83. b30.21, Transcript of Colonial Radio talk by Gladys Brooke, 27 March 1932; quoted in *Ballymena Weekly Telegraph*, 25 May 1929, p. 11.

28. BHTA, MPS83.b30.21, Colonial Radio transcript, 27 March 1932.

29. Dayang Muda, *Relations*, pp. 246–7.
30. Glassco, *Memoirs*, p. 167.
31. Ibid., p. 163.
32. *Ballymena Weekly Telegraph*, 25 May 1929, p. 11.
33. Ibid.; *TST*, 14 June 1929, p. 10.
34. See H. H. The Dayang Muda, 'My interview with the Pope', *TST*, 9 April 1930, p. 10.
35. *The Singapore Free Press* [hereafter *TSFP*], 27 April 1932, p. 7.
36. See Jamie Gilham, *Loyal Enemies: British Converts to Islam, 1850–1950*, London: Hurst, 2014, p. 13.
37. Her Highness The Dayang Muda of Sarawak, 'She didn't heed the gypsy's warning!', *The People*, 9 October 1932, p. 7.
38. *Malaya Tribune*, 14 November 1931, p. 3; Malayan Muslim, 'The Prophet's Tunic in Paris', *The Light* [hereafter *TL*], vol. 11, no. 5 (1932), pp. 1, 7.
39. An Islamic movement founded by Mirza Ghulam Ahmad (1835–1908) in 1889, regarded by some Muslims to be heretical and outside the fold of Islam. See Jamie Gilham, *The British Muslim Convert Lord Headley, 1855–1935*, London: Bloomsbury, 2020, pp. 61–2, 63–6.
40. Ibid., pp. 97–8.
41. In 1914, internal disagreement about the spiritual leadership of the Ahmadiyya Movement led to the creation of two rival Ahmadi groups: the 'Lahoris' and 'Qadianis'. See ibid., pp. 65–6.
42. Ibid., p. 155.
43. Ibid., p. 159; Gilham, *Loyal Enemies*, p. 201.
44. It is unlikely that Sheldrake gained a doctorate, though he might have been given an honorary one by an institution overseas.
45. Quoted in *Malaya Tribune*, 18 November 1932, p. 3.
46. Quoted in *TST*, 24 April 1932, p. 1.
47. Quoted in *The Muslim Review*, vol. 11, no. 2 (1932), frontispiece.
48. See photographs in *Daily Herald*, 19 February 1932, p. 4; *Birmingham Gazette*, 19 February 1932, p. 1; *The Illustrated London News*, 27 February 1932, p. 323.
49. Maulana Muhammad Ali's edition of 1917. See Khalid Sheldrake, 'The Flying Declaration of Islam', *TL*, vol. 11, no. 15 (1932), p. 2.
50. *TSFP*, 9 March 1932, p. 12.
51. Quoted in ibid.
52. Ibid.
53. *TST*, 24 April 1932, p. 1.
54. *TSFP*, 9 March 1932, p. 12.

55. Quoted in ibid.
56. Ibid.
57. Quoted in *The Northern Whig and Belfast Post*, 2 April 1932, p. 7.
58. *Daily Herald*, 20 February 1932, p. 9.
59. *The Auckland Star*, 9 April 1932, p. 3; *New York Times*, 20 February 1932, p. 17.
60. Quoted in *The Nottingham Journal*, 26 February 1932, p. 9.
61. Gilham, *The British Muslim*, p. 171.
62. Quoted in *The Nottingham Journal*, 26 February 1932, p. 9. South Shields had an established Muslim community comprising men from Yemen and Somaliland, some of whom settled and married local women. In fact, Gladys did not visit the Muslim communities in South Shields or elsewhere.
63. *Staffordshire Sentinel*, 19 February 1932, p. 7; *The [Dundee] Courier*, 24 March 1932, p. 4; *Edinburgh Evening News*, 19 February 1932, p. 10.
64. *TST*, 22 February 1932, p. 16.
65. *TSFP*, 9 March 1932, p. 12.
66. Repr. in *TL*, vol. 11, no. 16 (1932), p. 2.
67. Quoted in *TSFP*, 9 March 1932, p. 12.
68. BHTA, MPS83.b30.21, Colonial Radio transcript, 27 March 1932.
69. Ibid.
70. Ibid.
71. Ibid.
72. Ibid.
73. *TST*, 22 February 1932, p. 16; *The Sunderland Echo*, 24 March 1932, p. 9.
74. Quoted in *TSFP*, 9 March 1932, p. 12.
75. Quoted in *TST*, 1 May 1932, p. 1. Richard Halliburton (1900–39) was an American adventurer and author who circumnavigated the world in an open cockpit biplane between 1930 and 1932. He met Sylvia Brooke during the Borneo leg of the journey.
76. Quoted in *Belfast Telegraph*, 2 May 1932, p. 7.
77. *[Dundee] Evening Telegraph and Post*, 4 May 1932, p. 10.
78. *The Sunderland Echo*, 6 May 1932, p. 8.
79. *TSFP*, 17 May 1932, p. 6.
80. *Belfast Telegraph*, 2 May 1932, p. 7.
81. See Gilham, *The British Muslim*, pp. 148–9.
82. For example, *The Yorkshire Post*, 24 March 1932, p.10; *TL*, vol. 11, no. 15 (1932), pp. 1, 7.

83. Her Highness The Dayang Muda of Sarawak, 'Mayfair stoops to folly', *The People*, 6 November 1932, p. 9.

84. Her Highness The Dayang Muda of Sarawak, 'It's the truth', *The People*, 28 August 1932, p. 5.

85. Ibid.

86. Ibid.

87. Ibid.

88. Ibid.

89. Ibid.

90. BHTA, MPS83.b30.21, Colonial Radio transcript, 27 March 1932.

91. [Marmaduke Pickthall], 'A New Islamic Journal', *Islamic Culture*, vol. 6 (January 1932), pp. 156–7, quote at p. 156.

92. For example, H. H. Princess Dayang Muda Khair-un-Nisa Gladys Palmer of Sarawak, 'The Mission of Islam and the Church', *The Aligarh Magazine*, vol. 44, no. 2 (1934), pp. 147–50; Her Highness The Dayang Muda (Khair-ul-Nissa of Sarawak), 'Why I Embraced Islam', *The Muslim Review*, vol. 11, no. 5 (1932), pp. 23–30; H. H. Dayang Muda of Sarawak, 'Clergy or Freedom', *The Muslim Review*, vol. 14, no. 1 (1934), pp. 34–42.

93. Her Highness Khair-ul-Nissa, The Dayang Muda of Sarawak, 'A Message to the Malaya Muslims', *The Muslim Review*, vol. 11, no. 2 (1932), pp. 59–61.

94. *The Muslim Revival*, vol. 1, no. 1 (1932), front cover and pp. 76–7.

95. Her Highness Khairun Nisa, The Dayang Muda of Sarawak, 'The Sinister City', *TL*, vol. 11, no. 43 (1932), pp. 5–8; Khair-un-Nisa, 'Princess Sarawak on Islam', *TL*, vol. 12, no. 4–5 (1933), pp. 2, 15.

96. Habibullah Lovegrove, 'Prophet's Birthday in London', *TL*, vol. 12, no. 4–5 (1933), pp. 7–9. See also *The Islamic Review*, vol. 21, no. 3 (1933), pp. 85–7.

97. Conrad W. K. Simpson, 'To European Muslims', *TL*, vol. 12, no. 6 (1933), p. 3.

98. Khalid Sheldrake, 'Letter', *TL*, vol. 12, no. 8 (1933), p. 4.

99. BHTA, MPS83.b30.22, Conrad Simpson to Gladys Brooke, 7 March 1933. The Berlin Mosque and Mission was established by a former Woking imam in 1923–4.

100. BHTA, MPS83.b30.22, Simpson to Brooke, 7 March 1933.

101. Ibid.

102. Khair-un-Nissa of Sarawak, 'Princess Sarawak's Disclaimer', *TL*, vol. 12, no. 20–21 (1933), p. 11.

103. Ibid.

104. Khair-un-Nissa of Sarawak, 'Princess Sarawak's Disclaimer', *TL*, vol. 12, no. 27 (1933), p. 4. See also *TST*, 31 May 1933, p. 12.
105. Quoted in *TST*, 26 June 1932, p. 12.
106. Khalid Sheldrake, 'Dr Sheldrake's Letter', *TL*, vol. 12, no. 38 (1933), p. 7.
107. Dayang Muda of Sarawak, 'The Path of God', *Islamic Culture*, vol. 7 (October 1933), pp. 607–12.
108. Ibid., p. 609.
109. Khair ul-Nisa Sarawak, 'The Unity of God', *Islamic Culture*, vol. 10 (October 1936), pp. 505–20.
110. Quoted in *TST*, 3 January 1937, p. 5.
111. See Gilham, *Loyal Enemies*, Ch. 5.
112. *Sunday Tribune* [Singapore], 9 February 1947, p. 4.
113. See, for example, BHTA, MPS83.b31.1.56/.38/.41, Anthony Brooke to Gladys Brooke, 12 October 1945, 1 February 1946, 9 April 1946.
114. BHTA, MPS83.b34.3.11, Gladys Brooke to Datu Patinggi Abang Haji Abdillah, 27 May 1946.
115. See *TSFP*, 20 May 1948, p. 8; *TST*, 7 November 1948, p. 3.
116. *TST*, 13 June 1952, p. 1.
117. District Probate Registry (England and Wales), Will and Testament of Gladys Milton Brooke, 10 February 1952.
118. *The Coventry Evening Telegraph*, 12 June 1952, p. 1; *Sussex Express*, 21 May 1954, p. 8.
119. District Probate Registry, Will and Testament of Gladys Brooke.
120. *Daily Herald*, 5 October 1954, p. 4.

8. 'WE WERE NOT ANYTHING LIKE WHAT THEY IMAGINED!'

1. A typewritten transcript of Safia Jabir Ali's speech, labelled 'Address by Mrs Safia Jabir Ali', was consulted by the authors in the private collection of her son, Amiruddin Jabir Ali, in Mumbai. Most of it is reproduced with an introduction in Siobhan Lambert-Hurley, Daniel Majchrowicz and Sunil Sharma (eds), *Three Centuries of Travel Writing by Muslim Women*, Bloomington, IN: Indiana University Press, 2022, pp. 441–50. Additional extracts are available at: https://accessingmuslimlives.org/travel/address/, last accessed 7 April 2022.
2. For a more expansive introduction to Muslim women in cultures of travel, see Siobhan Lambert-Hurley and Daniel Majchrowicz, 'Introduction: Muslim Women, Travel Writing and Global Mobility', in Lambert-Hurley *et al.*, *Three Centuries*, pp. 15–27.

3. On the emergence of travel writing by Muslim women in Urdu, see Daniel Majchrowicz, 'Malika Begum's mehfil: Retrieving the Lost Legacy of Women's Travel Writing in Urdu', *South Asia: Journal of South Asian Studies*, vol. 43, no. 5 (2020), pp. 860–78.

4. Daniel Majchrowicz, *The World in Words: Travel Writing and the Global Imagination in Muslim South Asia*, forthcoming.

5. Siobhan Lambert-Hurley (ed), *A Princess's Pilgrimage: Nawab Sikandar Begum's A Pilgrimage to Mecca*, Bloomington, IN: Indiana University Press, 2008.

6. For examples, see part I on 'Travel as Pilgrimage' in Lambert-Hurley *et al.*, *Three Centuries*.

7. Siobhan Lambert-Hurley, *Elusive Lives: Gender, Autobiography and the Self in Muslim South Asia*, Redwood City, CA: Stanford University Press, 2018, pp. 59–60.

8. There is a voluminous literature on Muslim socio-religious reform movements. A useful overview explicit to women is Barbara Metcalf, 'Reading and Writing about Muslim Women in British India' in her *Islamic Contestations: Essays on Muslims in India and Pakistan*, Delhi: Oxford University Press, 2004, pp. 99–119.

9. Other themes are addressed elsewhere in our scholarship. For instance, women's preoccupation with food is examined in Siobhan Lambert-Hurley, '"Human or Not, Everyone has their Own Habits and Tastes": Food, Identity and Difference in Muslim South Asia', *Global Food History*, forthcoming.

10. On his career, see Aparna Basu, *Abbas Tyabji*, Delhi: National Book Trust, 2007.

11. Prince. Nawab also refers to a Muslim nobleman or regional governor.

12. H. H. Nazli Rafia Sultan Nawab Begum Sahiba of the State of Jazira, *Sair-i Yurop*, Lahore: Union Steam Press, n.d. [c. 1909], entry for 25 April 1908.

13. Providing an account of the first journey is Maimoona Sultan, Shah Bano Begum, *Siyahat-i-Sultani*, Agra: Muhammad Qadir 'Ali Khan, 1913.

14. See Sughra Humayun Mirza, *Safarnamah-i Yurap*, Hyderabad: A'zam Stim Press, 1926.

15. Begum In'am Habibullah, *Ta'ssurat-i Safar-i Yurup*, Lucknow: n.publ., 1937.

16. Begum Nawab Sarbuland Jang, *Duniya 'Aurat ki Nazar Men: Mashriq o Maghrib ka Safarnama*. Delhi: Khwaja Buk Dipo, Khwaja Barqi Press, n.d. [1934], pp. 168–80.

17. Iqbalunnisa Hussain, *Changing India: A Moslem Woman Speaks*, Bangalore: Hosali, 1940, p. 157.

18. Atiya Fyzee, *Zamana-i Tahsil*, Agra: Mufid-i 'Am, 1921, entries for 18 September and 10 October 1906.

19. Qaisari Begum, *Kitab-i Zindagi*, ed. Zehra Masroor Ahmad, Karachi: Fazli Sanz, 2003, p. 465.

20. Muhammadi Begum, 'Personal Diary for the Year 1935', entry for 17 February 1935. The original copy of this diary is in the private collection of her daughter, Zehra Masroor Ahmad.

21. Muhammadi Begum's autograph book is in the private collection of her daughter, Zehra Masroor Ahmad.

22. Muhammadi Begum, 'Personal Diary for the Year 1935', entry for 17 February 1935.

23. Ibid., entry for 4 September 1935.

24. Ibid., entries for 4–5 September 1935. A translation of these entries is available at: https://accessingmuslimlives.org/women/personal-diary-1935/, last accessed 14 October 2022.

25. Maimoona Sultan Shah Bano Begum, *Siyahat-i-Sultani*, Agra: Muhammad Qadir 'Ali Khan, 1913, trans. by Mrs G. Baksh as *A Trip to Europe*, Calcutta: Thacker, Spink and Company, 1914, quotation at p. 66.

26. Abida Sultaan, *Memoirs of a Rebel Princess*, Karachi: Oxford University Press, 2004, p. 52.

27. Image reproduced in Siobhan Lambert-Hurley, *Muslim Women, Reform and Princely Patronage: Nawab Sultan Jahan Begam of Bhopal*, London: Routledge, 2007, p. 179.

28. Amina Tyabji's speech to Akdé Suraya, handwritten in Urdu for presentation on 22 August 1894, in the private collection of Rafia Abdul Ali, Mumbai.

29. Atiya Fyzee, *Zamana-i Tahsil*, entry for 10 November 1906, translated in Lambert-Hurley *et al.*, *Three Centuries*, p. 299.

30. Siobhan Lambert-Hurley and Sunil Sharma, *Atiya's Journeys: A Muslim Woman from Colonial Bombay to Edwardian Britain*, Delhi: Oxford University Press, 2010, p. 164.

31. Ibid., p. 125.

32. Nazli, *Sair-i Yurop,* pp. 57–8.

33. Lambert-Hurley *et al.*, *Three Centuries*, p. 324.

34. Muhammadi Begum, *A Long Way from Hyderabad: Diary of a Young Muslim Woman in 1930s Britain*, ed. Kulsoom Husein, trans. Zehra Ahmad and Zainab Masud, Delhi: Primus Books, 2022, p. 26.

35. Khaliq Anjum, *Qazi 'Abdul Ghaffar, Ek Mumtaz Nasr-nigar,* New Delhi: Anjuman-i Taraqqi-i Urdu (Hind), 1996, p. 28.

36. Daniel Majchrowicz, 'Ideological Voyages: Nationalism, Colonialism, and Identity in the Works of Qazi 'Abdul Gaffar', in Roberta Micallef and Sunil Sharma (eds), *On the Wonders of Land and Sea,* Boston: Ilex Foundation, 2013, p. 147.

37. Partha Chatterjee, *The Nation and Its Fragments: Colonial and Postcolonial Histories,* Princeton, NJ: Princeton University Press, 1993, pp. 116–57. Useful for gaining this comparative perspective is Sanjay Seth's 'Nationalism, Modernity and the "Woman Question" in India and China', *Journal of Asian Studies,* vol. 72, no. 2 (2013), pp. 273–97.

38. Muhammadi Begum, *A Long Way,* p. 129.

39. Ibid., p. 130.

40. Lambert-Hurley *et al.,* *Three Centuries,* p. 300.

41. Ibid., p. 299.

42. Lambert-Hurley and Sharma, *Atiya's Journeys,* p. 151.

43. Muhammadi Begum, *A Long Way,* p. 34.

44. Ibid., p. 181.

45. Lambert-Hurley *et al.,* *Three Centuries,* p. 301.

46. Ibid., p. 351. *Karchobi* is elaborate embroidery of silver thread on silk, pointing to the fact that the sari mentioned here was that worn by Muhammadi Begum at her wedding. A *kurta* is a tunic-style shirt or dress worn by women, while a *shervani* is a long-sleeved coat with a stand-up collar that was adopted by Indian men as formal dress in the nineteenth century.

47. Lambert-Hurley *et al.,* *Three Centuries,* p. 351.

48. Ibid.

49. Ibid., p. 299.

50. Ibid., p. 448.

51. Begum Nawab Sarbuland Jang, *Duniya,* p. 4.

52. Begum In'am Habibullah, *Ta'surat,* p. 70.

53. On the challenge of maintaining a home and family in Britain with fewer or no servants, see Shaista Suhrawardy Ikramullah, 'Inglistan meñ naukaron ke halat', *'Ismat* (Delhi), vol. 59, no. 5 (1937), pp. 355–8, trans. in Lambert-Hurley *et al.,* *Three Centuries,* pp. 471–80.

54. Muhammadi Begum, *A Long Way,* 128.

55. Lambert-Hurley *et al.,* *Three Centuries,* p. 326.

56. Begum In'am Habibullah, *Ta'surat,* p. 70.

57. Muhammadi Begum, *A Long Way,* p. 59.

58. Begum In'am Habibullah, *Ta'surat*, p. 73.
59. Muhammadi Begum, *A Long Way*, p. 106.
60. Ibid., p. 35.
61. For a development of this theme, see Lambert-Hurley and Sharma, *Atiya's Journeys*, p. 91.
62. Leela Gandhi, *Affective Communities: Anticolonial Thought, Fin-de-Siècle Radicalism, and the Politics of Friendship,* Durham, NC: Duke University Press, 2006.
63. See Shompa Lahiri, *Indians in Britain: Anglo-Indian Encounters, Race and Identity, 1880–1930*, London: Frank Cass, 2000, pp. 72–6; A. Martin Wainwright, *'The Better Class' of Indians: Social Rank, Imperial Identity, and South Asians in Britain*, Manchester: Manchester University Press, 2012, Ch. 8.
64. 'Address by Mrs Safia Jabir Ali', reprinted in Lambert-Hurley *et al.*, *Three Centuries*, p. 448.
65. Begum In'am Habibullah, *Ta'surat*, p. 79.
66. Muhammadi Begum, *A Long Way*, p. 114.
67. 'English Translation of a Speech Delivered by Her Highness in the Ladies' Club, Bhopal, When Leaving India for Europe' in Anon, *A Brief Decennial Report of 'The Princess of Wales Ladies' Club, Bhopal*, Calcutta: Thacker, Spink and Company, 1922, pp. 81–4.
68. This transition is discussed in Siobhan Lambert-Hurley, 'Out of India: The Journeys of the Begam of Bhopal, 1901–1930', *Women's Studies' International Forum*, vol. 21, no. 3 (1998), pp. 263–76.
69. Maimoona Sultan, *A Trip to Europe*, p. 114.
70. Begum Sarbuland Jang, *Duniya*, p. 8.

9. NOOR INAYAT KHAN

1. Jean Overton-Fuller, *Madeleine: The Story of Noor Inayat Khan*, London: Victor Gollancz, 1952.
2. Shrabani Basu, *Spy Princess*, Stroud: The History Press, 2006. See also Arthur Magida, *Code Name Madeleine*, New York: W. W. Norton and Company, 2020.
3. See, for instance, the website of the Armed Forces Muslim Association, https://afma.org.uk/2018/03/08/true-british-muslim-heroine-noor-inayat-khan/, last accessed 11 June 2022.
4. This memory particularly stands out in Shaikh-ul-Mashaik Mahmood khan's mind: 'When [Noor] came to Holland staying with the Tuylls and visiting us on several occasions, our father, well aware of her proficiency in music and her interest in teaching the young, asked her

to give me some piano lessons. So she started with Mozart's Sonate Facile — not that facile for an innocent beginner. To smoothen my entry into that rich selection of novel notes, she began explaining the melodic and rhythmic course with an interpretation of rabbits frolicking all over those delicious notes/nuts, eventually resting a bit from their exertions in the second andante part in melodic peacefulness.' Personal correspondence with the author, 27 August 2022. The correspondence cited here and throughout this chapter was conducted with the author by email.

5. I follow here, at his suggestion, Shaikh-ul-Mashaik Mahmood khan's convention of rendering 'khan' in lowercase to emphasize its character as a hereditary title rather than a surname. An exception is made in the case of the subject of the chapter, who is widely known, in the media and in biographical works, as 'Noor Inayat Khan'.

6. Shaikh-ul-Mashaik Mahmood khan, personal correspondence, 14 June 2022.

7. For example, in the title of her retrospective obituary in *The New York Times*: Amie Tsang, 'Overlooked No More: Noor Inayat Khan, Indian Princess and British Spy', *The New York Times*, 28 November 2018, https://www.nytimes.com/2018/11/28/obituaries/noor-inayat-khan-overlooked.html, last accessed 11 June 2022.

8. Fuller, *Madeleine*, pp. 11–18; Basu, *Spy Princess*, p. 1; Magida, *Code Name Madeleine*, p. 13.

9. Shaikh-ul-Mashaik Mahmood khan, personal correspondence, 15 June 2022.

10. On Inayat khan's life, see Elisabeth de Jong Keesing, *Inayat Khan*, London and The Hague: Luzac and Company and East-West Publications, 1974; Elise Guillaume-Schamhart and Munira van Voorst van Beest (eds), *Biography of Pir-o-Murshid Inayat Khan*, London and The Hague: East-West Publications, 1979; Pirzade Zia Inayat Khan, *A Pearl in Wine: Essays on the Life, Music and Sufism of Hazrat Inayat Khan*, New Lebanon, NY: Omega Publications, 2001.

11. A follower of Sufism, or Islamic mysticism.

12. Or 'Saiyid', 'Syed'; a signifier of eminence used by Muslims who are descendants of the Prophet Muhammad; also, a title to denote a prince, lord or chief in Arab societies.

13. Gerry Farrell, *Indian Music and the West*, Oxford: Oxford University Press, 1997, pp. 147–55.

14. Shaikh-ul-Mashaik Mahmood khan, personal correspondence, 14 June 2022.

15. Noor Inayat Khan, *Aède of the Ocean and Land: A Play in Seven Acts*, Richmond, VA: Suluk Press, 2018.

16. Noor Inayat Khan, *King Akbar's Daughter: Stories for Everyone*, New Lebanon, NY: Omega Publications, 2012, pp. 226–7.

17. Claire Ray Harper, *We Rubies Four: The Memoirs of Claire Ray Harper (Khairunnisa Inayat Khan)*, New Lebanon, NY: Omega Publications, 2011, p. 137.

18. Unpublished MS in the collection of David Ray Harper. Noor underwent six months of telegraphy training in Edinburgh in 1941.

19. Unpublished MS in the collection of David Ray Harper.

20. Fuller, *Madeleine*, p. 50.

21. Noor Inayat Khan, *Dream Flowers: The Collected Works of Noor Inayat Khan*, Richmond, VA: Suluk Press, 2020.

22. Shaikh-ul-Mashaik Mahmood khan, personal correspondence, 15 June 2022.

23. Guillaume-Schamhart and Van Voorst van Beest, *Biography*, p. 180.

24. Fuller, *Madeleine*, pp. 118–9.

25. Shaikh-ul-Mashaik Mahmood khan, personal correspondence, 14 June 2022.

26. Fazlur Rahman, *Islam*, London: Weidenfeld and Nicolson, 1966, pp. 123–7.

27. Shahab Ahmed, *What is Islam? The Importance of Being Islamic*, Princeton, NJ: Princeton University Press, 2017, p. 31.

28. Shihab ad-Din Yahya Suhrawardi, *The Philosophy of Illumination*, trans. John Walbridge and Hossein Ziai, Provo, UT: Brigham Young University, 1999, p. 1.

29. Inayat Khan, *The Sufi Message of Hazrat Inayat Khan*, vol. 1, London: Barrie and Jenkins, 1960, p. 56.

30. Khaliq Ahmad Nizami, *The Life and Times of Shaikh Nizamuddin Auliya*, Delhi: Idarah-i Adabiyat, 1991, p. 125.

31. Makhdum Sharaf ad-Din Ahmad Yahya Manayri, *Maktubat-i sadi*, Patna: Khuda Bakhsh Oriental Public Library, 1994, p. 142.

32. See Roderic Vassie, 'Persian Interpretations of the Bhagavadgita in the Mughal Period: With Special Reference to the Sufi Version of 'Abd al-Rahman Chishti', PhD Diss., University of London, 1988.

33. See Thomas Dahnhardt, *Change and Continuity in Indian Sufism: A Naqshbandi-Mujaddidi Branch in the Hindu Environment*, Delhi: D. K. Printworld, 2007.

34. Khwaja Hasan Nizami, *Hindu mazhab ki ma'lumat*, Delhi: Halqa-yi Masha'ikh, 1927, p. 6.

35. Fuller, *Madeleine*, p. 60. Noor also composed an undated and unfinished vignette on the birth of the Prophet Muhammad, as yet unpublished.

36. A division, or chapter, of the Qur'an.

37. Inayat Khan, *The Sufi Message of Hazrat Inayat Khan*, vol. 5, London: Barrie and Rockliff, 1962, p. 20.

38. A lecture on the symbolism of *The Conference of the Birds* may be found in Munira van Voorst van Beest (ed), *Complete Works of Pir-o-Murshid Inayat Khan, Original Texts: Lectures on Sufism, 1923 I: January-June*, The Hague: East-West Publications, 1989, pp. 206–13.

39. For a detailed analysis, see Noor Inayat Khan, *Dream Flowers*, pp. 62–81.

40. Women's contributions to Sufism are explored in Margaret Smith, *Rabi'a the Mystic and Her Fellow Saints in Islam*, London: Cambridge University Press, 1928; Camille Adams Helminski, *Women of Sufism: A Hidden Treasure*, Boston, MA and London: Shambhala Publications, 2003; 'A'ishah al-Ba'uniyyah, *The Principles of Sufism*, trans. Th. Emil Homerin, New York: New York University Press, 2016; Rkia Elaroui Cornell, *Rabi'a from Narrative to Myth*, London: Oneworld Academic, 2019.

41. Guillaume-Schamhart and Van Voorst van Beest, *Biography*, p. 243.

42. Basu, *Spy Princess*, p. 195.

43. Ibid., p. 182.

44. Quoted in ibid., p. 179; Magida, *Code Name Madeleine*, p. 232.

45. Basu, *Spy Princess*, pp. 149–50.

46. Ibid., p. 159.

47. Ibid., pp. 160, 169–70, 189–91.

48. Thomas Carlyle, *On Heroes, Hero-worship, and the Heroic in History*, new edn, Oxford: Oxford University Press, 1946, p. 202.

49. Lara R. Curtis, *Writing Resistance and the Question of Gender: Charlotte Delbo, Noor Inayat Khan, and Germaine Tillion*, Cham, Switzerland: Palgrave Macmillan, 2019.

50. A survey of this kind is made in my introduction to Noor Inayat Khan, *Dream Flowers*.

51. Ibid., pp. 218–9.

52. Shaikh-ul-Mashaik Mahmood khan, personal correspondence, 20 June 2022.

53. Christa Kamenetsky, *Children's Literature in Hitler's Germany: The Cultural Policy of National Socialism*, Athens, OH: Ohio University Press, 1984.

54. Fuller, *Madeleine*, p. 111.

55. Reiko Ohnuma, *Head, Eyes, Flesh, and Blood: Giving Away the Body in Indian Buddhist Literature*, New York: Columbia University Press, 2007, pp. 266–7.

56. Curtis, *Writing Resistance*, p. 75.

57. Inayat Khan, *The Bowl of Saki*, Geneva: The Sufi Headquarters Publishing Society, 1936, p. 16.

58. Noor Inayat Khan, *Dream Flowers*, pp. 109–15.

59. Noor Inayat Khan, *King Akbar's Daughter*, pp. xvii–xviii.

60. Lee R. Edwards, 'The Labors of Psyche: Toward a Theory of Female Heroism', *Critical Inquiry*, vol. 6, no. 1 (1979), p. 33.

61. Carlyle, *On Heroes*, pp. 319–20.

AFTERWORD

1. Boris Johnson, 'Denmark has got it wrong. Yes, the burka is oppressive and ridiculous—but that's still no reason to ban it', *The Telegraph*, 5 August 2018, https://www.telegraph.co.uk/news/2018/08/05/denmark-has-got-wrong-yes-burka-oppressive-ridiculous-still/, last accessed 11 December 2022. A *burqa* is an enveloping outer garment worn by some Muslim women to cover their body and face.

2. Rowena Mason and Harriet Sherwood, 'Cameron "stigmatising Muslim women" with English language policy', *The Guardian*, 18 January 2016, https://www.theguardian.com/politics/2016/jan/18/david-cameron-stigmatising-muslim-women-learn-english-language-policy, last accessed 6 January 2023.

SELECT BIBLIOGRAPHY

Abd-Allah, Umar, *A Muslim in Victorian America: The Life of Alexander Russell Webb*, Oxford: Oxford University Press, 2006.

Abel, Richard L., *The Making of the English Legal Profession, 1800–1988*, Washington, DC: Beard Books, 1998.

Ahmed, Leila, *Women and Gender in Islam: Historical Roots of a Modern Debate*. New Haven, CT: Yale University Press, 1992.

Ansari, Humayun, '*The Infidel Within': Muslims in Britain since 1800*, London: Hurst, 2004, 2018.

Asmay, Yusuf Samih, *Islam in Victorian Liverpool: An Ottoman Account of Britain's First Mosque Community*, trans., ed. and introduction by Yahya Birt, Riordan Macnamara and Münire Zeyneb Maksudoğlu, Swansea: Claritas Books, 2021.

Aydin, Cemil, *The Idea of the Muslim World: A Global Intellectual History*, Cambridge, MA, Harvard University Press, 2017.

Ballhatchet, Kenneth, *Race, Sex and Class Under the Raj: Imperial Attitudes and Policies and Their Critics, 1793–1905,* London: Weidenfeld and Nicolson, 1980.

Basu, Shrabani, *Spy Princess*, Stroud: The History Press, 2006.

Caballero, Chamion and Peter J. Aspinall, *Mixed Race Britain in The Twentieth Century,* Basingstoke: Palgrave Macmillan, 2018.

Cates, Fatima E., 'How I Became a Mahommedan', *The Allahabad Review*, 11 September 1891, p. 142.

Cheruvallil-Contractor, Sariya, 'Women in Britain's First Muslim Mosques: Hidden from History, but not Without Influence', *Religions*, vol. 11, no. 2 (2020), pp. 1–12.

Cobbold, Lady Evelyn, *Pilgrimage to Mecca*, London: John Murray, 1934.

SELECT BIBLIOGRAPHY

The Dayang Muda of Sarawak, Her Highness, *Relations and Complications. Being the Recollections of H. H. The Dayang Muda of Sarawak*, London: John Lane, 1929.

The Dayang Muda of Sarawak, Her Highness, 'Why I embraced Islam', *The Muslim Review*, vol. 11, no. 5 (1932), pp. 23–30.

Gandhi, Leela, *Affective Communities: Anticolonial Thought, Fin-de-Siècle Radicalism, and the Politics of Friendship,* Durham, NC: Duke University Press, 2006.

Geaves, Ron, *Islam and Britain: Muslim Mission in an Age of Empire,* London: Bloomsbury, 2018.

Geaves, Ron, *Islam in Victorian Britain: The Life and Times of Abdullah Quilliam*, Markfield: Kube, 2010.

Gilham, Jamie, *The British Muslim Convert Lord Headley, 1855–1935*, London: Bloomsbury, 2020.

Gilham, Jamie, *Loyal Enemies: British Converts to Islam, 1850–1950*, London and New York: Hurst and Oxford University Press, 2014.

Gilham, Jamie and Ron Geaves (eds), *Victorian Muslim: Abdullah Quilliam and Islam in the West*, London and New York: Hurst and Oxford University Press, 2017.

Gilliat-Ray, Sophie and Jody Mellor, 'Bilād al-Welsh (Land of the Welsh): Muslims in Cardiff, South Wales: Past, Present and Future', *The Muslim World*, vol. 100, no. 4 (2010), pp. 452–75.

Guillaume-Schamhart, Elise and Munira van Voorst van Beest (eds), *Biography of Pir-o-Murshid Inayat Khan*, London and The Hague: East-West Publications, 1979.

Halliday, Fred, *Arabs in Exile: Yemeni Migrants in Urban Britain*, London: I. B. Tauris, 1992.

Horstman, Allen, *Victorian Divorce*, New York: St Martin's Press, 1985.

Hyam, Ronald, *Empire and Sexuality: The British Experience,* Manchester: Manchester University Press, 2017.

Inayat Khan, Noor, *Dream Flowers: The Collected Works of Noor Inayat Khan*, Richmond, VA: Suluk Press, 2020.

Inayat Khan, Noor, *King Akbar's Daughter: Stories for Everyone*, New Lebanon, NY: Omega Publications, 2012, pp. 226–27.

Khan, Shaharyar M, *The Begums of Bhopal: A Dynasty of Women Rulers in Raj India*, London: I. B. Tauris, 2000.

Lahiri, Shompa, *Indians in Britain: Anglo-Indian Encounters, Race and Identity, 1880–1930*, London: Frank Cass, 2000.

Lambert-Hurley, Siobhan, 'Out of India: The Journeys of the Begam of Bhopal, 1901–1930' in Tony Ballantyne and Antoinette Burton (eds), *Bodies in Contact: Rethinking Colonial Encounters in World History*, Durham NC: Duke University Press, 2005.

Lambert-Hurley, Siobhan, *Elusive Lives: Gender, Autobiography, and the Self in Muslim South Asia*, Redwood City, CA: Stanford University Press, 2018.

Lambert-Hurley, Siobhan, *Muslim Women, Reform and Princely Patronage: Nawab Sultan Jahan Begam of Bhopal*, London: Routledge, 2007.

Lambert-Hurley, Siobhan and Sunil Sharma, *Atiya's Journeys: A Muslim Woman from Colonial Bombay to Edwardian Britain*, Delhi: Oxford University Press, 2010.

Lambert-Hurley, Siobhan, Daniel Majchrowicz and Sunil Sharma (eds), *Three Centuries of Travel Writing by Muslim Women*, Bloomington: Indiana University Press, 2022.

Magida, Arthur, *Code Name Madeleine*, New York: W.W. Norton and Company, 2020.

Majchrowicz, Daniel, 'Malika Begum's Mehfil: Retrieving the Lost Legacy of Women's Travel Writing in Urdu', *South Asia: Journal of South Asian Studies*, vol. 43, no. 5 (2020), pp. 860–78.

Mernissi, Fatima. *The Veil and the Male Elite: A Feminist Interpretation of Women's Rights in Islam*, Cambridge MA: Perseus, 1991.

Monro, James. *Moslems in Liverpool*, Calcutta: Methodist Publishing House, 1901.

Muhammadi Begum, *A Long Way from Hyderabad: Diary of a Young Muslim Woman in 1930s Britain*, ed. Kulsoom Husein, trans. Zehra Ahmad and Zainab Masud, Delhi: Primus Books, 2022.

Overton-Fuller, Jean, *Madeleine: The Story of Noor Inayat Khan*, London: Victor Gollancz, 1952.

Perraton, Hilary, *A History of Foreign Students in Britain*, Basingstoke: Palgrave Macmillan, 2014.

Purvis, June, 'Using Primary Sources When Researching Women's History from a Feminist Perspective', *Women's History Review*, vol. 1, no. 2 (1992), pp. 273–306.

Purvis, June (ed), *Women's History: Britain, 1850–1945. An Introduction*, Abingdon: Routledge, 1995.

Rahman, Fazlur, *Islam*, London: Weidenfeld and Nicolson, 1966.

Robinson-Dunn, Diane, *The Harem, Slavery, and British Imperial Culture: Anglo-Muslim Relations in the Late Nineteenth Century*, Manchester: Manchester University Press, 2006.

Seddon, Mohammad Siddique, *The Last of the Lascars: Yemeni Muslims in Britain, 1836–2012*, Markfield: Kube, 2014.

Sharp, Matthew A., '"On Behalf of the Sultan": The Late Ottoman State and the Cultivation of British and American Converts to Islam', PhD Diss., University of Pennsylvania, 2020.

Singleton, Brent D., 'Brothers at odds: Rival Islamic movements in late nineteenth century New York City', *Journal of Muslim Minority Affairs*, vol. 27, no. 3 (2007), pp. 473–86.

Sultan Jahan, *An Account of My Life (Gohur-I-Ikbal)*, translated by C.H. Payne, London: John Murray, 1912.

Sultan Jahan, *The Story of a Pilgrimage to Hijaz*, Calcutta: Thacker and Sprink, 1909.

Vicinus, Martha (ed), *A Widening Sphere: Changing Roles of Victorian Women*, first pub. 1977, New York: Routledge, 2013.

Wainwright, A. Martin, *'The Better Class' of Indians: Social Rank, Imperial Identity, and South Asians in Britain*, Manchester: Manchester University Press, 2012.

Winrow, Gareth, *Whispers Across Continents: In Search of the Robinsons*, Stroud: Amberley, 2019.

Oral History Interviews

National Archive of Wales, MD789, Interview with Olive Salaman by Monique Ennis, 2006.

National Archive of Wales, MD790, Group interview with Olive Salaman, Selwyn Roddren, Betty Campbell, Monique Ennis and Sian Roddren, Undated (c.2000s).

National Archive of Wales, MD808, Interview with Olive Salaman and Betty Campbell by Selwyn Roddren and Monique Ennis, 2004.

NOTES ON CONTRIBUTORS

Editors

Sariya Cheruvallil-Contractor (PhD) is Professor in the Sociology of Islam at the Centre for Trust, Peace and Social Relations, Coventry University, UK. She is Chair of the Muslims in Britain Research Network. As a feminist sociologist of religion, she interrogates the power dynamics and societal hierarchies that determine how knowledge is produced and disseminated. She is author of several publications including *Muslim Women in Britain: Demystifying the Muslimah* (2012). In 2016–18, the British Academy and Leverhulme Trust funded her to lead the first exploration of the roles of women in Britain's earliest mosques.

Jamie Gilham (PhD) is an independent historian and biographer based in the UK and Taiwan. A Fellow of the Royal Historical Society (UK), his research focuses on the history of Islam and Muslims in Britain and Western travellers to the Middle East. He is the author of books including *Loyal Enemies: British Converts to Islam, 1850–1950* (2014) and *The British Muslim Convert Lord Headley, 1855–1935* (2020). He is co-editor of *Victorian Muslim: Abdullah Quilliam and Islam in the West* (2017) and editor of *Islam and Muslims in Victorian Britain: New Perspectives* (2023).

Contributors

Judith Bourne (PhD) is Professor of Law at St Mary's University, Twickenham, UK. Her research focuses on feminist law, first women lawyers, and race and the law. Her publications include *Helena Normanton and the Opening of the Bar to Women* (2016) and, with Caroline Derry, *Gender and the Law* (2018).

Pir Zia Inayat Khan (PhD) is an independent scholar in the US. He is also the Sufi lineage-bearer (*sajjada-nishin*) of his grandfather and Noor Inayat Khan's father, Hazrat Inayat Khan. He received his PhD in religion from Duke University and has written extensively about Sufism and the life and work of Hazrat Inayat Khan and Noor Inayat Khan. His publications include *Saracen Chivalry: Counsels on Valor, Generosity and the Mystical Quest* (2012), *Mingled Waters: Sufism and the Mystical Unity of Religions* (2017) and *Immortality* (2023). He is also the editor of *Dream Flowers: The Collected Works of Noor Inayat Khan* (2020).

Siobhan Lambert-Hurley (PhD) is Professor of Global History at the University of Sheffield, UK. A cultural historian of modern South Asia with particular interests in women, gender and Islam, she is co-editor of *Rhetoric and Reality: Gender and the Colonial Experience in South Asia* (2006), *Atiya's Journeys: A Muslim Woman from Colonial Bombay to Edwardian Britain* (2010) and *Three Centuries of Travel Writing by Muslim Women* (2022). She is the author of books including *Muslim Women, Reform and Princely Patronage: Nawab Sultan Jahan Begam of Bhopal* (2007) and *Elusive Lives: Gender, Autobiography and the Self in Muslim South Asia* (2018).

Hamid Mahmood is the founder of Fatima Elizabeth Phrontistery, an Islamic supplementary school (*madrasa*) in London. A teacher by profession, he is interested in the history of Islam and the West and is the co-author of a booklet about the Victorian British Muslim convert Fatima Cates entitled *Our Fatima of Liverpool: The Story of Fatima Cates* (2023).

NOTES ON CONTRIBUTORS

Daniel Majchrowicz (PhD) is Assistant Professor of South Asian Literature and Culture at Northwestern University, USA. His research considers the history and culture of Muslims and Islam in South Asia with an emphasis on Urdu literature, travel writing, popular culture and language politics. He is the co-editor of *Three Centuries of Travel Writing by Muslim Women* (2022) and author of the introduction to a new edition of Muhammadi Begum's diaries, *A Long Way from Hyderabad: Diary of a Young Muslim Woman in 1930s Britain* (2022).

Diane Robinson-Dunn (PhD) is Associate Professor in the History Department at the University of Detroit Mercy, USA and is a Fellow of the Royal Historical Society (UK) and a member of le Groupe de recherche Achac (France). She specializes in the creation of culture, or systems of meaning, in the context of fluctuating imperial and national borders from northern Europe to the South Asian subcontinent in the late nineteenth and early twentieth centuries. Her publications include *The Harem, Slavery and British Imperial Culture: Anglo-Muslim Relations in the Late Nineteenth Century* (2006, 2014).

Matthew A. Sharp (PhD) is an independent scholar in the US. He has a PhD in Near Eastern Languages and Civilizations with concentrations in Arabic and Islamic studies as well as Middle Eastern Literatures and Societies from the University of Pennsylvania. His work explores the exchanges and relationships between British and American converts to Islam and Ottoman state officials and Arab and Turkish Muslim intellectuals in the late nineteenth and early twentieth centuries.

Gareth Winrow (PhD) is a writer and independent researcher in the UK. He previously worked in Turkey for twenty years as Professor in the Department of International Relations, Istanbul Bilgi University. He has published extensively on Turkish foreign policy and on energy and security issues, and serves on the editorial board of the journal *Turkish Studies*. His books include *The Kurdish Question and Turkey: An Example of a Trans-State Ethnic Conflict* (with

Kemal Kirisci, 1997), *Dialogue with the Mediterranean: The Role of NATO's Mediterranean Initiative* (2000) and *Whispers Across Continents: In Search of the Robinsons* (2019).

INDEX

INDEX

INDEX

INDEX

INDEX

INDEX

INDEX

INDEX

INDEX